CAPTURED AT THE IMJIN RIVER

CAPTURED AT THE IMJIN RIVER

The Korean War Memories of a Gloster 1950–1953

by

DAVID GREEN

LEO COOPER

First published in Great Britain 2003 by
LEO COOPER
an imprint of
Pen & Sword Books Limited
47 Church Street
Barnsley
South Yorkshire
S70 2AS

ISBN 0 85052 959 X

A catalogue record for this book
is available from the British Library.

Typeset in 10.5/12.5pt Plantin by
Phoenix Typesetting, Burley-in-Wharfedale, West Yorkshire

Printed in England by
CPI UK

Contents

Acknowledgements   viii

Foreword   xi

1. Called up   1
2. Life with the Battalion : Preparations for War   12
3. Six Weeks at Sea   21
4. Korea : Our Baptism of Fire and an Historic March   30
5. A Touch of Frostbite   53
6. Close Encounters   66
7. A Battle Honour Won : Hill 327   80
8. Heesoon   88
9. The Battle of the Imjin River   93
10. The March   108
11. A Prisoner in Chongsong   115
12. A Failed Escape : The Cages and Slave Labour   131
13. Back to the Main Camp : The Chongsong 'Olympics'   143
14. Peace at Last! : Homeward Bound   162

Acknowledgements

I would like to express my warmest thanks to the Curator of the Gloucestershire Regiment War Museum and the Editor of the Gloucestershire Echo for all their help and for giving me permission to reproduce photographs and illustrations from their archives.

My best thanks too to three of my former comrades, Tony Eagles, Roy Mills and Morris Coombes for their contributions.

My sincere thanks to my publisher, Brigadier Henry Wilson of Pen & Sword Books, for his most cordial and encouraging enthusiasm for my story, and to my editor, Brigadier Bryan Watkins, who has shown just the same enthusiasm and interest. I am grateful to him for his concise editorial revision of my original manuscript and for the addition of historical background notes throughout the text.

Lastly, and most especially, to my darling and devoted wife Janet, who has always shown faith in me and for the long hours spent in setting my handwritten text into print.

Kelmscott   D.J.G.
Western Australia
1 January, 2003

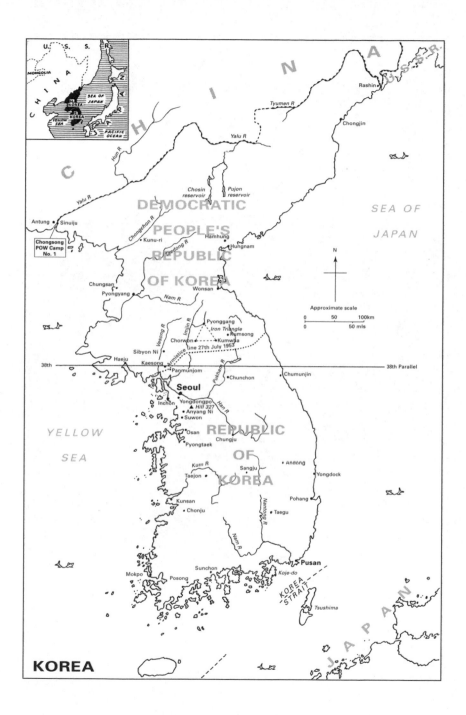

U.S.S.R.

MONGOLIA

CHINA

SEA OF JAPAN

N. KOREA

YELLOW SEA

PACIFIC OCEAN

Rashin

Tyumen R

Chongjin

Yalu R

Chosin reservoir

Pujon reservoir

Hun R

Yalu R

Antung • Sinuiju

DEMOCRATIC

PEOPLE'S

REPUBLIC

OF KOREA

Chongsong POW Camp No. 1

Chongchon R

Kunu-ri •

Taedong R

Hamhung

• Hungnam

SEA OF

JAPAN

Chungsan •

Pyongyang •

Nam R

Wonsan

N

Approximate scale

0   50   100km

0   50 mls

Yesong R

Imjin R

Pyonggang
Iron Triangle
• Kumsong
Chorwon • • Kumwha
line 27th July 1953

Sibyon Ni •

Armistice

Pukhan R

38th

Haeju •

Kaesong •

Panmunjom •

• Chunchon

• Chumunjin

38th Parallel

YELLOW

SEA

Seoul

Inchon •
Yongdongpo •
▲ Hill 327
• Anyang Ni
• Suwon

Han R

REPUBLIC

OF

KOREA

• Osan

Chungju

• Pyongtaek

Kum R

Taejon •

Sangju •

• Andong

• Yongdock

Kunsan •

• Chonju

Nantong R

Pohang •

Taegu •

Nam R

Mokpo •

Posong •

Sunchon •

Koje-do

Pusan

KOREA
STRAIT

Tsushima

JAPAN

KOREA

ix

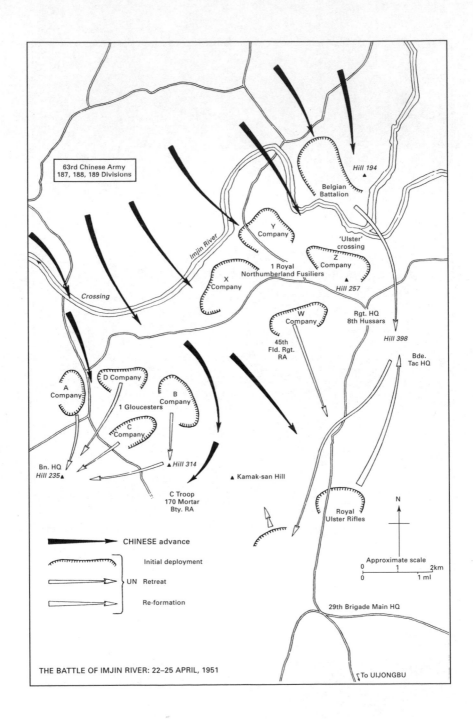

63rd Chinese Army
187, 188, 189 Divisions

Hill 194 ▲

Belgian
Battalion

'Ulster'
crossing

Y
Company

Z
Company

Imjin River

1 Royal
Northumberland Fusiliers

Hill 257 ▲

X
Company

Crossing

W
Company

Rgt. HQ
8th Hussars

Hill 398

45th
Fld. Rgt.
RA

Bde.
Tac HQ

D Company

A
Company

B
Company

1 Gloucesters

C
Company

Bn. HQ
Hill 235 ▲

▲ Hill 314

▲ Kamak-san Hill

C Troop
170 Mortar
Bty. RA

Royal
Ulster Rifles

N

CHINESE advance

Initial deployment

UN   Retreat

Re-formation

Approximate scale
0   1   2km
0   1 ml

29th Brigade Main HQ

THE BATTLE OF IMJIN RIVER: 22–25 APRIL, 1951

To UIJONGBU

x

Foreword

In this book I have set out to describe my life as an eighteen-year-old National Service soldier with the 1st Battalion The Gloucestershire Regiment in the early 1950s. The Battalion served in Korea with 29th British Infantry Brigade as part of the United Nations Force, under American command, which finally stalled the attempts of the Communist North and their Chinese allies to overwhelm South Korea and to bring it under Communist domination. We experienced great hardship at times and were involved in some very hard fighting, the Battalion being finally annihilated at the Battle of the Imjin in April, 1951. For all the hardship and dangers, there was one priceless thing which I can never forget: the wonderful comradeship of a soldier's life on active service.

This book is dedicated to my closest friend – my best mate – No. 22341335 Private Peter D. Hone, with whom I served from my first day in the Army. Pete was killed in the Imjin Battle, fighting heroically with his Bren gun against the hordes of Chinese soldiers who finally swamped our position on Hill 235, overlooking the Imjin Valley.

*　　　*　　　*

Despite the fact that over 142,000 United Nations soldiers, mostly Americans, were killed in Korea and that the Communist casualties, for which we have no official figures, must have exceeded that number by many hundreds of thousands, few people today seem even to know that the Korean War was fought or why. Certainly very, very few understand what an important part was played in that war by the British National Servicemen who formed so large a proportion of those serving in 27th and 29th British Infantry Brigades and their supporting arms and services. I, for one, am intensely proud to have been amongst them.

Taken prisoner during the Imjin Battle, I spent two and a half years as a prisoner of war in Chinese hands.

Pete Hone has no known grave, for when the Americans retook what by then had become known as 'Gloucester Hill', three weeks or so after the battle, they so blitzed the area that such bodies of our dead mates as were recovered were quite unrecognizable. They were cremated and their ashes buried in a United Nations War Cemetery in Pusan, each headstone bearing the inscription 'Soldier of the British Army'.

*   *   *

What little faith I had had in a God had been shattered by the sights that met our eyes when we arrived in Korea.

Now, over fifty years later, I have revisited the country and I marvelled at its progress. To see the happy faces of the hard-working people, and especially the children, has made me realize that the sacrificial efforts of the United Nations Force had not been in vain. Ironically, the situation in North Korea, whose Communist leader Kim Il Sung was chiefly responsible for the tragedy that hit the South, is still desperate.

1

Called Up

It was 9 March 1950, and a cold, windy spring morning, as I stepped off the double-decker bus at what was then called Cheltenham's LMS (London, Midland and Scottish Railways) station, clutching the little brown suitcase which my Mum had just bought for me at Boots The Chemists. I had come to catch the 8.45 train for Wiltshire which would take me on the first stage of my journey to Bulford Camp, on Salisbury Plain, and the start of a new adventure.

I had been called up for National Service in the Army and allocated to the Gloucestershire Regiment – known throughout the Army and thereafter as 'The Glosters'. Now I was off to report to the Wessex Brigade Training Centre at Bulford for my recruit training.

As the wind whistled through the sooty, corrugated roof, the Birmingham-bound train was busily getting up steam, its smoke billowing through the ancient bridge, engulfing me as I made my way to the southbound platform. At the foot of the steps a bespectacled, moustached, overweight porter-cum-ticket inspector held out his hand, his beady but kindly old eyes peering out over the inch-thick lenses. As he took my Railway Warrant, he grunted, 'Goin' to be a soldier, eh? Good luck to ya son'. Muttering my thanks, I glanced up at the big station clock which hung from the roof. With a 'clunk' the minute hand moved on to twenty-two minutes past eight. As I had often done in the past, I made my way to the only warmth and comfort available, the railway café and its inevitable cup of stewed tea. Stewed though the tea was, I knew I could rely upon finding a slice of excellent slab fruit cake, just like the cake we had on Sundays at the boys' home where I had spent a few correctional months as a fifteen year old and for which I had often been involved in a keen battle with the cards in the hope of winning some more.

As I sat there munching my cake, I looked back over the past few years, years which had certainly had their ups and downs. I reflected that today I was setting out on an entirely new life and one into which I was determined to put my heart and soul. All those blots on my copy-book (such as my recent spell in Gloucester jail for the theft of a camera which one of my mates had actually stolen – I had just happened to be with him – but I wasn't going to tell *them* that) would be water under the bridge and quite unknown to my new companions.

Before I had received my call-up papers, I had been growing increasingly unsettled and bored, constantly seeking something I could really get stuck into. Meanwhile, I had been working as a builder's labourer, a job that kept me very fit but lacked any sort of challenge or prospects. I had even been toying with thoughts of the Foreign Legion. Now things were going to be different – but just how different I never guessed.

Looking back over fifty years, I suppose I was a pretty typical product of my age group: born in 1931, one of two boys in a family of seven, the oldest of whom, my brother Eric, was already serving in the Royal Navy. By the time I was called up, Eric had long since completed his twenty-two years service and had left the Navy as a Chief Petty Officer after a very tough war in which he had twice been torpedoed and had been involved in a number of major battles. He found it impossible to settle in 'Civvy Street' and drifted from one labouring job to another, his life hopelessly overshadowed by drink. My mother, bless her, looked after him like most mothers would.

She had battled her way through life from the start, having come from a very large family of foundry workers in the Black Country. At times she could be as hard as nails but with a heart of gold (in capital letters!). Dad was a very hard working jobbing gardener, a job he loved but which earned him pretty poor and rather irregular money. He was a great reader of gardening books, ancient history and the Bible. Being a Christadelphian, he always believed that God would provide, giving his mate (Dad) all the energy he needed throughout the hours of daylight to produce a great variety of fruit, flowers and vegetables in our garden – which, for a family as short of ready money as ours, was a tremendous asset. His religious philosophy persuaded him that as far as the development of his sons was concerned, this was a matter to be left to the tender mercies of the Good Lord, which must account for much of the unruliness of my teens. He had two besetting sins, as far as Mum was concerned: he smoked a pipe and he charmed the ladies of the district.

However, I loved my Dad. With Eric away for so many years at sea, I was very much 'Daddy's boy' and would do all I could to help him by getting him bean- and pea stocks for the garden and wild briars from the woods as rootstocks for his roses. His granddad had been a full-time poacher, which probably explains my own love of my forays into the woods and countryside with my mates, all armed with our deadly long-bows, firing arrows tipped with six-inch nails which we had flattened by placing them on the railway. On his mother's side, he was descended from a Huguenot family who had escaped to England during the French Revolution in the late eighteenth century. He was a very intelligent man and I am sure that, in different circumstances, and given the oppor-tunity, he would have gained a Master's degree. Like me, he was a keen sportsman and, when young, had played rugby union and boxed; he and I would often have a little spar in the kitchen, despite his being short and bow-legged, with a well-filled stomach!

Fights in the school playground were a regular feature of my life, not least with those boys who pestered my younger sister Ruth. I suppose that, as the only boy at home, surrounded by a bevy of sisters, I felt that I had to show the world how tough I was and had built up a reputation as a scrapper. With the benefit of hindsight, I now realize that I had an inferiority complex as long as my arm. Though no hooligan, trouble and I were never far apart. However, of this I was sure: though, as a family, we were humble and always poor, we were a happy-go-lucky lot with the best Mum and Dad in the world.

As I pondered on all this, comfortable in the knowledge that the relief driver and fireman of my train were sitting just by the door, waiting to have their billies filled from the steam tea urn, the urn itself began to rattle and the floor to vibrate. The screeching of brakes and the crashing of coach buffers told me it was time to move – the 8.45 was in.

I soon found an empty compartment and put my little brown case up on the rack, sitting myself by the window. If the plush red upholstery did smell like an empty coal sack, it was none-the-less very comfortable.

At Gloucester City most of the passengers got off but a few got on. One, a lad of about my age, slid open the carriage door and slumped into the seat opposite me.

'Hiya!' he muttered.

I nodded in response. As he settled down, I noticed that he too had a little brown case, just like mine. He was about my height, just under six feet, but quite solidly built. He had dark brown hair and a large, jutting chin. From the look of him, he was clearly not enjoying life.

After a while, he pulled out a packet of Woodbines. 'Wanna smoke?'

'Yeah mate. Thanks.'

'Where ya going?' he asked, adding, 'I've been called up for the Army, the Gloucesters, Bulford Camp'.

'Same 'ere!'

3

We began to talk. His name was Pete, Peter Hone, an apprentice printer from Gloucester and none too pleased to have had his apprenticeship broken in the middle.

Despite his glum looks, there was something about him that made me feel that we would be mates. As we talked on, the feeling became a conviction and by the time the train drew up with a squeal of brakes at Amesbury, our destination, we had already become friends.

We alighted to see a number of other lost souls, all wearing a slightly apprehensive look. As we began to drift towards the exit, a smart-looking Corporal, armed with a clipboard, gestured to the flock to group together. Our transport, a 3-ton army truck, stood on the other side of the fence and its driver began to let down the tailboard. As the noise of the departing train died away, the Corporal began to call the roll of our names in alphabetical order, gesturing to the first lad, Alan, to get into the truck. 'Move!'

That short, sharp but very effective command was our first taste of authority, an order we would learn to respond to again and again over the coming ten weeks, responding more rapidly each time. Those who hounded us would be mentally hung, drawn and quartered by us all as we lay in our 'pits' at night, planning the perfect murder, which would be slow and painful. Discipline was a matter quite alien to most of us and was something we had yet to understand.

As the last of us embarked, the driver and Corporal lifted the tailgate and pinned it in with an almighty clang – we were off and our new life had begun. As the truck rattled along, I took stock of those around me. On average we were a reasonably well-built lot. One or two were a bit small and others, like Pete and I, were fairly tall. As budding infantrymen, we consisted mainly of non-tradesmen, builders' labourers, farm workers and the like. We had one obvious misfit, who sat on a large suitcase, surrounded by several others. He even had a travelling companion bag round his neck! A right mummy's boy!

As we left Amesbury, the landscape opened up and became flatter, for we were now on the outer edges of Salisbury Plain. The driver began to slow down and we saw that we were about to pass a bunch of about forty lads of our own age, running three abreast, with a very athletic companion at their side. He was shouting out encouragement, such as, 'Get the lead out of those bloody legs boys. Only another five miles to go.'

The lads were dressed in what we would learn to call 'PT kit' – blue shorts, white vests, khaki socks and, now, ammunition boots – the soldier's term for his ordinary army boots. The whiteness of their bodies emphasised the look of strain and exertion on their faces. This sighting had the effect of straightening out a number of backs and a mental

4

reassessment of one's own body and its capabilities. I secretly congratulated myself on my own physical fitness, thanks to my love of sport and the long hours of heavy manual labour which I had been putting in on the building site. This sort of thing wasn't going to worry me, I thought, rather boastfully. Later, I would think back to that piece of vanity as I toiled away, running in a new pair of army boots which were fast blistering my heels to ribbons.

The Wessex Brigade Training Centre was a typical wooden-hutted army camp, the by-product of the need in the fairly recent war to produce adequate barracks and hospitals at maximum speed and minimum cost. Later some brick buildings, such as a church and a gymnasium, had been added. The overall result was functional and not too uncomfortable.

The truck stopped at the guardroom, where the Corporal booked us in and we were told to dismount. As we did so, shouts of command could be heard from the barrack square – our introduction to the joys of 'square bashing' and something with which we would all too soon become very familiar.

We were now led to one of the hut complexes, known as 'spiders'. Each consisted of a number of barrack rooms, sticking out from a central corridor which housed the NCO's rooms, an office and a central toilet block. Each barrack room contained forty beds and steel lockers.

On being invited to grab a bedspace, Pete, my new mate, and I managed to get ours just inside the door. Whilst all this was going on a tough-looking Corporal, in well-washed khaki denim overalls, his boots and brasswork gleaming, announced that he was Corporal Cox.

'You'll be seeing a lot of me over the next ten weeks. If I do my job properly, you'll hate my guts. If you're lucky, you'll end up like this bloke here.'

Stepping to one side he pointed to an immaculately turned out young soldier in battledress and a blue beret, his Glosters' cap-badge and brasses shining with reflected light. '2233742 Private Bishop, trained soldier, who will be showing you lot the ropes.'

Hate Cox we certainly did. Nothing short of perfection was good enough for him. His bark was fearsome and his bite was worse. However, by the end of our training, when we came to pass off the square, we all realized how much we owed him. He had turned the rabble that we had been into a squad of well-drilled, smart, disciplined young soldiers. We realized too, by then, what a pride he took in us and that behind the ferocious exterior lay a very warm heart and a great sense of humour.

After a quick run-down on what lay ahead and what would be expected of us, we were dismissed to the NAAFI Canteen, having missed dinner in the Dining Hall. 'Back at 1500 hours', barked Corporal

5

Cox, as Bishop shepherded us on our way in a string of shambling groups.

The NAAFI was quite a modern brick building at the far end of the barrack square. As Pete and I stood in the queue, remarks about the girl wiping the tables were being passed. 'Not a bad bint that. I bet she does alright.' Some bloke asked her, 'Lately, love?' She looked up with a smile and in a Welsh accent replied 'Nightly!' That brought a few laughs. She was a bit of alright and could take a joke and make one. We would very soon find out that you needed to have a laugh and a bit of a joke in there. It was about the liveliest place around. What was more we would be spending about half our twenty-five shillings a week in there on fags, the odd cup of tea, a very occasional pint of beer and quite a bit on cleaning materials – blanco for our webbing, boot polish, Brasso and so on.

Back in the billet at 1500 hours we were soon marched off to the Quartermaster's Stores where a Colour Sergeant and about ten soldiers kitted us out in record time with our bedding and uniform. They had obviously done this so many times that they could do it in their sleep. They certainly kept us moving, quite an experience for some of us! We were already beginning to find out that from now on we not only did what we were told but we did it fast!

Bishop helped us to stow this mountain of kit in our lockers and showed us how to make up our beds – he was obviously Cox's 'winger' and attached to our squad for the meanwhile. As he and another soldier were doing all this, we went off in threes to the camp barber. Bang went my treasured Boston hairstyle!

That evening most of us sat round the pot-bellied stove, having had our first army meal – a great improvement on what many of us had had to live on at home – and nattered away, getting to know each other. Already a feeling of comradeship was beginning to build up. By the end of the ten weeks it would have reached a pitch that would leave an indelible memory with us for the rest of our lives. There's nothing like a shared experience, particularly one of being chased unmercifully, morning, noon and night, to create such a bond.

Pete sat glumly on the bench beside me, staring at the stove and obviously still resenting the break in his apprenticeship which this strange, and to him crazy, way of life was causing. Yet every now and then an occasional glimpse of the cheerful side of him, which I would come to know so well, would sneak through.

As we nattered on, it began to dawn on me that for some blokes, who came from very poor backgrounds, perhaps living with a widowed mother and with few prospects of a decent job, this wouldn't be at all a bad way of life. As for me, it was the exciting challenge I had been looking for and I was determined to make the best of it, looking forward to what the future might hold. Here, at last, was something I could really get stuck into and I was quietly confident that I could make a go of it.

Despite that confidence, like all my new mates, I found those first few weeks of training pretty hard going. I had thought that all my work on the building site, mixing concrete and barrowing around to the points where it was needed, must have made me pretty fit but I soon found that what we were now going through was different – even the business of learning to march. Poor old Pete, his co-ordination was just plain hopeless and he simply could not manage to make his left arm swing forward as he stepped out with his right foot. Corporal Cox hammered him unmercifully, which only made matters worse, as some of the lads thought it all a bit of a joke. And that wasn't all: he could not learn to salute – he would put up his right arm shoulder-high and then bend his head down to meet it. Meanwhile, his feet would be all over the place. This posed us quite a problem because until we had passed the saluting test, we were not allowed out of camp. After four weeks, during which we were confined to camp anyway, we were all bursting to get out into the real world.

There was nothing for it but for me to get to work on him, pretending I was an officer and getting him to salute me. At times I felt I would never win. It was hopeless. At others, we would have a good laugh when I pretended to be an ATS officer, swinging my hips at him. He knew just how he would salute her! At long last he got it right and passed his saluting test at the guardroom.

Truth to tell, we had little time for forays into Salisbury or the local villages for we were kept at it from Reveille to Lights Out. Corporal Cox had only one standard – perfection in all things and especially turn-out. So what little spare time we had was mostly taken up in 'buffing up' our kit – blancoing our webbing, polishing brass and working up our best boots to a mirror-like finish – all done with a hot spoon and lashings of spit and polish, as Bishop had taught us. What is known the world over as 'bullshit' quite baffled me at first, but I gradually came to realize that it was all part of teaching us to develop that perfection that Cox so worshipped and to learn the meaning of unquestioning obedience to orders. Truth to tell, it was all just as well, for we had precious little money to spend. Nine of my twenty-five shillings went home to my poor mother and by the time such other swindles as 'barrack damages' had been taken away, a couple of pints in the NAAFI on pay day, the odd bar of chocolate and a couple of packets of ten fags each week was the sum of my self-indulgence. What little was left over soon went on cleaning materials and writing pads. When the fags were gone, I was driven to picking up tab ends – but I had been used to that since I was a small kid.

Great emphasis had been placed upon physical fitness from the first day of our training and we all knew that the day would very soon arrive on which we would find ourselves out running in PT kit and boots, like the struggling squad we had encountered on the hills behind the camp on the day of our arrival. And come it did!

Until you had to run over them, the hills looked very attractive. One had had a huge Kiwi cut out on its face, by the New Zealanders during the war. It was now looked after by the local inhabitants, in their memory, and our barracks were named after it. There were some nice little villages on the hills and the local housewives would gather to watch us toiling by to the accompaniment of their ribald cracks. Perhaps they fancied us virgin soldiers – if they did, it was of little concern to the suffering squaddies.

Every Saturday morning we did that three-mile run around the hills – up one side, along the top and down back to the camp. It was a killer and we'd come in falling all over the place, to the slave-driving jeers of our super-fit instructors, who had been hurling insults at our tormented bodies all the way round. I can hear Pete now: 'Jesus Christ, what are they doing to us, the sadistic bastards?' Little did we know how grateful we would be in a few months' time for that fitness which we had acquired at Bulford when, as soldiers at war, we were being driven to the limits of our endurance.

But Saturday was Saturday, Sunday was different. With Pete released at last, we skipped our way down the road from the guardroom towards the stop for the Salisbury bus on a lovely sunny morning. We hired a rowing boat on the river and were soon making our way upstream, with me at the oars and Pete holding the rudder. I suddenly saw a gleam in Pete's eye and it was clear that the boat was heading across the river. What was more, Pete clearly intended that it should be so. Even as I was cursing him in fairly obscene terms for incompetence, the bow struck the bank and I lay on my back in the bottom of the boat. As gales of girlish laughter struck my ears, I looked up to find the prettiest of sights, straight up the girl's skirts. Tearing my delighted gaze away, I then saw that there were in fact two very pretty girls laughing at us and clearly anxious to get to know us. Needless to say, within minutes they were tumbling into the boat beside us. The smell of their perfume sent shivers down my spine and I decided that today was going to be a very good day. And so it was.

After a short trip up the river, we took the boat back and found a nice little café for tea. The two girls came from the Tidworth NAAFI, not far from Bulford, and they had clearly decided to spend the rest of their Sunday with us. We next went out to Stonehenge, which lay close to the road to Amesbury. It was here that the highspot of the day occurred, although Pete's feelings on the matter were a bit mixed. He had taken himself to the little wooden loo from where he emerged a few minutes later, covered in sand and with his pants still round his ankles. The almost hysterical screams of laughter from the two girls might well have been heard back in Salisbury! Quite unmoved by his state of undress, they rushed forward and began to brush him down, combing his hair and generally putting things to rights. Pete had by now decided that he could take quite a lot of this and immediately cheered up. It transpired that whilst still seated, he had pulled a large handle beside him, only to release the load of sand intended for the oversize bucket above which he had been seated!

Having sorted out Pete, we walked the two miles to Amesbury and took the Tidworth bus, Pete and I dropping off at Bulford. Sadly, we never managed to arrange another day with Anne and Margaret and so we did not see them again – but we never forgot them. It had indeed been a day to remember.

★　　　★　　　★

Our training progressed. The weeks seemed to fly by, so fast that it was hard to realize what an astonishing change had come over us all. We had begun to take a real pride in our turnout, our bodies and minds were now attuned to instant reaction to any order and we were beginning to feel pride in our soldierliness – the spirit of 'Corporal Cox's young Glosters' was tremendous, our comradeship within the squad had developed by leaps and bounds as we had toiled together over the past weeks, learning to accept the demands of a disciplined life and to take the rough with the smooth, not that there had been much of the latter!

One of the first things that 'Coxic', as we had begun to call him, had done was to give us a talk on the history of the historic regiment of which we had now become members.

In 1881, the 28th (North Gloucestershire) Regiment of Foot, first raised as Colonel Gibson's Regiment of Foot in 1694, was amalgamated with the 61st (South Gloucestershire) Regiment of Foot to become the Gloucestershire Regiment. The 61st had been converted to that title from being the 2nd Battalion 3rd Foot (The Buffs) in 1758.

No other regiment of the British Army carries more Battle Honours on its Regimental Colour than the Glosters. The tradition by which its members wear two cap badges, back and front, is unique and commemorates the gallantry of the 28th foot at Alexandria in March, 1801. Attacked from both the front and rear, the two ranks of the Regiment fought back-to-back. What had seemed to some of us to be a trifle odd about Private Bishop's head-dress when we first saw him in our barrack room, now became something that meant a lot to each one of us.

As our own proficiency on the drill square improved under Coxie's persuasive tuition, we could see later intakes making their first stumbling attempts to march and began to feel something of the old soldier in ourselves. Needless to say, from time to time we had to be reminded pretty sharply, in Coxie's eloquent barrack language, that we still had some way to go!

Towards the end of our training, a sports day was laid on at nearby Tidworth and an evening's boxing in our own gymnasium at Bulford. Because I had been used to jumping hedges, wire fences and even five-barred gates, since I was a kid, I had entered for the 200 yards hurdles. I also put my name down to fight as a welterweight in the boxing tournament.

The hurdles were a disaster. I might have realized that jumping various rustic obstacles from sideways on bore no relevance to the carefully-paced, head-on approach to hurdles. By the time I had bowled over my third hurdle, I had become a non-participant, feeling pretty stupid.

However, the boxing was a different story. I had had my first boxing lessons from coloured American soldiers during the war when I had got myself a job as general errand boy, boot cleaner and kitchen hand in their anti-aircraft camp outside Cheltenham. There, very often playing truant from school for days on end, I often earned more in a day than poor old Dad earned in a week. The nine months I spent in the boys' home, where sport was the chief item on the curriculum, had also given me more experience, as there were some useful boxers amongst the others lads. Whilst still a schoolboy, I had become a member of the boxing team of a local youth club. We took part in the Schoolboy Championships of Great Britain and I reached the final of the Western Counties preliminary rounds in Bristol. There a tough-looking Bristol boy, who clearly came from a boxing family, had won a points decision over me, though it was plain that the crowd thought I had been robbed. At Bulford my fate was much the same. I reached the final but lost on points to a very experienced Welsh boxer several years my senior. However, I did win the prize for the best loser. That performance even won me a heart-warming pat on the back from Coxie who observed, 'Oh Green, good bit of boxing the other night.' At that stage I had not yet tumbled to the pride Coxie took in his squad and the personal pleasure my award had given him – 'One of *my* boys, you know.'

At last the time drew near for our Passing-Out Parade, an event to which we were all looking forward and for which Coxie had been making us ready with plenty of additional drill. By now we were as determined as he was that we would put on a first class show. Once that was successfully accomplished, we would be Trained Soldiers and our move to join the Battalion in sight.

Fate now took a small hand as far as I was concerned. We had all been through a Personnel Observation Selection Test under the Educational Sergeant to assess our suitability for technical training. Having managed to persuade him that none of us knew a nut from a bolt, we sprinted off in a race for the NAAFI, to get first in the queue. Thinking I was taking a short cut, I slipped between the corner of a hut and a telephone pole, not realizing that a steel bar connected the two. Although no bones were broken, I was very shaken up and put in the sick bay for observation. This meant my missing the Parade. Happily, the window of my ward gave me a grandstand view of the parade ground and on the day, I stood looking out, determined not to miss a moment of it. As I heard the band playing 'To Be a Farmer's Boy' and the crunch of ammunition boots on the tarmac, the lads swung into view. With bayonets fixed and arms swinging in perfect unison, they looked a million dollars. A great lump came into my throat and to my astonishment, a torrent of tears rolled down my cheeks. Thank God I was alone.

I had always been one of the crowd before; now, for the first time, I was seeing all my mates as an outside observer. At once I saw how that rabble of fat, sloping-shouldered, slouching youths that had been our squad only ten weeks ago had become an immaculate, well-drilled platoon who marched with the swing of trained soldiers. The metallic soul-stirring sound of steel-tipped boots on the tarmac. Then there was Pete. Who would have thought that so recently he had found drill almost impossible to master and had been the source of so much laughter? Now, with his arms swinging in perfect unison with the rest, he looked every inch the fighting man he would later prove himself to be.

At the head of the squad, his head high and chest out, marched Coxie. He too looked as proud as a peacock. This was his squad, they were his boys and their faultless marching and turnout were due to him. All was now forgiven the man who had shaped and moulded us. A great bloke!

If at that moment those lads had been marching to face the hell of a Monte Cassino, Dave Green would have been there with them. Now, at last, I understood what it had all been about and how much the comradeship of my mates meant to me. No matter what the future might bring, those blokes and the times we had together would never be forgotten.

2

Life with the Battalion :
Preparations for War

Now trained soldiers, we were only waiting for our marching orders to join the Battalion. Meanwhile, we were granted a short leave of, I think, six days.

Pete and I set off together for Gloucester where he wanted to take me to meet his married sister and to visit the printing works where he was apprenticed and his father was the foreman. Unfortunately, his father was away when we got to the works so, having met his sister, I jumped on the Cheltenham bus and made my way home.

When I got there, I found my brother Eric was living there and seemed to be going through one of his better patches though, no surprise to me, he had commandeered my bike! Mother was padding round the house in my football stockings and Dad, whose fine voice was letting rip on 'Abide with Me' as he got ready for chapel, was wearing one of my hand-painted ties! For once, his Sunday suit was not in the pawnshop as everyone had got a job and there were a few bob in the kitty.

The six days sped by. All my old mates were off in the Services but it was good just to be with the family and, despite having purloined all my kit, they were delighted to have me home. I think Mum was secretly very pleased to see the impact that my training had already had upon me and to know that I was so determined to really make a go of my time in the Army.

I found that she had been saving the nine bob a week that I had allotted her from my pay. That was a laugh! I didn't have the heart to ask her for the bus fare from Andover to Bulford that I would be needing when I went back – so I walked the ten miles back to camp. It had been a great week but, like all good holidays, I was looking forward to seeing Pete and my other mates again.

Next morning we found that our posting orders were in and within a few days we were off to Roman Way Barracks in Colchester to join the Glosters. We were made very welcome and found ourselves in a completely new world. As Coxie has said to us before we left, 'Take a good look at yourselves, lads. Never ever again will you look so smart!' He was right. To our surprise, discipline, though never slack, was a bit more free and easy and hair a bit longer and there was a real family atmosphere about the Battalion. We soon decided that this was going to be a bit of alright, though we laid a bit low at first whilst we learned the ropes and mastered the slang of a regular battalion. My name being Green, I had to be 'Dodger', for that was the nickname of all Greens in the regular army, just as Millers were 'Dusty' and Whites 'Chalky'.

Colchester has been a garrison town since Roman times and, as in all garrison towns, there was friction between the various regiments and between the soldiery and the local lads. As always the root causes were booze and a shortage of women. Our principal opponents were the Ulster Rifles and on most pubs or cafés there were notices banning one regiment or the other, for we too had our fair share of hooligans in the Glosters. We also had a lot of fun.

Pete and I were both posted to C Company, he to 8 Platoon and I to 9. This meant that during the coming weeks, whilst the Battalion was having to carry out a lot of external assignments, as is always the way when serving at Home, we did not see a lot of each other. I found another Dodger Green in 9 Platoon and we soon became mates. He came from the Birmingham area and had already served one engagement of three years in a different regiment. After only a few weeks in Civvy Street, he had re-enlisted. Well over six feet tall, with light brown hair and good looks, he was much admired by the girls – which didn't worry him one tiny bit! I always said that the reason we got on so well was that we shared everything – mine! Not only did he never have any fags but he seldom had much of anything else – boot polish, Brasso, soap or blanco. Like many regular soldiers, he was a master scrounger, always with a charming grin.

Despite the numbers away from barracks on external chores, we had RSM's Drill Parade every Friday morning; nobody, but nobody, was excused. Regimental Sergeant Major Jack Hobbs was a formidable figure. In his peaked cap and Sam Browne belt, with his gleaming pace stick under his arm, he was indeed lord of all he surveyed. A former prisoner-of-war in Germany, he was a very human man but woe betide any Smart Alec who thought he could put one across him. Our great Jack never missed a trick. Under his sharp eye and masterly handling of the Battalion on the Square, we were one big family with a tremendous feeling of regimental pride and belonging.

After RSM's inspection and the removal to the guardroom at the double of all those found to be in bad order, there followed a bit of drill with the band crashing out all our favourite marches, ending with the march past to the regimental march, 'Kinnegad Slashers'. Jack knew his battalion and he never overdid those drill parades but, whilst we were at it, he looked for one hundred per cent. So, inevitably, a number of culprits, deemed 'Idle', would be doubling away to the guardroom to join those already mustered awaiting sentence. This would usually be a couple of days 'jankers', mounting behind the guard in full kit, grass-cutting, kitchen fatigues and the like. Only the truly idle got it right in the neck with extra drill on the square in full marching order and a 60lb pack on their backs. This was an experience not easily forgotten and usually acted as a lightning cure!

Every battalion has its characters and Bernie, a middle-aged, red-headed bloke with a freckled face, was one of ours. God alone knows where he came from but he had an armful of service stripes and it would not have surprised me if it had turned out that he was what the Army calls a barrack rat – that is to say, he had been born a soldier's son.

In the small hours of one morning he had been found creating a distur-bance in the cookhouse where he had wandered looking for some supper. Drunk as usual, he had fallen into a bath of custard, just made by the duty cook for the following day. He was smothered in the stuff.

In the pub on the following night, we held a Kangaroo Court, Corporal 'Whacker' Walker being the presiding judge. Bernie was sentenced to be hanged from the regimental flagpole, outside the guard-room, until presumed dead. He had until closing time to consume his last drink.

'Time, gentlemen, please' was not an expression used in that estab-lishment. It was not appreciated. It was a case of 'Out you lot', from an ex-paratrooper who had demonstrated on more than one occasion that he meant what he said.

Bernie was duly fallen-in between two escorts. With Whacker Walker in front, we all fell in behind.

Then it was 'Prisoner and escort, by the left, quick march! Sing up lads, let's 'ave ya!'

With a will, we struck up one of the Battalion's more unprintable songs:

'We are the heroes of the night.
We'd rather fuck than fight."

With Bernie being cajoled by Whacker, it was 'Bernard! Nice and tidy now. Step out. Get those arms swinging. Head and eyes to the front!' Then, 'Smile, Bernard, you only die once!' and 'All together now lads. With Bernard. Just for Bernard. He's going to die!'

On we marched to the guardroom where we found Sergeant Taffy Morgan, the Guard Commander, was in on the secret.

Beneath the flagpole, Bernie stood with the halter round his neck. The 'Padre' – Lance-Corporal 'Smudger' Smith – read his epitaph. 'This 'ere man, born out of wedlock, coming from his mother's womb, kicking like a young heifer, 'as bin a constant source of discomfort to all 'ho 'ave 'ad the misfortune to meet 'im. Who bist us to judge?'

Just as we were about to take up the slack on the rope, Sergeant Morgan appeared at the door of the guardroom and shouted, ''ang on! We've just 'ad a call from the 'ome Office to say that 'is Majesty 'as granted Bernie a reprieve, but 'es got ter knock aht a couple of chunes on the old mouth organ.'

Bernie was lapping all this up. He always had his mouth organ about him somewhere and could often be heard playing unknown airs of his own composition. Opening with one of these, he was then led into songs more appropriate to the occasion.

After we had rendered a few of the popular army songs of the day, each more unprintable than the last, and our numbers had swelled with numerous late arrivals, all a little the worse for wear, we decided that it was time we hit the sack. In line, with our arms linked, we gave a full-throated version of that well-known wartime classic, 'Bless 'em all!'

As back to our billets we crawled and Bernie was led off to his abode, it became very obvious that our little bit of fun had disturbed the entire camp. Ah well! It was great whilst it lasted!

What a character Bernie was! I did not see him again for some time but will never forget the day, months later and after we had arrived in Korea, when one of our forward patrols in Seoul, the South Korean capital, had found only one living person. Who was it? Why, none other than Bernie, of course, swimming in a vast vat of beer!

The tasks we were sent out on varied from the plain boring and dreary, such as guarding an ammunition dump, to the mildly entertaining, as when Corporal Hawkins and I were sent off in a truck delivering meat and groceries around the Redhill area in Surrey, because of a strike in the big London markets, from where we loaded up in the small hours each morning. Surrey is a lovely county and we really enjoyed ourselves. It would have been better still if Corporal Hawkins had been a better map reader – 'Where the 'ell are we?'

I shall always remember the stretch we did at Lakenheath, a big RAF station being used by the Americans. There was some suspicion of sabotage against the high octane fuel stocks and, until the RAF could organise their own additional security arrangements, C Company 1 Glosters would oblige. We were spread out in pairs around the perimeter, living in bell tents. I was paired with my new mate Dodger. Needless to say, we made a real pig's ear of erecting the tent, largely due to my trapping Dodger under the canopy and then laughing about it. As we wrestled on the grass, Corporal 'Whacker' Walker, our section Corporal, arrived to brief us on our duties. Whacker was well known to be a bit of a bastard, especially when he'd had a dram or two, and he now proceeded to give us a rousing bollocking, reminding us that we were soldiers and not Boy Scouts. What I had not known, until then, was that there was no love lost between Whacker and Dodger, who had served together in another regiment where it had been Dodger who was the NCO. Apparently, the charming Dodger had pinched Whacker's girl and had never been forgiven for it. Dodger hated Whacker's guts.

Dodger was pleasant, a little shy with women but physically strong and with a tough exterior. Underneath, he was . . . well, sensitive. Whacker on the other hand, was all man. A dedicated and ambitious soldier, the Army was his life. Some months later, I discovered that, bastard or no, Whacker was the bloke to have around when the bullets were flying. He was tough, through and through.

Having delivered his bollocking, he was just about to leave when he remembered that he had to tell us that the Mess would be open at 1730. Neither of us had ever been in an RAF dining hall before and the array of goodies we found there was beyond belief – better than our own Officers' Mess. I was always known as 'Swill-bin' but Dodger could leave me standing. Without further ado, we got stuck in!

It was a pretty dreary assignment, apart from the super grub, but it did lead to my firing my first shot in anger. Some idiot on a scooter failed to halt on my challenge and our orders were that in such cases, we should fire. I fired and, happily, missed. I don't know who was the more frightened, him or me. Anyway, he disappeared into the night and that was that.

From Lakenheath we went off to Thetford for an ammunition guard. Boring though that was, there were masses of pheasants to chase through the thick bracken, which impaired their take-off, but apart from a few tail feathers, my score was nil! However, I could sit out in an adjoining hayfield or on the banks of a shallow river and enjoy the sun whilst I dreamed of home and what life was going to hold in store for me – never for one moment coming within a mile of the truth.

Back in camp, Pete Hone came back into my orbit again. He too had been doing the rounds of chores, with 8 Platoon, although his were even drearier than mine.

Whilst we had been away, we had been pretty well out of touch with the news, although there was a buzz going round about a war starting up in the Far East in a place called Korea, which few of us could place on the map. It seemed that 27 Infantry Brigade from Hong Kong had been sent to join the Americans there and rumour had it that another brigade would be joining them. When reservists began to appear in the Battalion it seemed pretty clear that the brigade would be ours – the 29th. So now we would be fighting alongside the Ulster Rifles, instead of with them in the Colchester pubs.

★ ★ ★

Few people today have any real knowledge of the story of the Korean War, especially of the events of the second half of 1950, during which the whole scene was dramatically changed by the arrival of massive Chinese forces to reinforce the army of the communist North, which was beginning to take a severe beating. In order that my readers may have some idea of the situation in which the Glosters would find themselves when they arrived in Korea, it is necessary for us to have a quick look at the progress of the war up to November, 1950.

At the Potsdam Conference in 1945, the Allies had agreed on the principle of establishing an independent Korea, until lately so firmly under Japanese control. A joint Soviet/US commission was established to begin the work of rehabilitation and, later, to oversee free elections. Inevitably, the Soviets took on the northern half of the country and the Americans the south. The dividing line was the 38th Parallel of latitude, hereafter described throughout my story as 'the 38th Parallel'.

Typically, the Soviets lost no time in establishing a puppet Communist government under a man named Kim Il-Sung and to build up Soviet-type and -equipped North Korean forces. By 1948, the year in which the Soviets withdrew from the area, they had created an army of some 90,000 men with 200 tanks and 2,000 guns, including medium artillery. They had also produced an air force of 210 combat aircraft. Earlier in that year, the United Nations had announced that they would be sending a UN Commission to oversee free elections throughout Korea in the coming year. The Soviet response had been a flat rejection of the idea and a refusal to allow the Commission to enter North Korea. So the elections were going to be confined to South Korea. Meanwhile, the Americans had created a very different type of army to Kim Il-Sung's. Little more than a gendarmerie designed for border control and the support of the police in internal security situations, it had 70,000 men under arms but relatively few heavy weapons and no air arm. Clearly, if it ever came to blows between North and South, the Americans would have a job on their hands. After the 1949 election, a National

17

Assembly was formed and an elderly, dogmatic politician, Syngman Rhee, appointed first President of the Republic of Korea (ROK). Kim Il-Sung's reaction was to declare a Peoples' Democratic Republic embracing both halves of the country. Clearly a clash was now only a matter of time.

Syngman Rhee was a dedicated right-wing nationalist and the oppressive nature of his rule created great resentment and unrest in South Korea. In consequence, a second election was held in 1950 and a significant opposition to Rhee emerged. The Americans were uneasy about the situation and it was apparent that the emergence of the opposition in the National Assembly might lead to American political moves to influence the position and to gain commercial advantages. Realizing this, Kim Il-Sung struck before these American moves could begin. On Sunday 25 June, 1950, he launched a full-blooded attack across the 38th Parallel, taking both the South and the Americans by surprise. President Truman reacted at once and a small American battle group had arrived in Korea by 1 July. Ill-trained and -equipped, it was virtually non-effective and was swept to one side by the advancing Communists. Three American divisions from General Walton H. Walker's 8th US Army were then despatched, with more to come. On 13 July, General Walker assumed command of all ground forces in Korea. Meanwhile, General MacArthur had been designated as the Supreme United Nations Commander and at once made his presence felt.

Over fifty nations offered military support to the UN Force, the largest contribution being from Britain which, in addition to significant naval forces, sent 27 Infantry Brigade, under Brigadier Coade, from Hong Kong. They arrived in late August and were at once committed to the untidy battle being fought to establish a strong perimeter round the port of Pusan, where General Walker had his logistic base. 27 Brigade had been principally involved in internal security duties in Hong Kong and was in no shape for the sort of warfare to which it had been committed, ill-equipped and in-adequately prepared. They were in for a very tough time, made all the tougher by an American 'blue on blue' air strike which killed sixty of the Argyll and Sutherland Highlanders.

In mid-September, General MacArthur launched a brilliant amphibious operation at Inchon on the west coast only about 35 miles south of the Parallel, using a force designated as X Corps and including the 1st Marine Division. Its success swung the whole pattern of the campaign and enabled General Walker to break out of the Pusan perimeter. From then on the 8th Army and what was left of the ROK Army swept northwards and by 1 October had crossed the 38th Parallel. Within three weeks they had entered the North Korean capital of Pyongyang. Then the story switched to 'all change' once more.

Mao Tse Tung, the Chinese Communist leader, had grown uneasy about the possible threat to his own borders which the UN Forces' advance seemed *to him to offer. He secretly ordered a large force of Chinese 'volunteers' to go to the aid of Kim Il-Sung in order to 'resist American imperialism'. On 25 October, Chinese troops were in action. About a week later, Chinese fighters were flying in the airspace over the Yalu River.*

★   ★   ★

Rumour had now become reality. Our platoon commanders broke the news to us and gave us a talk about where and why we were going. We National Servicemen were told that if we wanted to go with the Battalion and with our mates we would have to sign on for three years as regulars.

As is always the case when a battalion mobilizes in peace time, there were quite a lot of blokes ineligible to go on operations overseas for one reason or another, mostly medical. This and the need to bring the Battalion up to its full War Establishment, were the reasons for the influx of reservists. Naturally, our officers were keen to take as many of us as would sign on.

Pete and I signed on the dotted line immediately. Innocents that we were, thoughts about fighting with live ammunition against men whose only aim was to kill us never entered our heads. Our minds were full of the glamour of a luxury cruise to the Far East, the sun, the mysterious East and the thought of those geisha girls with whom, we had been assured by some of the old sweats, a bar of chocolate would work wonders. Needless to say, the extra one pound eighteen shillings a week, to which we would now be entitled, was something beyond the dreams of avarice after scratching along on the miserable pittance of twenty-five shillings upon which we had had to manage until then.

To my delight, I had been selected for training as a sniper and, with about eight others from the Regiment, went on a course at Fingringhoe near Clacton-on-Sea. According to our instructor, we had been chosen for our stealth and agility across country. One test of our skills was a 1,000 yard crawl over open ground, whilst spotters watched through binoculars for any signs of movement. After all my years out poaching with the lads, this was meat and drink to me. We learned all sorts of useful tricks and techniques and I passed the tests with flying colours. For some reason, perhaps because I was the youngest on the course and still, as yet, a National Serviceman, I was not selected and went back to my Company in Colchester.

There I found the flow of incoming reservists had almost become a flood. Most were pretty disgruntled, particularly those who had been Japanese or German prisoners of war and were nearing the end of their reserve liability. It certainly struck us youngsters as being grossly unfair to pitch these blokes into this new emergency.

19

Before I had gone off to Fingringhoe, I had got to know one of the first reservists to arrive. His name was McIntyre and he was already in the battalion cells for getting involved in a fight with the local police. I was on guard one night near the cells, where Mac was the only prisoner. I kept him supplied with fags, impaled on the end of my bayonet! Mac was a good bloke who tried very hard to keep clear of authority. Content to do just what was required of him, he only wanted to be one of the lads. He was a tough casual-looking chap, usually with his beret on the back of his head, except, of course, on parade. A builder's labourer from Peterborough, he was one of those who were recalled during the last few months of their reserve service. I have no doubt that the fight he had been involved in was due to his drowning his sorrows in one of the Norwich pubs.

Our brigade had a great advantage over 27 Brigade, who had gone to Korea with no special winter clothing or equipment; rumour had it that they were already suffering from the cold in Korea which, as we would soon find out, was bitterly cold in winter. We, however, now received all sorts of new kit. Then, after a bit of special training, we were sent on embarkation leave.

Dad had been a conscientious objector in the First World War and had even spent a short spell in prison. Being a land worker may have helped with his release, but I am afraid it caused a good deal of turmoil in his family as two of his brothers went to the war, one being killed in France when he was only nineteen years old. So, perhaps, it was hardly surprising that Dad was a bit bothered about my going to Korea.

One evening, as I was getting ready to go out, he came into the scullery and said, 'You don't have to go, our Dave.'

'Where's that Dad?'

'Korea.'

I had not told him, or anyone else, for that matter, that I had volunteered. The truth was that I could not wait to get on my way.

'Don't worry about that Dad. I want to go. In any case, I expect it will all be over by the time we get there.'

1. The Gloster Regiment Athletic Team. Col. Carne sits 5th from the left in the front row. RSM Jack Hobbs sits 7th from the left in the front row. The author stands 3rd from the left on the top row.

2. Our first day on the *Empire Windrush*. Pete Hone is 7th from the left on the back row. The author stands beside him, 8th from the left on the back row.

3. The *Empire Windrush*.

4. C Company aboard the *Empire Windrush*. Back row: McIntyre 5th on the left, the author 2nd on the right. Centre row: Stan Lea 1st on the left, Matt Walwyn 4th on the left. Front row: Danny Kaye 2nd on the left.

5. National Servicemen on their way to Korea (photo taken in Japan).

6. Lieutenant Colonel James Carne VC, DSO, DSC (USA) who commanded the Glosters throughout Korea.

7. POWs enjoying a supply of tobacco after a seemingly long spell without.

8. Camp gymnastics: the author can be seen kneeling third from the right.

9. The Chongsong Olympics: Crawford putting the shot.

10. Chongsong POWs: the lack of a suitable diet is beginning to show.

11. The Company barber in action!

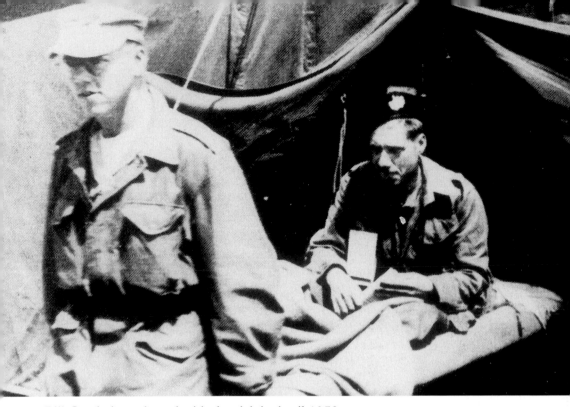

12. Bill Cox being released with the sick in April 1953.

13. This photo of the author (centre) with two US soldiers was taken the day before his release from Chongsong.

S.S. ASTURIAS Gross Tonnage 22,444 tons

14. The SS *Asturias* on which the author returned to England.

15. Homeward bound aboard the SS *Asturias*. The author stands on the higher deck on the extreme right.

3

Six Weeks at Sea

I stood with Pete and Reg Coltman, a 'K' Force volunteer from Cheltenham, aboard the troopship HMT *Empire Windrush*, a former German 'Strength Through Joy' ship taken as reparations at the end of the last war. We had boarded in the late afternoon and, having been allocated to our troop decks, were now enjoying the warm autumn evening in the stern of the ship, looking out over Southampton Water.

To say I was elated would be an understatement. I would not have missed this for the world – the smell of the sea, the harbour lights and the hooting of the sea-going ships. Pete, Reg and I embraced the moment.

Reg had been with the regiment in Jamaica, so trooping was no new experience for him. Like so many lads in the Army, he had found it impossible to settle in Civvy Street and, in a mad moment, had decided to get back with his mates. Now he was reliving his first trip on a trooper and whetting our appetites with tales of his experiences in Jamaica. We had been told that it would take about six weeks to get to Korea: through the Med, down the Suez Canal and Red Sea, across to Aden, Ceylon, Singapore, Hong Kong and so to the port of Pusan in Korea. It was a trip that people would pay hundreds of pounds to enjoy – and we were getting paid for it!

As we listened to Reg, a voice over the tannoy system instructed those with yellow tickets to 'proceed to the cafeteria now'. We had yellow tickets.

I could hardly believe the sight that met our eyes when we got there; the so-called 'cafeteria' was like a first class restaurant and it was clear from what we could see from the plates of those already eating that the

21

food was of the same order. Something told me that 'Dustbin Dodger' was onto a good thing.

Our Company troop deck was on G Deck, the lowest of all. It also accommodated the 'brig' or cells. Hammocks were in two-tier rows, hung from tubular steel poles. The floor, walls and ceiling were all of rivetted steel, the hum of the engines vibrating continuously through them. In all likelihood, G Deck, which lay right forward, below the waterline, with no portholes and the seas pounding the plates on both sides, was the least comfortable part of the whole ship. Not that this worried us landlubbers one bit. In our euphoria, we would cheerfully have slung our hammocks from the rigging if told to.

On the tide, the ship sailed, our captain manoeuvring her (all nice things are feminine!) with gentle skill through the mass of shipping in the harbour, the other ships hooting farewells to their Saxon warriors as we lined the rails of the upper decks. As we passed the Isle of Wight and came out into the open sea, we drifted back to our decks to sort out our kit and master the art of slinging and occupying our hammocks, an exercise which created a good deal of hilarity as blokes got in one side and fell out the other. However, it was not really as difficult as all that and we soon mastered the art and were swinging peacefully with the movement of the ship.

Our days always started with a fairly hefty slice of physical training (PT) but from then on, apart from the odd fatigue, our days were pretty much our own. I was utterly fascinated by the sea and spent my days either in the forward or after end of the main deck, staring out towards the horizon, trying to identify any ships we encountered. Or else I would watch the fish chasing our new webbing equipment which was hung out in the sea on string lines to bleach – this lot did not need blanco, which was a source of relief.

I was quite unaffected by the movement of the ship but poor old Pete suffered agonies of sickness from Day One. As we approached the Bay of Biscay and the seas began to mount, he became virtually part of the furniture of the tarpaulin-covered lid of the central hold. Even there he found little solace, but he did his best to eat and retain his meagre diet of dry bread.

Quite apart from my natural love of fresh air, the appalling smell of vomit on the troop decks kept me on the upper decks. Pete was by no means the only sufferer. At night I would creep up the iron stairway with my blankets in search of a suitable roost. This habit led to my first charge. I woke one morning to find myself being liberally doused, in what I had thought to be a safe spot, with a 4-inch fire hose as the crew began to wash the decks. The man with the hose was as astonished as I!

'God, what yer doin' there?' My only reply, as I lay there, soaked, in my underpants, was 'Jesus Christ!'

This broke the ice and we all fell about laughing as his mates, who were wielding the big bass brooms, helped me to my feet. Of course, my blankets were absolutely soaked and there was no way I was going to be able to dry them before the ship's inspection, a fairly rigorous affair, at 10 o'clock. Everybody tried to help but there was no disguising the wet stain on my hammock, in which the blankets had to be stowed.

That little lark cost me two days' pay.

My favourite spot in really rough weather was in the forepeak, which I now realize was a pretty silly place to be as the forty-foot waves crashed over the bow-rails as the ship headed into them, but I loved every minute of it. It gave me a feeling of belonging and made me wish that I had lived in the days of sail, climbing bare-footed up the rigging, body in tune with the roll of the ship, to the crow's nest, just as we youngsters used to climb up to the rooks' nests in the tall, swaying elms, throwing out the eggs for our mates to catch in their jackets, held out below.

In calmer weather we would laze on the open decks, reading or writing letters, sometimes enjoying the glimpses of land as we rounded the coasts of Portugal and Spain.

No Cunarder, the good ship *Windrush* averaged about 14 knots, a pleasant speed. As we approached The Rock (of Gibraltar), all eyes were searching the horizon for our first sight of this historic fortress. In fact, we did not actually berth there but lay out in the narrow straits between Gib and the coast of Africa. After a wait of only about two hours, we passed through the straits and into the Mediterranean.

As we hugged the coasts of Algeria and Tunisia, I was taking in all the sights and wondering about these strange countries and what sort of animals roamed there. The sea, and especially the porpoises which now followed us constantly, often racing ahead of the ship, and the flying fish, all fascinated me. There was an atmosphere of a pleasure cruise about the whole ship, officers and men making the most of every-thing and getting a good tan. Korea was furthermost from our minds. Bullshit and discipline eased. The nights were warm with slight breezes and clear, star-studded skies, encouraging the lads to come up on the upper deck to witness the beauty of our planet – something most of them had overlooked until then, having been too busy trying to earn a living.

We now learned that the Government had increased the spell of National Service from eighteen months to two years – so bang went that three years' regular engagement and the three guineas a week to which Pete and I had so looked forward. I had already increased my allotment to my Mum, so was now left with nine shillings a week. I hadn't the heart to cancel it and so spoil her enjoyment of putting that bit of money in a bank for her little boy. Bless her, the only bank she knew was Uncle Harry's pawnshop!

As we approached Italy, one old stager said to a youngster beside him, 'Them be the lights of Naples. I was there in '44 on the old vino. Them Italian women . . . shag 'em all night for a packet of fags.'

We lined the rails as those lights twinkled and began to fade away, reflecting over the quiet waters and conjuring up romantic thoughts about all those beautiful women over there, just waiting to get their lovely hands on us randy so and so's! What a hope! Never mind, in a few days we'd be getting a run ashore at Port Said for a few hours.

Alexandria lay to starboard, the place where our great regiment won the honour to wear its back badge in 1801. I was immensely proud to be a member of my regiment. As Coxie had told us at Bulford, we had more battle honours on our Regimental Colour than any other in the British Army. We were proud, too, to be men of Gloucestershire. Despite the injection into our ranks of reservists and 'K' Force volunteers from many other counties, mainly 'Us bist cum from the Forest, Gloucester, Cheltenham and Bristol. Oh ay ole butt!'

Port Said, when we got there, was a bitter disappointment. Before the time came for us to run ashore, we had a full dose of the traditional Port Said treatment with the bum-boat men. Pete and I decided to try a pineapple, never having seen one outside a tin before. We sat near the rails in a quiet spot and started to gnaw at the thick skin like a couple of lions, only to find that our poor lips were no match for that fibrous outer layer and were soon quite sore. Pete threw his away in disgust. 'Spend half me time spewing up and, now, when I can eat, I can't fucking get at it!'

I slapped him on the back and laughed. 'Never mind, mucker, you'll be alright tomorrow. We'll be going ashore!'

A half smile came over his dejected face as he said, 'No fucking bints, though, they reckon them Muslims lock 'em up.'

As we sat enjoying the warm desert breeze which wafted the still air and looking out to the shore, not wanting to miss a minute of our first foreign call, we were joined by Mac and a couple of other mates. They had brought some beer, which we shared as the occasional call of the *muezzin* drifted across from the minaret of a local mosque, piercing the very air, sometimes loud and then just an echo.

The next morning broke with a shower of instructions about our trip ashore coming over the tannoy. We learned that much of Port Said had been put out of bounds to servicemen, thanks to the depredations of our brigade cousins who had already passed through in two troopships and who had painted the town red. So, in short, Port Said was a bit of a washout. Some of our mates said that there were still some colourful areas if you only knew how to find them – which we didn't.

On we went, down the Suez Canal where we saw boys diving for pennies, distant views of the pyramids, and were invited, traditionally, to 'Get your knees brown' by airmen from the RAF stations along the canal.

Our next port of call, which was equally uneventful, was Aden. Then, at last, we were back in the open sea and heading for Ceylon.

A boxing tournament had been laid on and I entered as a welterweight. I won both my first two fights on technical knockouts but, as is the story of my life, was beaten narrowly on points in the final. The winner did not lay a single punch on me worth remembering but his gangling ability to evade a fight and certain death gained him the necessary points. I was not altogether surprised to learn later that he was the referee's batman! After those first two fights, many of my comrades had reassessed their opinions of me and I had become 'The Blonde Bomber', 'Dodger the Slodger' and 'Killer Green'. I did not particularly like being called 'Killer'. What cheered me immensely was the last fight of the day, between my mate Dodger Green and Lance Corporal Smith, who 'did come from the forest proper'. God only knows how he got that stripe. It was a grudge fight and must have been the mismatch of the century! Dodger had never got on with 'Smudger' Smith and, in a fit of temper, agreed to a grudge fight, even though he was at least a foot taller than Smudge and probably weighed half as much again as he did. Frankly, I cannot believe either of them had been in a boxing ring before although there was lots of play acting from Dodger in the warm-up time as he performed what looked like some form of Saint Vitus's dance in his corner. Smudger was a real country boy, I believe a reservist in his early forties, but without much between his ears. However, what he lacked in brain he more than made up for in guts. Dodger opened up with a swinging, clearly telegraphed right which was neatly ducked, sending Dodger into a sort of pirouette which Smudger took to be a golden opportunity to attack his back, finally deciding to jump on it! We spectators were in fits as the referee tried in vain to disentangle the gladiators. The bell got no response and amidst those flailing fists no one could tell who was who. Finally, tired of catching the overs, the referee decided that discretion was the better part of valour and jumped out of the ring, leaving the two warriors to get on with it. After about five minutes the two exhausted scrappers decided that enough was enough. Still exchanging insults and certainly not friends, they climbed out of the ring to loud cheers from the lads. Whatever it did for them, it certainly gave us five minutes of hilarious entertainment!

The heat when we reached Aden had to be experienced to be believed, well up into the nineties, which brought most of us up on deck to sleep on the hatches in our boxer shorts. Above us was the officer's open deck and as night fell, a number of the younger ones, mostly National Service, fresh-faced and straight from college, would appear at the rail above our heads accompanied by the nurses who were coming out to Korea with us, and ladies from the ship's staff, the gentle breeze, which blew after dark, blowing up their skirts and putting all sorts of ideas into the minds of the watching lads below.

Our almost idyllic voyage soon brought us to Colombo, the capital of what was then still called Ceylon, and one of the largest man-made harbours in the world. There we got the same bumboat treatment we had received in Port Said, although the range of the exotic fruit they had on offer was rather wider. Here it was decided that we would show the flag and so two companies, including our own, together with the band, marched through the city. It was quite a casual affair but it seemed to brighten up life a bit for the locals with whom we exchanged 'Hello Johnny's' and sang along with the band.

On we went across the Indian Ocean with the Bay of Bengal to port, as we headed for the Straits of Malacca and Singapore. Although Korea was far from our minds at that time, training did begin to pick up a bit and we had rifle practice from the stern of the ship. I never went much of a bundle on the Lee Enfield rifle, the Bren gun being my preferred weapon. A beautiful piece of machinery which I could fire quite accurately from the hip, though, as we would soon find out, Errol Flynn tactics were sheer folly when the fighting was for real. Pete too loved the Bren and could use one to good effect.

Singapore gave us our first taste of the mysterious East though we would find that, as in every other port of call, the two other battalions of our 29th Brigade, the Ulster Rifles and the Northumberland Fusiliers, had queered our pitch by painting the town red on their way through. Nevertheless, we were able to get around much more than we had in Port Said. Warm, tranquil air breezed through the busy streets, neon signs flashing invitingly and beautiful girls with split skirts adorning their slim bodies slipped past us, giving Pete and I shy smiles. We, who had shared a bottle of 'Tiger' beer were anybody's.

Unfortunately, girls of the night in Singapore had seen many good-looking servicemen and seamen from the big wide world, most of them with far thicker wallets than ours – and money was the number one priority. We drifted through the many attractive shops buying little gifts and memorabilia and bargaining with the sloe-eyed salesgirls. Bumping into a couple of our reservists, we got carried off to the world-famous Raffles Hotel, named after the founder of Singapore, and there we enjoyed a splendid evening with a lot of our mates, sipping our beer and singing the good old army songs, with the whole place joining in.

We finished the night with a chariot race back to the ship in half a dozen rickshaws, pulled by equally enthusiastic, athletic rickshaw wallahs. Well rewarded and praised for their efforts, they stood with us as, each propping the other up, we sang 'Now is the hour', joined by the *Empire Windrush* male voice choir, who lined the ship's rails. A good night had been had by all!

All good things come to an end and soon we were off to make our way through the South China Sea to Hong Kong. As we sailed, things began to get busier aboard the *Windrush*, weapon training and lectures inter-larded with spells of pretty vigorous PT, filled our days and evenings. The luxury cruise atmosphere had gone, yielding reluctantly to thoughts of Korea and of the challenges we would soon be facing.

Our wills were now drawn up – something to which I, for one, had never given a thought but now made me realize, for the first time, that all this was for real and that war was no longer for us just a word. It was a little thing but when I heard Whacker Walker being asked for details of his next of kin by the officer who was supervising the exercise and Whacker replied 'None, sir' I felt, all of a sudden, that I now understood him much better, his toughness and his drinking, and I wondered whether Dodger, in pinching his girl some years back, had not done something much more significant than he realized at the time.

Green by name and still pretty green by nature, despite over a month's experience of life at sea, I had not yet hoisted in that oldest of nautical lessons 'Never spit to wind'ard'. So it was that when emptying the company dustbin over the ship's side, straight into a wind bordering on gale force, the bin was ripped out of my hands like a feather and went ricocheting down along the ship's side, probably frightening to death the blokes slumbering in their hammocks within the hull's inner walls. That little disaster cost me three days' pay. As I was now making an allowance of fourteen shillings a week to Mum, three sevenths of twenty-five bob left me with Sweet Fanny Adams. Of course, Pete, who was the best mate any bloke ever had, helped me out, but it was a black week.

Unlike Singapore, Hong Kong, always described with such enthu-siasm by those who had served there, struck me as having a somewhat anomalous air. Somehow, the British colonial influence seemed to have tainted the natural friendliness of the Chinese people, many of whom were desperately poor and lived in a mass of little sampans in a vast concentration of small boats which were home to them, in all weathers, and a hotbed of crime. In Hong Kong the rich were extremely rich, and the poor were close to the breadline. One of the busiest commercial ports in the world, Hong Kong harbour was packed with shipping whose seamen thronged the streets at night. It was also full of the ships from the Royal- and United States Navies, whose crews, of course, added to the activity of the nightlife of both Victoria, the island which is Hong Kong proper, and Kowloon, the main port and centre of commercial activity. To these could be added the troops of the garrison and such, like ourselves, who were passing through and hell bent on having a good time ashore – insofar as our meagre pay would allow. By day, the open water between Kowloon and Victoria was thronged with junks, with their picturesque hulls and big lugsails and with the families of their owners playing on the decks, grandma being propped up against the high stern – the contrast between ancient and modern was extraordinary.

For me, our visit to Hong Kong was ruined by a piece of my own carelessness. Pete had lent me his watch a few days earlier and, thoughtlessly, I had left it in the washroom after getting ready to go ashore. Although I went back to collect it only minutes later, it had gone. Although poor old Pete had said, 'Forget it, mucker', I was really upset, for I knew that his family had given it to him on his embarkation leave. It seemed that every shop window was displaying outrageously-priced timepieces, glaring at me. I vowed that, one day, I would get him a new one!

Back in the South China Sea once more, it began to sink in upon us, as yet pure, young lovers of the night that it was getting colder and colder as we headed for Pusan, the main port of South Korea. We dived into our second kit bags and out came our heavy duty sweaters, string vests and gloves – the last of our illusions about luxury cruising having been blown to tatters!

Into the teeth of the increasingly bad weather, the good old *Windrush* battled on. I had got really fond of that old tub. She had a lot of character and standing in my favourite place in the forepeak, as she rolled and pitched into the waves, my now longish blonde hair blowing in the wind, I developed a real sense of belonging. I should miss her after we disembarked in a few days' time.

2 November was my 19th birthday, though I kept that to myself. We had never made any fuss about birthdays in our family and, in any case, much as I enjoyed the company of my mates, I kept myself to myself. Now, musing about the all too often mis-spent days of my youth, I had come to realise that, in many ways, I had become a different person. I now belonged to a military family with a tremendous family spirit of which we were all intensely proud. For the first time I understood that the Regiment was more important than me and that loyalty to my mates had become a matter of sovereign importance. If it came to the push,

28

their interests and safety would now take first place in my hitherto rather selfish life. In the fighting in which we would soon assuredly become involved, these things were going to matter. That wonderful Glosters' spirit was going to carry us through, no matter what was demanded of us.

4

Korea:
Our Baptism of Fire and an
Historic March

So this was Korea. The hilly coastline loomed forbiddingly as we coasted slowly into the drab port of Pusan on a cold, grey misty 9 November.

This was going to be no picnic! The Chinese hordes that we were going to slaughter, according to one of the Battalion's senior officers – known affectionately by us all as 'The Mad Major' – were massing on the Yalu River, the border between Manchuria and North Korea. We had now arrived at what must, at that time, have been the gloomiest port in the world, to be greeted by a pantomime of coloured American soldiers, rattling through 'When the Saints Go Marching In' followed by a handful of jazzed up Vaudeville numbers. They were joined, so it seemed, by the wind and a percussion group of loose corrugated iron sheeting on the roofs of the dreary-looking go-downs or warehouses. What a dump!

The band stopped, to the cheers of the bedecked ship's passengers, and some highly decorated officer took the stage. His barely audible words of welcome took off in spasms with the wind. Finally, he introduced a Korean representative, a doll-like figure dressed in white with a high-rimmed, black head-dress and a whispy beard.

Harmonious chords of 'I want my Mummy' swept through the ship. We had arrived!

Disembarkation now got under way. We made for the ramshackle-looking go-downs, dodging the heavy showers of rainwater which fell steadily from their leaky roofs. Mustering in companies and platoons on the platform of the marshalling yard, we stood gazing at our next mode of transportation, an incredibly ancient steam train with its long line of uninviting carriages.

After we had been allocated our places on the train, I and one other bloke from my company were detailed to help with the loading of compo* ration boxes, stacked on the platform and destined for the forward or goods section of the train. Always on the lookout for felonious gain, in the mild confusion that existed at the time, I found it easy to slip one of the two boxes that I was carrying into the willing hands of Dodger Green, who was standing ready at our carriage window.

The fatigue over, I returned to our platoon's compartment to find that boxes lined the undersides of the wooden seats. They were draped in issue blankets, ensuring at least some creature comforts for what promised to be a pretty spartan journey.

At last, everything having been loaded, the poor little engine got its considerable burden into motion. They say that combined prayer can move mountains and an awful lot of prayer must have been going aloft as, by jerks and bounds, we slowly began to move into the darkness of the night.

Coming as we all did from the northern hemisphere, we were well used to cold, but not Korean cold, a joy once experienced never forgotten. However, with everything closed tight and the warmth of ten mens' bodies wrapped in their blankets creating a bit of a fug, things got a little better but, nevertheless, it was clear that we were in for a pretty uncomfortable night. Of course, it was not just a matter of the cold. Sitting upright on hard wooden seats was a far cry from our snug hammocks on board ship, particularly as there were endless intermittent jolts from the poor old engine up front and we seemed forever to be coming to a short halt and then lurching on again. It is in situations like this that the wonderful comradeship of a platoon enables the soldier to take such discomfort in his stride and even to see the funny side of it all.

Daybreak gave us our first glimpse of the Korean countryside. In the South it is sparsely populated and almost entirely given over to agriculture. Dotted with many hills, which average about 500 feet, all the valleys are a mass of paddy, whilst the lower slopes of the hills are terraced. A weak winter sun penetrated the misty ground air, rays of its

* Compo: Composite rations. An excellent balanced ration developed during the Second World War. Normally packed in a box for 14 men for one day, they catered for almost every need of the soldier in the field, including cigarettes and chocolate – even loo paper!

light revealing the dishevelled but grinning figures of 9 Platoon in our carriage.

Our discomfort throughout the night had, in stages, led to ingeniously developed solutions to the worst of our problems. Dodger and I had piled up our large compo boxes to create a sort of pyre between the seats, padded with our big packs and kitbags. Lying head to toe, occasionally changing our positions by instinctive movements, we had found comparative comfort. It had been our first lesson in making the best of things. We had also discovered how untying your bootlaces not only gave relief to swelling feet but also helped to keep them warm. The close proximity to one another developed 'mateship' still further and 'mucker' and 'rotate' would come more and more into our vocabulary.

'Oow, what are whee going to have for breakfast, Greeny? Oow, what have we here? Best bully beef, beans? No? You don't fancy that?' 'We 'ad it last night. Oh dear!'

Dodger was propped up, half out of our makeshift bed, digging through one of our two opened boxes, making out that we were in some sort of first class hotel and mimicking our Platoon Commander, Lieutenant Waring, a well-educated National Serviceman for whom I actually had a lot of time and respect, as indeed I had for the other officers in the Battalion.

Whilst this charade was going on, the train went into a series of jerks, buffeting the carriages throughout its length. Finally, we came to a grinding halt and a message came down the train that we could get out and stretch our legs. The cooks would make a brew. Our little engine, which conjured up pictures of George Stephenson, would supply the boiling water.

Over to our right we could see a small village of wattle and mud cottages with thatched roofs which seemed to invite a visit. It was only about 100 yards away.

Pete now joined Dodger and me from the next carriage and together we walked across. It was good to be limbering up on terra firma once more after six weeks at sea. The stony soil was carpeted with a short, sharp cane stubble, the remnants of the recent maize harvest. A group of Korean women gathered round what looked like a well, their white-clad, pantalooned figures giving off a whiter than white glow in the warm sun. We approached them as they chatted with wide grins whilst they drew their water. One was deftly washing rice in a couple of dried-out gourds, swishing the water around and skimming the husks that had floated to the top over the edges. After some humourous exchanges, we managed to establish that we were *Yongu* (English) and were heading *cho-gi* (north). They responded by placing their hands over their ears and saying in their gutteral voices 'Boom! boom!' with even broader grins covering their friendly faces. As we walked on, we were drawn to an open-sided building in which we found two young girls, one of whom tried to hide as we approached but was goaded out by her braver companion. Fresh, healthy and pure-faced, they were self-consciously pounding grain to make flour. This was done by means of a heavy three foot log attached at one end to a horizontal pole which was itself supported in the middle by a short, vertical pedestal. At the other end to the log was a footrest for the operator. Pressure applied by the operator's foot raised the head of the log which was then allowed to fall into the receptacle holding the grain, made from a large hollowed-out log. With their white-scarved heads bowed over their task, they worked away, giggling and making remarks to one another.

To their delight, Pete and I took over. Every time I got my act out of sequence, I got a nice little dig in the ribs, punctuated with gales of happy laughter, which of course made me do it all the more!

Dodger, meanwhile, was looking on in his usual pompous fashion, making his thoughts known as he compared one girl with the other. Next year's seed maize hung from the rafters along with bunches of dried-out red peppers. The countryman in me had really come alive once more and if one of those lovely sloe-eyed beauties had said 'Stay here with us,' Dave would unhesitatingly have said 'I will.'

It was time to go and as we said our goodbyes, their sad eyes looked up from those bowed heads with shy, gentle smiles. It had been a nice encounter. Here, at least, was peace and, it seemed, as yet untouched.

We scrambled back into our carriages and RSM Jack Hobbs paced the length of the train, ensuring that doors were shut and that all platoons were 'present and correct'.

The Korean train crew had restocked the little train with fuel and water from the village and off we went once more, the engine seeming to have benefitted from its rest and pulling its considerable load with a new-found authority.

On we went through the same, never-ending series of hills, sparsely covered with low scrub and small saplings. Some had terraced paddy on their lower slopes and, occasionally, a white-clad peasant could be seen amongst them in his baggy rolled-up pantaloons.

As we made our slow approach through the outer suburbs of the city of Taegu, the scene began to change. Here, signs of turmoil could be seen – the bullet-ridden remnants of a train, just like our own, lay pushed or blown on its side, its rusting underparts exposed to the elements. A distant viaduct, its centre blown out, shouldered the now gloomy sky.

As I looked, the old railway porter's words came back to me. 'Good luck to ya son', rang a bell in my memory. Doubtless an old soldier himself, those words, which I had accepted so carelessly at the time, were probably charged with memories of scenes such as these and the fighting that had created them.

The train had now stopped in a very battered station. The stench of human excrement wafted through the open carriage window, tainting the keen midday air. A little boy in a tattered khaki coat and battered cap was standing there trying to barter his wares – cone-shaped newspaper bags filled with roasted peanuts in their shells. An equally ragged old lady was plying some form of rice cake wrapped in a cabbage leaf and now joined him. Money had little significance.

Dodger pulled a tin of mepacrine tablets out of one of the compo boxes. Had we been in a malarial area, like Malaya, those tablets would have been important to us but here in Korea, where no such risk existed, they were useless.

'OK? You change?' he said, holding the tin out to the little boy who at once snatched it out of his hand in exchange for a bag of peanuts. Seeing my disapproving looks, Dodger then gave the kid a tin of bully beef and a tin of dark chocolate.

'I was only joking', he humoured with a grin from ear to ear. We had already had our fair share of bully but it can make a very good meal on an empty stomach, as we would later discover.

I brushed the rice cake aside. Peanuts in their shells we could eat but not that. Dodger dug out another couple of tins for the old lady, who was pathetically grateful.

Looking out through the shattered walls of the station we could see buildings, once majestic but now standing as mere shells of their former selves, silent witnesses to the comings and goings of defeated armies.

★   ★   ★

After the fall of Pyongyang to the UN forces, the North Korean Army began to surrender in droves and no less than 135,000 prisoners were taken by McArthur's troops, who were now pushing on to the Yalu River. Recognising the potential threat to their own territory, the Chinese counter-attacked sharply, scattering the 6th ROK Division. On 5 November just four days before the 29th Brigade arrived in Pusan, McArthur announced that a new situation had arisen and that he was now faced by a new, fresh army. However, his requests for permission to bomb the bridges over the Yalu were refused and he was ordered to close up to the river, an operation which he estimated would involve the clearance of 60,000 Chinese troops. He was also instructed to make arrangements for elections to be held throughout Korea under UN auspices. To enable him to do this, he planned another amphibious landing by General Almond's 10 Corps – this time on the east coast at Wonsan. Meanwhile, General Walker's 8th Army would close up to the river. D-day for both operations was 24 November.

The Chinese were well prepared and had 300,000 men facing McArthur's 205,000. On 26 November, they counter-attacked against the strung-out UN troops, sweeping down the hills which flanked the valleys in which the road-bound 8th Army was packed, nose-to-tail.

After only four days of fighting, the UN forces were in full retreat, because of the imminent danger of being outflanked. McArthur decided to cut his losses and to withdraw all the way back to the 38th Parallel. He was greatly assisted in this by the fact that the Chinese had to call a halt to enable their logistic support to catch up.

By 13 December, the Eighth Army was back on the Imjin River, with the British 27th and 29th Brigades, who had played a vital role in covering the withdrawal, on the western end of the line.

On the east, Almond's 10 Corps had begun its evacuation through the port of Hungnam after bitter fighting in which the British Royal Marine Commando Group had greatly distinguished itself as it fought alongside the magnificent American 1st Marine Division.

The tide had turned.

★   ★   ★

Early in the war, the South Korean ROK Army and the Americans had been pushed right down to the area of Taegu, where we were now halted, and the ravages of the fighting were becoming increasingly evident. Twisted, discarded railway lines littered the unused tracks and burned out carriages lay half buried in bomb craters. Signal wires, dangling from broken poles, were suspended in mid-air. All had been prime targets for the Americans' bombers when they first joined the conflict as the spearhead of the UN Force.

Off we went once more, chugging slowly along to Taejon over towards the west coast and in the great bend of the Kum River. Here the smell of human excrement was almost overpowering and it was a great relief when we chugged on yet again. After another three days of stopping and starting, by the end of which we had gorged all that was left of the contents of the compo boxes we had scrounged at the start of our seemingly endless journey, we arrived at our destination, Suwon, which lay some 50 kilometres south of the southern capital, Seoul.

If Taegu station had seemed a wreck, it was as nothing compared to the station at Suwon, which had virtually disappeared, its remnants strewn everywhere, with a large heap of wreckage gathered in tangled disarray beside the only useable track.

After sitting on those wooden seats for day after day, it was with some relief that we found ourselves beavering away to get the train unloaded and stacking ammunition, ration boxes, support weapons and our personal kit in neat piles, the latter by companies and platoons. All would soon be collected by American trucks, our own transport having yet to arrive at Pusan.

All this was being done under a moonless sky as it was still the early hours of a bracing, frosty morning. For most of us the activity was more than welcome and helped to loosen up our cramped limbs but, inevitably, there were any number of professional scroungers who walked up and down the dark platform looking busy but doing nothing.

The trucks arrived and were soon loaded to the hilt in an orderly fashion, their coloured, gum-chewing drivers looking on morosely, totally disinterested. Within a couple of hours they were all on their way, as were most of the senior officers and NCOs who would be acting as the Battalion Advance Party and getting the place ready for the companies. No trucks for us, we were going to march! However, it seemed that it was only about six miles to the University which was to be our temporary billet.

Left to our own devices, a subdued quiet reigned at first as men collected into groups and began to move towards a fire that had been lit in a forty-gallon oil drum at the far end of the platform. Then a strong tenor voice began to sing:

> 'Where be that blackbird to?
> I know where ee be,
> Ee be up in the tuddy field,
> An' I be aader he.'

That and the fire were enough to get us going – not that it ever took much to get us off the mark! A small, bow-legged figure was silhouetted in the light of the now ferocious fire which had been enlivened with a draught of petrol. Sparks, flying skywards, rained down upon us as if to welcome us to this strange and foreign land.

Small wonder that we got into our stride so quickly for if there was anyone in the Battalion who could generate a party spirit it was Archie Coram, the singer who was so intent upon slaying that unfortunate blackbird. A regular soldier from Exeter, he had served in many campaigns and was truly one of the Regiment's characters. Every inch the countryman, it needed little imagination to see that short, bow-legged figure, topped by those bright, laughing eyes set astride a great hooked nose, driving his cows, thumbstick in hand, to milking. 'Ooh aahh! Archie. Give it um!'

So on he went, stamping those short legs and shaking his fist:

'Ee sees I and I sees ee,
We both sees one and t'other.
With a whopping great stick, I'll knock ee down,
Blackbird . . . I'll 'ave ee!'

Joined now by everyone around him, Archie broke into '. . . and they call I Buttercup Joe.' Our Archie fitted that bill to a T. He could always rely on having a wealth of musical talent from us Glosters to accompany him. Now a mouth-organ had joined the fray as the soaring sound of those Gloster voices chased the sparks from the fire up into the darkness. To anyone hearing us that morning it must have left with him an unforgettable memory as we left our dhobi mark on Suwon station: 'The Glosters were here!'

Our platoon sergeants returned as dawn was breaking and soon had the companies formed up and ready to march the six miles to the University with full pack and rifle. It was now so long since we had done anything even resembling a march that those six miles were going to be enough – particularly with that full pack. However, breaking into song once more, we swung along and soon reached the southern gate of the only walled city in South Korea, through which we passed, to find that Suwon was almost a city of the dead, the inhabitants mostly having long since fled south, driven not so much by the North Korean soldiery as the devastating power of the United States Air Force.

We found the University to be spacious and quite adequate for our purpose. Lightly built, it had concrete outer walls and long internal corridors flanked by large lecture rooms which were ideally suited for our orderly billeting – not that we had the luxury of a bed, or even a mattress, to lie on, just a hard concrete floor. There was no shortage of fresh air, which poured in through the great apertures where the windows had once been.

The cooks, who had come on ahead with the Advance Party, had settled in and they produced a very welcome breakfast. A considerable quantity of mail, which had been building up, was now dished out but Pete and I were out of luck. I suppose it was just that we both came from big families who were either too busy to write or not very good at putting pen to paper. Whatever the reason, we had become used to not getting regular mail but, now, being so far from home, this time it was rather different and we felt sorry for one another. Shrugging our shoulders, we moved off to a quiet corner, away from 'My sister's getting married' and

37

'Our kid's got hisself into trouble again' and the old soldier's joking cry of 'After you with the sports page!' Few people who have never been to war realize the importance to the soldiers of their family mail. As time goes on, it becomes more and more important and the disappointment of missing out when the mail arrives becomes more and more intense. Fortunately, this is a problem which the Army does understand.

To introduce us to the problems of manoeuvering over the Korean terrain and, not least, the difficulties of preparing defences in such rocky surroundings as we would find in the hills, an exercise had been laid on for the following day. It turned out to be a right balls up.

Our company was to prepare a defensive position on a particular hill, our first job being to find it! I don't know how far we marched but it was a long way. Our Company Commander, Major Walwyn, for whom I had great admiration, footslogged it all the way with us. He refused to ride in his Land Rover, which was driven by his batman at the rear of the column. Seeing his Major limping, this bloke drove up to suggest that he should get in the vehicle. This suggestion produced a string of swear words and outright rejection of such a dastardly offer. How I loved to hear him swear in his beautiful Oxford English accent!

'Go away, you fucking silly man. Bloody exercise is good for your system, isn't it, Private Green?'

As he said this, looking at me with his mischievous, blue-eyed smile, I could not help thinking what a good-looking chap he was. Middle-aged 'been around' wrinkles on his bronzed features made him look just like David Niven and British to the core. Rather than give in to his blisters, from which most of us too were suffering, he would gladly have swapped his not-so-badly-blistered foot for a twin to his more painful one. Thoroughly enjoying himself on this day out with his blokes, he was singing the most unprintable soldiers' songs at the top of his voice!

At last we found our hill but our troubles had only just begun. Like good soldiers, we cussed and swore as we dug into the rocky soil, our only comfort being the pack of 'beautiful' bully sandwiches issued to us with our breakfast in camp by the grinning cooks. To add to our joy, the steady drizzle now turned into pouring rain. We sat the night out in our foxholes, the rain coming in under our ponchos and trickling down our backs. Of course, this was only kids' stuff – playing at war. How different it would be in a real war situation under attack, not from the other companies, who were supposed by now to have found us and were probably lying knackered not far away, but by hordes of Chinese.

However, those other companies never appeared. In fact, they were lost! So 'Here endeth the first lesson' and we all went home!

The next exercise was more successful. This time, it was we who were attacking an imaginary hill outpost – but with a difference. Carefully monitored live fire was aimed just over our heads or just in front of us as we advanced, to give us at least a taste of what it was like to be under fire in such a situation. Another feature of this exercise was the introduction of what was called a 'winkling group' and 'Muggins' played a large part. I had to carry a circular napalm canister, known as a 'Life Buoy' flame thrower, on my back. Its purpose was to burn out any well-dug-in resistance. The only snag to all this was that no one would volunteer to be my Number Two or, for that matter, to be anywhere near me! The only casualty from its use was the vegetation on the hillside.

Whilst we were exercising like this, many thousands of so-called Chinese 'volunteers' were massing north of the Manchurian border. Sadly, they were without their girlfriends, the only Chinese that Pete and I had come all this way to see.

Pete had by now become a very different lad from the rather morose and bewildered boy who had joined with me at Bulford in March, only eight short months previously. To many people's surprise, he was now showing his true stripes and taking immense pride in his Bren light machine-gun, which both he and I rated as the best personal weapon. Complete confidence in the reliability and effectiveness of your weapon is a matter of life and death when the bullets start flying in earnest. Throughout the six years of the Second World War, the Bren had proved itself a winner under all circumstances and we were convinced that it would now do so again. Within a matter of days we would be able to put our confidence to the test.

During their swift advance into North Korea, the UN troops, which had included what was now redesignated the 27th Commonwealth Brigade* had swept through all the major towns and cities lying on the only two roads of any consequence leading north (which came to be known as the MSR [Main Supply Route] and the Secondary Road) and were now sitting on the Manchurian border, contemplating the prospect of crossing it to mop up what was left of the North Korean Army. However, the newly-established presence of the *Chingwa* (the so-called Chinese volunteers) in massive strength had effectively changed the situation.

Meanwhile, bands of North Korean guerillas, which had either been swept aside or ignored during the main advance, were making a nuisance of themselves in the areas of Sibyan-Ni, north of Seoul, and Kaesong, which lies just north of the 38th Parallel. It was now decided

---

* The 3rd Royal Australian Regiment and 2nd Princess Patricia's Canadian Light Infantry had joined the Middlesex and Argylls.

that the 29th British Infantry Brigade should deal with them. That meant us!

Moving up from Suwon, through the outskirts of a sparsely populated Seoul and then through Kaesong, the Battalion occupied positions on an apron of high ground called Sinanjui, being spread out thinly across its bowl-shaped centre. C Company was on the left flank.

By now our platoon had been completely re-formed, consisting of regulars, reservists, a 'K' Force volunteer and a single National Service man – me. My 'buddy' or dugout mate, was David Kaye, known to us all as Danny. A very handsome, dark-haired, well-built figure of a man, he came from Nottingham and had volunteered for Korea, being still only twenty-three. He was well educated and had high moral standards. A better mucker and mate would be hard to find, so I was extremely lucky.

Sergeant McKay, our platoon sergeant and a former Gordon Highlander, had given us the honour of a nice forward position on the forward slope of a gully which overlooked the easiest, and perhaps only, means of access to our high ground.

Danny and I took it in turns with pick and shovel, for digging into that rocky ground was no easy matter. During our short spells of rest, we surveyed our territory, which seemed to me to be very exposed. I tried to work out the quickest and safest way of retreat, back to the rest of the platoon, safely dug-in on the reverse slope, well out of sight. Willingly would I have swapped our position for one now housing those supposedly experienced soldiers. Maybe they thought that I could run faster or perhaps Sergeant McKay thought that his one and only National Serviceman and 'K' Force volunteer were expendable. Run? You must be joking!

That night I took first watch. We were on a fifty percent stand-to. Danny was in our painstakingly created sleeping quarters in our L-shaped trench, a poncho covering the roof. Fortunately, there was a three-quarters moon, giving us reasonable observation to our front, which sloped down into the bottom of the gully and then up on the other side. Earlier, I had seen men silhouetted on the skyline over there. They were from the next-door company and some distance away.

A good hour passed. Never having been in such a serious situation before, I listened for every little noise and flurry, watching every shadow until I got double vision. All of a sudden, I saw three figures coming down the slope from the direction of the next-door company. As I strained my eyes, trying to identify them, my finger on the trigger of my rifle, taking first pressure, my mind was in a turmoil, wondering whether or not to challenge them. I had never seen a North Korean soldier. If these were Koreans, I might be able to challenge and shoot one but the other two would get me. They scrambled into our gully and began to come up, passing no more than twenty yards to my right and heading for our platoon position. As they veered slightly towards me, I saw that they must be ours as one was a peak-capped officer. It was too late to do anything now so I just held my breath and kept still.

That officer had been within a hair's breadth of meeting his maker. What a disaster that would have been. Phew! I needed a cigarette!

Stooping down into the bottom of the trench, with my overcoat pulled over my head, I tried to light one. A broad Scots accent cut the air beside me.

'What the fuckin' 'ell are yu doin' dun there?'

Sergeant McKay was dancing around, waving his arms like a dervish.

'You'se 'ad it, matey! Sleeping on guard is a court martial offence!' My plea that I was lighting a fag fell on deaf ears as he strutted off, still cursing. I thought, 'Up you. You want to try it here, mate!'

Danny could have slept through the bombing of Coventry. I shook him.

'Time to get up, mucker!'

'Get up? I only just got to bed.'

'That was two hours ago, Danny!'

He put me in mind of my sister Mary, who had adamantly refused during the war to get out of bed for anything or anybody during the air raids on Cheltenham.

We got safely through the rest of that night and the next day. I tried again to explain to Sergeant McKay what had happened. As usual, the rest of the platoon were on my side. Hughes, a reservist from Norfolk, said 'Garn, Sarge. He's only a young 'un, poor little sod! What else is a bloke supposed to do? We all 'ave a sly drag, including you. Only way to keep awake.' So that was the last I heard of that!

On the next day we were to go on a recce patrol in company strength. Some guerillas were suspected to be lying up in the hills in a spot which was ideal for an ambush of UN logistic transport. C Company was to check this out.

We were taken in three-ton trucks to within a mile or so of the suspect spot and dropped off there to continue on foot. We advanced cautiously in single file on each side of the road. A couple of carriers with mounted machine-guns, from Support Company, brought up the rear.

As we passed through a little village, we saw a badly wounded Korean leaning against a bale of straw. A typical peasant, he had cropped hair and the traditional white peasant garb. He was sitting in a pool of blood from a large wound in his left thigh, which was still bleeding. He was quite alone. We learned that he had been shot in the act of planting what was believed to be a mine and acting suspiciously in the area of a bridge in the forward area. A carrier which had gone up to investigate was blown up when its commander decided to cross the river, not by the supposedly mined bridge but by the ford beside it. Those guerillas were a crafty lot!

At the mouth of the next valley, the Major held an 'O' Group.* He had decided that we should cross the bridge and then split into two groups. We were to fan out and advance across the paddy fields to a point where the surrounding hills converged on either side of the road. The exit to the valley was very narrow and the hills on the left, which virtually overhung the road, were to be especially routed out.

The advance across the paddies was without incident and we began our ascent up the hills on the left. The hillsides were covered with scrub and young saplings. As we approached the top, the going got steeper with loose shale underfoot. Danny was somewhere on my left with the rest of the platoon except for Jock McKay, who was on my right.

As Jock and I reached the top, we came across a bedraggled group of about thirty guerillas, sitting around their fire. Jock at once opened fire with his Sten gun whilst I engaged a man standing not twenty yards away, firing my rifle from the hip. He just stared at me as he dropped, his hands still in his coat pockets.

As I attempted to find a fire position behind cover, the ground gave way under my feet and I began to slither down the slope on the shale. As I fell, I caught a fleeting glance of the man I had shot at. He was still on his knees, blood covering his tunic.

By great good fortune, my boot became entangled with a large shrub and this broke my fall and left me in an almost horizontal position, suspended in its growth. My cap comforter and the sweat from my forehead were blinding me and the bolt of my rifle was covered in grit, which I attempted vigorously to blow away.

I couldn't see anything of the rest of the platoon but there was plenty of automatic- and single-shot fire. Expecting some reaction from the enemy, I got into a fire position and stayed put. As I lay there, sweating profusely, I could not help laughing at poor Archie Coram who I could now see on a little mound out in the open to my right at the base of the hill. Bullets were ricocheting all around him, coming, so he thought, from our blokes on the other side of the road. Half-turning, he was shouting, 'You silly sods! It's me! Stupid bastards! Oy! Pack it in!'

Across the road behind us, the other platoon had obviously run into trouble. A broad Brummie voice was shouting, 'They've blown moy leg orf!'

* 'O' Group: Orders Group

Through a gap in the trees, I could see movement from the direction of the voice, which was still crying for help. A figure fell through the scrub some fifteen feet to the road below.

They were clearly pinned down. The guerillas had now withdrawn to higher ground and were beginning to take a few shots at us as well. Archie scooted for cover like a startled hare. I thanked God he was unhurt. Seeing what had happened to him, I was thankful that we had not been seen crossing those paddies. We would have been sitting ducks. Even though it would have taken some time, our best approach would have been to traverse through the hills on either side to take them by surprise, though, in all truth, Jock McKay and I certainly surprised that gang sitting round the fire.

Things had quietened down and I was able to disentangle myself from my life-saving bush. What remained of the enemy had fled, taking some of their wounded with them.

A message now came for us to regroup in a shallow dip further down our side of the road. This we did, drawing fire from the higher ground as we did so. We then gave support to the other platoons who were still pinned down. Bullets skimmed off the road like infuriated hornets, sending fragments of rock around our ears. Lieutenant Waring lay at my side. I marvelled at his coolness. He was no older than I but quite unmoved by the whole affair. He calmly raised his head to check our position.

'See there, Green', he said, pointing at the puffs of smoke from the shots coming our way. I gingerly lifted my head and saw what was clearly a group of the enemy on the next ridge.

'OK chaps, two o'clock right; 200; group of enemy on that next ridge. Fire at will.'

We each pumped a couple of magazines into the area and figures could then be seen moving back. The incoming fire grew increasingly sporadic until all that was left was the occasional single shot. The day was won.

We all began to help with the wounded as the remnants of the two platoons began to emerge from their positions. Remembering the Brummy bloke, I made my way to the area in which he had fallen and found him spreadeagled across a flattened bush. He was still conscious. His right leg was smothered in blood from thigh to foot. His face was covered in bloody handprints. He had clearly grasped it in his pain. I attempted to rip his trousers away from the wound but the blood oozing out of the soggy material made this difficult. I could see a neat hole on the outer side of his knee where the bullet had entered. Getting out my field dressing to place on the wound, I stupidly tried to support his leg by putting my hand under it. The poor lad let out a scream of agony, his eyes rolled upwards and he became almost unconscious. Only then

43

did I realize that the leg was completely shattered. Only a thin strip of flesh was holding the two halves together. The other wounded were being attended to for much more minor wounds and I shouted for help. A medic came over and at once sent me off to find a piece of wood which could be used as a splint. He then gave him a shot of rum, stuffing the water-bottle with the remainder into his blood-covered hands.

By now help had arrived. A three-ton truck was parked up on the road and a wounded Korean prisoner sat nearby. He was dressed in a conglomeration of khaki gear with light fawn trousers, sand shoes (or 'pumps' as we then called them), a long tunic with brass buttons and a pile hat with ear-flaps, which hung down each side of his yellowish face. A typical Asiatic, he was quite resigned to his fate. He told an interpreter that there had been about 200 of them and that they had been issued with five rounds of ammunition apiece. Their long, ancient-looking rifles, their bayonets looking like short swords, had been piled in a heap.

Lucky old us! I would not have staked a day's pay on our chances on our survival, piss-poor shots though they were, had there been more of them.

A dead guerilla had been brought in for good measure and Lieutenant Waring reproachfully told me to leave the body, which I had rolled over for a better look, to see if he was the one I'd shot. I had only fired that one shot by instinct, and could not tell whether it had been fatal or not.

It had been a fairly sharp baptism of fire for us and those of us who had taken part and come through now felt that we were proper soldiers. Jock McKay was thanking his lucky stars that he had not been leading 7 Platoon, whose sergeant had been shot through the head and killed.

Back we went to our old position and things went on much as before. We made little improvements to our dugouts – a shelf for loaded magazines and grenades and a solid roof of logs over the sleeping pit.

The two hours on, two hours off, business was a bit much, so much so that I quite often found myself falling asleep, only to be woken by a smouldering mitten, set on fire by the burning stub of a cigarette.

A dear old lady in England had adopted our platoon and sent us out warm socks and mittens to help keep out the cold, God bless her. Danny kept in touch with her. May she rest in peace for ever. Such contacts mean a hell of a lot to soldiers far from home and living under really tough conditions.

As I took my turn on guard, the events of that day's fighting which we had just been through would often go through my mind. I would say to myself that anybody attempting to get up our by now thoroughly slippery slope, would have seasoned Dave Green, guerilla fighter, to contend with. 'Yeah, I was there at Sibyoni. Gave 'em 'ell we did!'

The cookhouse was down at the rear on flat ground. I vowed that once

I got clear of Korea, I'd never eat bully beef again. Day after day, it was dished out in one form or another. Mind you, the compo steamed treacle pudding was smashing and there were plenty of boiled sweets and bars of dark chocolate too – just the job to help you keep awake on guard on a cold night. Little did I realize how nostalgically I would be looking back on these luxuries in a few months' time.

One day, a spot we had often passed before caught my attention. What looked like the form of a body was defined in the snow in a small, sparse thicket. On closer inspection, it turned out to be the body of a youngish Korean man, his severed head, with its shock of long, raven-black hair, at his side. It looked as if he had been executed with a sword. Dead bodies were commonplace enough but this one was mysterious and stayed indelibly in my mind.

New orders now came through. We were to form a rear guard for the now retreating UN Forces. They had been pushed back by the Chinese, who had crossed the Manchurian border on 26 November, not by road but across the hills on foot, thousands upon thousands of them, hell bent on cutting off the UN Forces in chunks. They were making a pretty good job of it too. 27 Brigade were in the thick of it up there. Some Turkish units, which had been thrown in within a week or so of landing, had almost been annihilated.

This was going to be no guerilla hunting expedition but real war and about as tough as it comes. I, for one, thanked God that we had at least had a day under fire at Sibyoni, for it had had a remarkably strengthening effect upon the confidence with which our platoon went about its business.

A trek of some 80 to 100 miles now lay before us. When we boarded the waiting trucks next morning, each had a sizeable brew can dangling below the tailboard. The weather was atrocious, blinding sleet and snow, and the occasional hot drink was going to be a must.

As usual, I made myself comfortable at the tailboard end so as not to miss the sights – not that one could see much in that weather. Danny and a lad called Stan Lea, a reservist who came from Coventry, were beside me – we usually sought each other's company. Stan was a pleasant bloke, not all that much older than us, who always had a smile to brighten our days. Next to him sat his trench buddy, Dymock, an unassuming regular soldier of about Stan's age. He came from Southampton and was always particular about his personal hygiene. He would shave in his tea if necessary. His turnout was impeccable and he took endless care to ensure that his uniform, even his greatcoat, did not get creased in the wrong places. He had a delightfully dry sense of humour but a smile was the most you would get from him – he didn't like creasing his face either!

'Ave ee got a light, boy?' The high pitched sing-song voice was that of Hughes from Norwich, a small man in his forties. He and his buddy, Gravenell, a rugged, lofty West Countryman, with size 13 boots and a voice to match, were like chalk and cheese but good mates, nonetheless. They were sitting together opposite us and the chatter rattled on as we went on our bumpy way. The floor of a three-ton truck is not the most comfortable place upon which to be seated at the best of times and when traversing a heavily pot-holed road, it's hell. A short break to enable us to 'ease springs' in the bushy roadside came as a welcome relief for both reasons.

Our bladders duly emptied, amid a good deal of raucous competition to see who could pee the furthest, we clambered back into our trucks and on the convoy went, only to stop again at what looked like a pretty permanent American camp. Our Company Commander wanted to use the telephone. The soldiers there, it seemed, were celebrating, possibly Thanksgiving Day. A row of overflowing rubbish bins, which stood just near our trucks, were overflowing with the leftovers of the day. Like poor Cinderellas, our blokes were into them. It was just an appalling waste of good food, luckily untainted and lying on clean packing material, refrigerated by the freezing winter air. Feeling rather shamefaced, I helped myself to an oversize turkey leg, the likes of which I had never seen in my nineteen years. However, my natural dignity got the better of me and I decided to stick to my bully sandwich.

On the move once more, we all burst into one of our favourite songs, 'Down by the Old Mill Stream', our beautiful singing utterly wrecked by Hughes and Gravenell, who were oblivious to the outside world and had their heads together, producing the most earsplitting caterwaul.

The windscreen wiper on the truck behind us had its work cut out swishing away the driving snow, the clear arc of the glass revealing the peering, concentrating driver labouring at the wheel and occasionally turning to his mate, whose tipped boots were all that could be seen of him. Who, in God's name, would want to be a driver out here? Many trucks had already gone over the side of the steep, winding hill roads, thanks to the incessant ice and snow. As we neared Pyongyang, progress became very slow as the southbound traffic was filtering its way through on a road hardly wide enough for two vehicles. At last we got through and entered what was left of the North Korean capital. The few remaining inhabitants looked like business people making their preparations to depart. They wore a mixture of Asian and Western dress – all except one, a girl in black, high-heeled shoes, black stockings and skirt, all topped with a fur coat and hat, possibly from whatever Russian Commission had been left behind when the Soviets had baled out in 1948. There was a definite Russian influence prevailing, perhaps even having its roots in the days before the Japanese occupation. It all rather reminded me of a documentary film I had once seen about Tashkent.

Once again, as we drove through the narrow streets on our way out of the city, we encountered American troops going in the opposite direction and heavily laden Korean trucks with immense loads and precariously balanced bodies on top.

We ploughed on through the slush, stopping and starting until finally we were forced to stop altogether. As far as the eye could see, an impassable mass of humanity was stretched out in front of us, gradually disappearing beneath a rapidly darkening, threatening sky.

The stretch of the Taedong River upon which we were to take up our positions still lay some distance to the north-east. There was nothing for it, we would have to finish our journey on our feet. Dismounting, we marched in single file, keeping about 20 yards from the churned-up road in order to avoid the slush spewed out by the passing American trucks. American soldiers on the southbound convoys shouted at us, 'You're going the wrong way, buddy!' boosting our morale no end. Leaning into the cold Siberian wind, with temperatures as low as minus 40 degrees, with ice forming around the mouths of the hoods of our windcheaters, we pressed on, passing a unit of thoroughly dejected Turks. Flashes of the newsreels of the Russian front in the early 1940s entered my mind. We passed a Korean truck, keeled over, its load scattered and injured passengers trying to revive a lifeless body, to no avail.

At long last, the frozen Taedong River lay ahead, the bridge crossing to our left overlooking the city behind us. On the other side of the river, the whole valley lay open before us, with the MSR cutting its way through the hills to the north. Trucks laden with military paraphernalia were moving slowly south. Abandoned equipment was scattered about here and there. As we prepared to spend the night on the open ground, fires in the burning city lit the sky and ammunition dumps exploded. Fully dressed, bootlaces untied, I crept into my poncho-covered sleeping bag. My rifle, now my friend, lay beside me. Surprisingly, I felt positively luxurious and secure as my body warmed the flakes of snow that floated down, melting on my eyelashes, which were about all that was exposed to the starry sky above me. The Americans had sent a message to say that they would be blowing up great quantities of supplies, including food. If we wanted any 'Grab it!'

C Company lay on an open hill, with a clear view for miles. The river still had enough men on the wrong side of it to tangle with the Chinese, including the whole of 27 Brigade and two of our companies. The bridge was packed with high explosives and ready for demolition, once those men had been withdrawn. 8 and 9 Platoons of C Company,

1 Glosters would be the last to leave, together with the small handful of sappers who were there to fire the demolition.

Waking in the morning, my finger still crooked in the trigger guard of my rifle, I felt flakes of condensation crumble as I propped myself up on one elbow. Snow-covered human forms stretched across the brow of the hilltop. To my front, the valley and the river were shrouded in a white mist.

Later, I learned that one of our men, a reservist, had accidentally shot himself in the hand. If lucky, he'd be home for Christmas! Unless, of course, the wound was deemed to have been self-inflicted. That would be quite a different kettle of fish!

A couple of trucks had been acquired to scour the city. The airport had been abandoned and all disabled aircraft, plus everything else on site, had been destroyed. There was going to be nothing, and I mean nothing, left of Pyongyang but burning rubble. Here was history in the making, like the burning city of Troy. Kids in the twenty-fifth century would be saying, 'He was here, Dave Green!'

By late afternoon, the mist had cleared and so too had the convoys, with the exception of a couple of trucks, stuck halfway down the road to the bridge. The front one, its bonnet cover up, had figures bent over it, including some from a jeep which stood beside it. All were clearly working frantically to get the truck mobile again. Meanwhile, rumours that the Chinese were racing on foot down the next valley began to put some urgency on our moving out. As darkness fell, we heard that they were crossing the frozen river on skis made from maize stalks. At last the lights of the troubled truck, running on about two cylinders, which we had willed down that last stretch, could be seen as it approached the bridge, triumphant blasts of its horn echoing through the valley.

We had long been ready to go but before we left we had another visitor. 'Bed check Charlie', as it was known by 27 Brigade, was a Russian biplane that cut its engine, soaring onto its target, which in this case happened to be our side of the bridge. It silently dropped its minuscule bombs, restarted its engine and took itself off. There were a number of explosions on impact, each about the calibre of one of our Mills 36 Grenades. No one was hurt and nothing damaged but what it did do was to warn us of the proximity of the enemy.

With a roar, the bridge was blown. We didn't see it, we were far too busy making our way downhill to the ruined city. But we certainly heard it.

As we reached the road, the sapper party passed in their Land Rover, wishing us luck. We were going to need it! That sense of history again became prominent in my mind. As we trudged through the burning streets, thoughts of Napoleonic defeat went through my mind. Was ours a defeated army? No, we were just making a tactical withdrawal!

An eerie silence prevailed, broken only by the crackling of the dying embers of the shattered buildings and the tramp of our marching feet through the deserted city. At least we could now say that 8 and 9 Platoons of C Company, 1st Glosters, were the last Western troops to set foot in Pyongyang for many years to come.

We realized that what we were now engaged in was no Sunday School outing. Not only had we one hell of a march ahead of us but we were all deeply conscious of the fact that the enemy, now in the next valley, might at any time be sweeping down in hordes to cut us off. This cheerful thought encouraged us to learn the gentle art of urinating on the march as we pushed steadily on at a rhythmic pace. Luckily for us, though we did not know it at the time, having reached Pyongyang, the Chinese had a short halt to allow their supplies to catch up.

As we marched I could hear Jock McKay, who was bringing up the rear, well knowing, old soldier that he was, that before many miles were covered there would be a job for him coping with the stragglers. He was singing away to himself, his old regimental song:

'A Gordon for me. A Gordon for me.
If you're nae a Gordon, you're nae good to me.'

Poor old Jock. He'd done his full stint with the Gordon Highlanders, of whom he was intensely proud and with whom he'd seen his fair share of war. Having managed to settle himself in a steady job as a postman in his beloved Highlands, he was pretty disenchanted at having been so rudely uprooted and then put into a regiment of Sassenachs at that! I couldn't help thinking to myself that, since we were all now in the shit together and he was one of us, he might have substituted 'Gloster' for 'Gordon' in his little ditty. We could even have joined him in it!

Some hours later, with a Chinese behind every tree and in every shadow, that rhythmic movement began to crumble. The weight of a small pack and rifle, cutting into our shoulders, meant a constant re-positioning of straps and a change in the carrying of one's rifle, one way or another. Every now and then a metallic clatter would be a tell-tale of spare gear being slung – reasons to be accounted for later, as if that was of any consequence to us at that time. Our once tidy, rhythmic marching had gradually disappeared. We had done 30 mile forced marches in training but they were as nothing to this slog. It had become a case of every man for himself.

Pete, who had been in front with 8 Platoon, had now straggled back and I had taken him under my wing.

'Come on, mucker, soon be there.'

'Soon be fuckin' where?'

Our feet were blistered and to stop would mean curtains.

'What was that school in Gloucester you went to, Pete? Hatherley, wasn't it? They were pretty bloody hopeless, weren't they, turning out blokes like you?'

'Whadya mean? We played rugby, not that cissy game you played. I'm going to have a rest. Fuck 'em.'

I grabbed his shoulder, dragging him down the road. Had we only been able to sing, the going would have been easier but to have done so would have been a sure pointer for the enemy. The soldier's prayer, which a veteran on the *Windrush* had taught me, came into my mind:

> *'Stay with me God, the night is dark,*
> *The night is cold, my little spark of courage dims,*
> *The nightmare road is long.*
> *Be with me God and make me strong.'*

It might have been written for us!

For what seemed like an eternity I dragged Pete on. There were times when it would have been so much easier just to have packed it in. I had taken his small pack, which he had tried to throw away, and we battled on. How well I remembered him showing me photos of his family which he kept in that pack! It was encouraging and even made me laugh to hear Pete say to a group of his platoon that we actually overtook:

'Keep it up, muckers! Won't be for long.'

We had left our positions at 1900 the previous evening and night had long since passed and we were still going. Word was passed that there was a good hot meal waiting, just down the road. 'Just down the road'. It was always 'Just down the road'. But somehow the words offered some sort of hope. Otherwise, our deranged lot, who were all supporting each other in small groups, would have been quite ready to throw in the towel.

Somehow, we made it. We had marched for hours and hours, non-stop, covering, we learned later, an unbelievable 60 miles.

There was more to come! Whacker Walker, who had been given his orders by some officer, came over, dejectedly relaying his message, for he knew just what response it would produce:

'Dig in.'

There was no need to look at the mens' faces to know how that was received – with utter incredulity. Needless to say, that hot meal had been a myth. Feeling more like zombies than soldiers and ravenously hungry, there was no way that any of them would comply.

I dug in alright, in disgust, under a big tarpaulin laid out to dry. I couldn't have cared less if a herd of wild elephants had stampeded through. I was knackered. Nevertheless, when I emerged a few hours later, I was glad to see that no one had dug in and no one had eaten. I was even gladder to see what a narrow escape I had had – vehicles had been driving over my tarp whilst I was in residence!

On the following day, still very sore, we dug into the solid ground, only to be told that we were moving back to Kaesong, still as part of the rearguard to the withdrawing UN Forces. Apparently, the idea now was to draw the Chinese forward, stretching their supply lines and enabling the greatly superior UN air forces to create havoc against them.

So, once again, we were on the move but, fortunately, in the comfort of a nice three-ton truck. We hadn't been long on the road when we seemed to have caught up the rear of the columns of local people fleeing from the approaching enemy. They were a pitiful sight. Some had even lost their flimsy, slip-on rubber shoes in the mud. With temperatures well below freezing, their plight was indescribable. Men and women with 'A' frames on their backs, packed with enormous loads. Children were staggering with babies on their backs. A few of the more fortunate had ox-carts but it was no picnic for any of them. Most were starving, all were frozen and none had any certain future. As we stood in the back of our truck, we looked on with a feeling of guilt as we rolled forward in the slipstream of these poor people who had scrambled out of the way of our leading trucks. But what could we do? The scale of the tragedy seemed unending.

We came to a small town. As we approached the town square, which was about the size of a large football pitch, we saw a Korean in a khaki uniform and clutching a rifle, emerge from the crowd on one side of the square, doubling what seemed obviously to be a civilian prisoner. He was tall and skinny with longish black hair, shoeless and dressed in the traditional white peasant garb. Around his mouth, in his unshaven whispy growth, we could see what we took to be either the remains of a quickly devoured rice meal or the results of an epileptic fit. We guessed that he had attempted to escape. One of our blokes jokingly gestured to the guard to shoot him, whereupon the guard pointed to the square.

There, out in the middle, a few hundred yards away, another guard stood with about another fifty prisoners, all standing in ranks, with heads bowed. As the new prisoner was delivered to him, the poor wretch fell on his knees before him. Then, after a short pause, he got up and began to run towards the distant hills, with his arms flailing. He was literally running for his life, which ended with a calmly raised rifle and a shot in the back. As he lay in the snow, another shot jolted his body and he was dead. The joker, visibly shaken, looked first at me and then at Danny. This was Korea, what could we possibly do?

I looked at my rifle and, for a moment, a mad thought entered my mind, so angered was I by what we had seen. To hit a standing man several hundred yards away from a moving truck was the height of improbability and, as I instantly realized, worse, an act of total irresponsibility which, if successful, could carry a very severe penalty. In any case, the guards were standing in front of the luckless prisoners, so the idea was a non-starter anyway.

Very soon we were well clear of the town but from the numerous shots that we heard echoing in the distance, we were left in no doubt about the fate of those unfortunate souls.

'You were only joking, mate', we consoled the wretched jester. Ashen-faced and full of remorse, all he could mutter was 'Bastards.'

5

A Touch of Frostbite

North of Kaesong once more, we dug our weapon pits. A very large blister on my right heel, a legacy from The March, had turned a nasty shade of blue and my foot had swollen so much that I was no longer able to get a boot on. Jock McKay took one look at it and told me to report sick, which I gladly did.

'Pack your kit and be back here at 1100 hours', said the Medical Officer. 'I'm sending you back to hospital to get this sorted out.'

As I hopped my way past the queue waiting outside the RAP*, I waved my ticket in the air with a loud shout of 'Yippee!'

With just one kit bag and a packet of sandwiches, I boarded the truck that was to take me to the makeshift American holding centre for transportation to Pusan. My rifle and second kit bag had been taken off me to await my return.

That night I shared the floor of what had once been a cinema with a number of American walking wounded. Next morning I duly queued with a bunch of GIs** waiting to board a truck for the railhead. To my surprise, the bloke in front of me proved to be an officer – something that just could not happen in the British Army where the old dogma that familiarity breeds contempt holds sway, for officers to mix with Other Ranks is 'just not on'. He turned to me and examined my battle dress with interest. When he got to my regimental shoulder titles, he read out, in his rich, American accent, 'Glou-ces-ter-shire Regiment. And what Gook did you take those from?' he said, pointing at my plimsolls – the

---

* RAP: Regimental Aid Post.
** GI: American term for an Enlisted Man.

53

only form of footwear I could bear on my frostbitten foot. He obviously thought I was a seasoned warrior from the fighting in the north.

As a truck started backing up to our line, he looked at me and then at his kit bag. 'Be back in a jiffy, buddy', he said and took off. The steps of the truck were lowered and we began to board. No sign of my officer so I took his kit bag with me, assuming that he had left it for me to look after whilst he was away for 'a jiffy'. The truck shot off as soon as it was loaded and I was left holding the baby. What could I do? Throw it out of the back? Hopefully, he would follow and come to find me. Meanwhile I hung on to it, wondering, with my inquisitive mind, just what it contained.

An Australian soldier, who had been waiting in another queue, had spotted my British uniform and had slipped across to join me. Sitting himself down at my side he greeted me:

'G'day bloke!' He was a good old 'dinky di'. He had been up on the Manchurian border with 27 Brigade. A splinter from a grenade had penetrated his right eye, which was covered with a black patch, giving him a rather piratical appearance. Apart from his slouch hat and insignia, we were dressed alike. He was a lot older than me but was as interested in England as I was in Australia.

We arrived at the railhead and were soon on a train heading for Pusan, smoking American cigarettes and chewing gum. 'When in Rome . . .'

We had each been issued with a couple of boxes of C6 rations. These had a little burner upon which to heat the various cans, a tin opener, cigarettes and a packet of chewing gum.

My newly-arrived cobber had taken a lot of photographs of the fighting up north but admitted that many of them had been taken on delayed time exposure, the camera being slipped quickly from its cover onto a suitable rock. No matter how they were taken, I found them extremely interesting.

Most of our fellow travellers were either suffering from minor wounds or some illness. Like most Americans, they were very friendly and generous. We soon found that they had a great deal of respect for British and Aussie soldiers, so we felt very much at home with them.

My Aussie mate was delighted to find that I was familiar with both poker and crap ('Come on, seven or eleven, baby!) with both of which I had become indoctrinated by my American friends in what were known as the 'Yankee' Camps during the war years. 'Yankee' is a name the Americans dislike and, having respect for them, I never used it in their company if I could help it, but that was the name given and used by all and sundry. Those hutted camps were dotted all over Southern England from 1942 onwards as the invasion forces for Normandy grew and as more of the United States Air Force arrived to carry out their costly bombing raids over Europe. As I have described in an earlier chapter, those camps were heaven on earth for youngsters like me, truants from school and delighted to earn good money for little jobs.

Rolling the dice down the central aisle between the carriage seats, my new-found mate really looked the part, had it not been for his uniform. There he crouched, a big cigar hanging out of his mouth and chewing gum as he crooned to the dice 'Speak to me baby'.

Eventually, my curiosity about the contents of the officer's kit bag, which was still beside me, got the better of me. So, rogue that I am, I took a look inside. All that it contained was a feather down sleeping bag and a beautiful goathair pile hat – both of real quality.

After many stops and starts, we pulled into a delapidated railway station in Pusan. A horde of kids, who had been sitting in their gangs around the fires they had lit between the lines, came to greet us. I guessed that they must be living in the many derelict carriages strewn around the place. Like alley cats dressed in oversize military gear, many had the wizened faces of old men. We gave those kids the treat of their short lives – enough C6 rations to keep their little army going for some while.

A number of trucks were waiting to take us to the large American military hospital nearby. When we got there, I could hardly believe my luck when all our clothes were taken away for de-lousing and cleaning and we were issued with a complete US uniform, including underclothes, boots, kit bag – the lot.

A pretty young American nurse gave me a shot in the arm. She didn't see many 'Limeys' and, unless my vivid imagination was seriously astray, I could tell that she took a fancy to me. Then, after a nice shower, clean pyjamas and new slippers, it was into bed, without the nurse, I'm sad to say, but another did come to dress my foot, which had grown no worse.

My Aussie friend was no longer with me, probably having gone to a surgical ward where that eye of his would get sorted out. Frankly, I was perfectly happy to stay where I was, enjoying the unaccustomed luxury of it all. However, I could not get those kids at the railway station out of my mind. Like English kids around the Yankee camps during the war, they were looking for anything they could scrounge or steal. Poor little devils, my only wish was that they could share the same treatment as we did.

It wasn't long before I discovered two other Glosters in the hospital. One, a real cockney, had wasted no time in seeking me out. Bill Cox, tall and slim, with that slick city look of 'seen it all, mate', was a real wide boy. Although he could walk, if he were to be believed, he had every unknown or undiagnosable disease going. That was for now, but he would have no problem fixing that too, for in truth, there was nothing

55

wrong with him, but he was a master of the art of convincing malingering. He'd simply got fed up with the discomfort of life in the field in the Korean winter and had decided that a nice spell in dock would be the thing for him. When he'd had enough of that, he'd be off back to his mates in time for Christmas!

'Bit of orl right 'ere, Tosher', he said, sitting on my bed and quipping the shapely nurse in her tight smock, as she stretched to adjust a light fitting.

'Wot yer got then?' he said, pointing at my bandaged foot. ''Ere, I'll soon make that better'. Picking up a slipper, he swatted the blanket around my foot.

'Missed! Come 'ere. Don't worry, I'll get it', he mused.

I thought to myself, 'We've got a right character here!'

After a bit more banter, he stood up. 'Oops, me back's gorn agin! Better get back or I'll miss me orange juice. You know wot I mean, Tosh?' Then as he limped away, he threw over his shoulder, 'Shrapnel's playing up a bit.'

My first meal was breakfast. The luxury was unbelievable. Steaks, as many as you wanted, eggs, smoked frankfurters, creamed corn. There was a choice of single cartons of a wide variety of cereals and, in little tins, grapefruit, pineapple and apple juices – and all served by beautiful Japanese girls. My mind went to Pete – this lot would be just his handwriting!

Bill had reappeared, still cracking jokes, and we stood together at the counter where I inhaled the rich aroma of strong coffee, something I had always associated with wealth.

We found a table and put down our well-laden plates, only to see the lot collapse when I accidentally kicked one of the table legs. Somewhat embarrassed, as help came from all directions, we left the scene, filtering off into the crowded room to start again. Our re-enactment, 'Take Two', found us tucked well away, lost in the large mess with our refuelled plates. There were no flies on us!

Another couple of luxurious days passed and my foot was healing much too quickly for my liking. However, I was moved to another ward, or should I say billet, and all my kit was handed back to me. The free issue GI uniform was mine for keeps! I had become an out-patient!

I felt a bit uncomfortable in my new abode as the bloke in the next bed was an American officer, who was treated by the GIs as just another 'buddy'. Opposite, in every sense, was a Turkish soldier. His uniform fascinated me. It was a very coarse version of British battledress but the gaiters were actually attached to the trouser-leg!

I had packed my own uniform away in my kitbag along with the rest of my kit, including the newly-acquired sleeping bag. I fastened my

Gloster's cap badge to the goathair cap and was now a UN soldier! The sight would have given my Commanding Officer apoplexy and me about three months in the glasshouse*. In my well-fitting GI uniform and my highly original headgear, my army belt and GI boots, I thought I looked just the part. On my first venture out into Pusan, I was challenged by the sentry on the hospital gate when I returned. Not knowing what was required, I answered 'Friend', to which he replied 'Oh, French! OK buddy carry on. Qui passe!' And so it went on. I could come and go as I pleased.

Whilst foraging around during that day, I had met a little Korean boy who wanted to buy anything, such as cigarettes, clothes or whatever.

In my pidgin Korean I told him, 'No worries son. Tomorrow I'll meet you here.'

My Korean cannot have been that bad because, when I arrived at his pitch next day, there he was. I had a kitbag full of goodies and he had plenty of US dollars. I found it as easy as falling out of bed to replace this stuff from the Quartermaster's stores. Of those in charge there, I never saw the same face twice.

We soon had a thriving business going, my little friend and I. God knows where he sold it all, but he always wanted more. Within days I had a wad of money – US dollars, British BAFSVs** and Hong Kong dollars.

One night I got a lift into town from a GI ambulance driver who drove first to a sleazy dock area where he told me he had to meet someone.

'Don't ya worry, buddy, me and you are goin' to have a ball.'

Stopping the ambulance, he reached over his seat to pick up a package.

'Hang on there, Limey.'

Across the street stood a tall sinister-looking Gook, dressed in a black smock and a black-brimmed Tibetan-looking hat. The two exchanged parcels.

On his return, the driver openly told me that he was supplying penicillin to this bloke and being handsomely rewarded. I thought, 'Yeah, but who is he supplying it to?' I didn't like it one bit.

Back in the city centre, we sat in a little café where we had a choice of about four different coloured moonshine concoctions. Suspiciously, all smelled the same. Petrol with meths; petrol with paint thinners; who was to know and who cared anyway? Taken in a glass the size of a large

* Glasshouse: Military slang for a Detention Centre.
** BAFSVs: British Armed Forces Special Vouchers. Token currency issued to troops on campaign overseas.

thimble, you either knocked it back or sipped it. The second course was quite definitely not recommended – it was horrible!

The American wasn't a bad bloke. He seemed to know everyone, where to go and, like most of his compatriots, very generous with his ill-gotten cash. I thought I had plenty but he could afford to use his for toilet paper.

'I'll take you to a whorehouse', he promised. This sounded like a good idea for it was an experience I had yet to explore. Sure enough, that was where we ended up but not before visiting a couple of other watering holes and drinking more than was good for us. In some back-street shack, I found myself with a young, plumpish but quite attractive Korean girl. She made love to me more than once whilst I, with my inebriated brain, was trying to figure out what in the hell was going on.

The very next day, I had a pain in my private parts. I had all the symptoms of a venereal disease. Had it been a few days later, it would have had me worried. As it was, I kept the problem to myself, too embarrassed to see the doctor or even tell Bill, of whom I had not seen very much lately, as he was still in the main part of the hospital.

Where I was now billeted, we had our own little mess hall and I kept very much to myself, not mixing with anyone in particular and keeping a pretty low profile. My foot had healed rapidly and I had stopped going to the out-patients' ward. There was so much coming and going that the staff seemed to have absolutely no control and I realised that I could stay on and continue to enjoy life for a bit longer. Each night I would creep into bed. Next morning, up with the lark, I would wash and shave, sweep my bedspace and that of the American officer and make my bed, then away for the day! I think the officer thought I was one of the staff. I called him 'Sir' and avoided him like the plague. Very much the loner, I was thoroughly enjoying myself. However, I took good care not to get involved with the ambulance driver again and kept well away from the Happy Havens! Most of those I encountered simply could not fathom who the hell I was. Dressed in what I called my United Nations outfit, I looked more like Davy Crocket than Davy Green!

An incident which disturbed me very much was my encounter with a poor little kid as I was crossing a bridge. Dressed in rags, with size ten boots on his bare feet, he came screaming up to me, beating my legs and wailing. I could tell that the uniform I wore signified to him the cause of all the horrors that his poor little soul had endured. I just stood there, looking up to the skies and blaspheming against the so-called heavens and their so-called God.

'What's this poor little kid done to deserve this?' I cried as he ran off, still wailing.

What little faith I had, I had always sought for more. Both Mum and

Dad were deeply religious but I have to confess that, over the years, I had challenged their faith many times. That little scrap of tortured humanity, and all the other suffering kids I had seen, made my blood boil. Life just was not fair! My little spark of faith had grown very dim indeed.

Some would say that at just nineteen, I was still only a boy and that my solitary excursions had a good measure of risk attached to them. Not that I thought about that at the time – which goes to show how immature and naïve I still was. But I had always prided myself on my ability to take care of things. However, one night, which will always be engraved on my memory, I had a close encounter.

I was looking around a small shop when I noticed the woman who owned it saying something to one of her children and pointing at me. The kid came out with an apprehensive look on his face, giving me a final glance as he ran off up the street. Almost at once, two shifty-looking Koreans came into the shop, one standing by the door, the other speaking with some agitation with the woman.

By now I was fully switched on to the situation. Sure enough, they made towards me, the one in front putting his hand inside his jacket from which appeared what was unmistakeably the handle of a large knife. Shaping up to them, I shouted, '*Spraken de Deutche*', which always sounded pretty good to me. God knows how or why that came out from me then but German always sounds authoritative. Even my bastard version worked like a charm. I had frightened them to death! They shot out of the shop door and the woman ran out of the back. My ego boosted no end, I stood over the counter and shouted at the figure I could see skulking against the darkened background.

'Don't you try fucking the British around, lady.'

Pointing at my cap badge, I added, 'Britisher . . . me! *Englisho!*' and with a two-fingered 'V' sign I left the shop only to run into another fracas almost immediately.

'Whew! Watch it Dave!'

A big American ship was in dock. On board were the survivors of the US cavalry units who, with the help of the British 41st Royal Marine Commando, had escaped through Hungnam, on the east coast, after being cut off further north by the Chinese. A couple of these cavalrymen, who were only about my age, had grabbed an old street vendor around his neck and were throttling him and shouting, 'You gooks killed my buddies, you motherfucker.'

The poor man was old enough to be their grandfather and was obviously as blameless as I. So, jumping from the frying pan into the fire, I shouted, 'Hey, come on you blokes. Leave him alone, he's only an old man and your buddies' deaths were nothing to do with him.' I pleaded with them, taking their hands away from his throat – not aggressively but in an understanding way.

'Come on fellas. Leave him alone!'

They had clearly been out on the town and, swaying in the breeze, they were patently the worse for wear. The least intoxicated one, with his arm around his mate, said, 'Let's go, buddy. Shape up and ship out.'

Ship out they did, staggering down the street and shouting obscenities at everybody and everything, including a lamp standard. Meanwhile, bowing profusely, the grateful old man, with his whispy beard, was beginning to make me feel that I possessed some sort of divine power. Much later, with the help of a flagon-sized bottle of hooch which I had picked up from a back street shop window, I had become convinced that I had. If I had run into those two drunken Americans again, they could have knocked me over with a fly-swatter.

Down in the dock area, where the tops of the big ships could be seen towering above the roofs of the large warehouses, I became aware of the sound of a multitude of voices and decided to investigate. Still clutching my bottle, I entered a door and discovered that the voices were coming from the other side of a ten-foot partition wall. Taking a last swig at the poisonous muck, helped down with a handful of Lifesaver sweets, I took a running jump and grabbed the top of the partition. With the strength of Samson, I somehow pulled myself up onto it. There I saw spread before me some hundreds of Korean refugees. Much to their amusement, I lowered myself down into the midst of this throng.

Rubbing the heads of the little kids, as though I were some incarnation of the Queen Mother, I dished out my Lifesavers and cigarettes.

'*Me Yongu* (English). We'll save you. The great English warriors are here', I cried, almost pounding my chest like some latter-day Tarzan. That stuff had certainly gone to my head. I was as pissed as a newt.

The next thing I remember was being out in the street once more, desperately grabbing one leg after the other, trying to make myself walk, though where to, God only knows. I was almost paralytic, plastered as I had never been before.

My saviour, in the form of a smiling Korean soldier or policeman, though for all I could comprehend he might well have been Genghis Khan, took my weight and, with my arm wrapped over his shoulder, we staggered along. By now my speech was completely incomprehensible, even to me, and my kind friend finished up with me over his shoulder, cheerfully carrying me for what seemed like miles.

How he knew where to take me remains a mystery to this day. I awoke with a king-sized hangover which my now fragile body took more than a week to recover from. Incredibly, I was in the right hospital and the right bed!

With my tail between my legs, this little lamb swore that never again would he wander from the fold. I sought solace with my old friend Bill. Believe it or not, we came to the conclusion that the time had come to abandon this life of ease, luxury and debauchery and move on. Christmas was near and we both wanted to rejoin our mates, like the good soldiers we were.

We made our decision known to the right authorities, who gave us our discharge papers and arranged for us to be transported to the Commonwealth Transit Camp, just outside Pusan. There, in stark contrast to the delights of the hospital, we shared a bell tent, which looked as if it had been one of a hundred others but had been left in its solitary and dingy glory when all the rest were taken away. Pitched at the far end of the camp, in low ground, from which you could just about see the administration buildings run by the Australians, it suited us down to the ground. Out of sight, out of mind. It was luxury when compared with our dugouts in the line. Our one companion was a lone British Commando. We learned from him that the only Aussies running the place were an Adjutant and a private soldier, who we had yet to encounter. Left to our own devices, eat or starve were the choices before us. There would be no handouts here.

Our tentmate lay on his bed, made up on the bare ground reading a book. A carton of beer stood beside him, with the compliments of the US cavalry soldiers who his Commando had helped out of Hungnam. No doubt he had come off that ship in port and was a bit of a hero.

I had not had a drink since that awful night – even the smell of that terrible hooch was still with me for over a week. So my interest in alcohol was in suspense, for the present at least. Back in my Glosters uniform again, I paid a final visit to Pusan, with a kitbag full of the US gear for which I had no further use – a complete uniform, boots and all – and sought out my little friend. Payment? A big grin from ear to ear and a can of American salted peanuts!

On my way back to the camp, I encountered another little kid who had set up by the roadside. He was selling apples – something for which Korea is famed the world over. Peanuts and apples made a meal fit for a king, cleansing my body and soul. I went on my way back to camp on Cloud 9. I felt great and as free as the wind.

I dived into the tent. There lay home-loving wide boy Bill who at once dived into the box I was carrying. Apple in hand, he peered down to see what other goodies it contained.

'Bleedin' apples!'

'Yeah, Daddy Christmas', I replied.

'I'm starvin' Tosh! he went on. 'These sodding Aussies have got fuck all. Poxy 'ole this is.' He looked a dismal sight.

'Errol Flynn 'ere,' he went on, pointing to our Commando friend's empty bed space, 'reckons there's a Yankee Ordnance Dump dahn the road where we can get fixed up. Ee's gorn aht with 'is cronies.' Doubtless those cronies were some of the survivors of the 2nd US Division who 41 Commando had done so much to help, getting them out of one hell of a tight hole, as they were getting engulfed by a swarm of Chinese.

Errol Flynn was right about that Ordnance Dump and, next day, a big American staff sergeant was telling us to help ourselves and saying, 'You Limeys are makin' a name for yourselves out there.'

You could tell he had seen little of that 'out there'. He probably couldn't even imagine what was going on. What's more, he didn't want to know. Who could blame him?

Stacked to the roof were boxes of one-man C6 rations, which I had first encountered on the train going down to Pusan.

'There ya go, Whitey, that should see you right', he drawled, as he pushed half-a-dozen packs under my arm. I wasn't too struck by being called 'Whitey'. I'd been called some names in my time, such as 'Snowball' and 'Blondie', but Whitey seemed to smack of some sort of albino. However, who was I to look a gift horse in the mouth? He certainly meant no offence and, like most Americans, could not do enough for us.

'We've bin orf ter see the Wizard, the wonderful Wizard of Oz', sang Bill as we marched off down the road back to that lonely tent.

'Abaht ten days' rations 'ere, Tosher', he said, and couldn't praise enough the generosity of our long-lost cousins from across the Pond. 'The good old Yanks, mate, always 'elped us out of the shit. 'Ave a snout son.'

At about ten o'clock next morning, our plans to get back to the Regiment suffered a bit of a setback as we breakfasted on mixed fruit, hamburgers heated on our little burners, and crackers. Just as I was about to light up a good old 'Lucky Strike', we were rudely disturbed by a brash private of the Australian Army.

'Gidday. What are you blokes supposed to be doing 'ere? Where do ya come from?'

We had not informed anyone of our presence in the camp.

This little bantam cock hardly matched up to our expectations of a 'Digger', apart from his slouch hat, being all of five foot nothing. However, what he lacked in height, he more than made up for in aggression and persistence. As for our reasons for being there, he was not going to be happy until we'd seen his Adjutant. Anyone might have thought that he was heading a couple of stray sheep as we crossed the field to the admin block, with his little legs going two to our one and his arms waving like windmills.

Following his directions, we went into a little office where we were soon explaining our itinerary to a casual and bemused officer, who was more or less telling us not to 'take any notice of this little runt' as the runt continued to go on like an old woman. He told us that a couple of trucks were coming through shortly and we could get a lift in one of them to the railway station at Samrangjin and then take a train. Apparently, our brigade was now just north of Seoul.

Sure enough, the trucks appeared next day and, packed and ready to go, we got our lift.

Samrangjin station was like all those we had already seen. As day began to change to night, we boarded a northbound train. A handful of Korean passengers were already aboard. There was no problem about tickets or ticket inspectors, for neither existed. The train was either going north or south, the driver and his mate being in sole charge on the line.

It looked as if they were doing some repairs to the underside of the train, making frequent trips to the only light, apart from their lamps, which came from a large fire in a tumbledown railway hut.

We soon made ourselves comfortable, each of us to a long wooden seat. With kitbags for pillows and a good old British Army greatcoat, arms folded and hands tucked into our sleeves, bootlaces untied – what more could a soldier ask for?

As we reminisced over the previous day's events, we had a good laugh about that silly little Digger.

'Right arse'ole that little cobber, eh Dave? Grovelling little bastard. 'E wants to get up norf wiv 'is mates.'

'You'd soon put one on 'im, wouldn't ya Bill?' I joked.

'No worries! 'It 'im wiv me 'andbag!' he scoffed.

Morning came and we were still sitting in our depressing station although a fresh fall of snow had lent it an air of slight respectability. The snow clinging to the carriage windows added a little warmth to the interior. One of the Korean passengers went over to the hut in which the train crew had spent the night and returned, gesticulating, and saying, 'Soon OK, choo-choo-choo!'

An hour and a half later, choo-choo-chooing, we were on our way north bound for Taegu. We shared, or rather gave out, breakfast to our Korean companions, who were overcome by our generosity and fascinated by the little burners from the C6 packs, which we showed them how to use.

Taegu had a bit more going for it in the way of buildings and as the train was having its usual long stopover, we had a bit of a walk round. We came across a nice-looking Korean girl selling roasted peanuts in their shells and swapped some with her for a packet of fags. Meeting a girl like that was unusual for, in most of the places we had been to so far, the girls were kept in hiding. She was about my age and her eyes sparkled as she smiled.

When we got to Taejon, or what was left of it, we learned that the train would be stopping there overnight. As we did not want to spend a night in that junkyard and we had time in hand, we jumped on the southbound train back to Taegu. In holiday spirits we sang:

> '*Spiving around the West End, in all the spiv hotels,*
> *Living a life of ease and luxury . . .*'

Back in Taegu, we stepped off into the dark, chilly night, our vaporised, warm breath dissolving into thin air. We made our way towards the still intact building from whence flickered the tell-tale light of a fire. The building's occupants, Korean refugees, beckoned us into its shell. Needless to say, the windows and door had long since gone. An unbelievably wrinkled old man, as thin as a stick, the sight of whom made Bill say that he'd 'seen more fat on a greasy chip', tended the fire, packing in the unburned ends of railway sleepers. The large arched stone fireplace would not have looked out of place in any English country pub. Its heat soon melted the large snowflakes as they were blown in by the wind. There was plenty of room, so we cleared the broken glass and rubble on the paved floor with our boots and sat ourselves amongst the refugees.

'Good on yer, Grandad!' greeted Bill, as he grinned at the old man, who responded with an upward movement of his wizened, outstretched arm towards the fire. The old chap was crouching in oriental fashion with his back to the wall. He wore a fur hat, with the untied earflaps hanging down each side of his wrinkled face, and smoked a very long-stemmed pipe with a tiny silver bowl.

In an opposite corner sat our friend the peanut girl. Her face was very attractive in the light of the fire and her now hatless head of raven black hair shone in the glow. Beside her sat another girl of about the same age. The other occupants of the room were three middle-aged couples, their pathetic bundles of worldly possessions at their sides.

Both Bill and I, having had experience of wartime England, felt a strong sense of sympathy towards these poor people. Bill had been evacuated, with his nametag pinned to his coat, to Wales. At the latter end of the war, he had joined the Army. As for me, I had spent many a night under the stairs or the kitchen table whilst Cheltenham was bombed and certainly knew what it was to have an empty stomach.

'What do you reckon then, mate?' I said, knowing full well how he was thinking. If we were going to eat, we were all going to eat together.

'Wot we got left, Dodger?'

A quick check revealed that we had two and a half C6 packs each. One pack contains more than enough rations for a single man for one day, so we were loaded.

'It's Christmas!'

Our newfound friends sensed what was happening as we dug into our kitbags. Like Huskies in the Arctic, even their hats bristled! They sat themselves, with legs crossed, in a semi-circle as we shared our wares with them. Their happy faces gave Bill and I great satisfaction. This might be a Christmas such as we had never known before, but Christmas it was and a very merry one too!

6

Close Encounters

Lieutenant General Walker, the UN Ground Forces Commander and Commanding General of the US 8th Army, was killed in a jeep accident on 23 December. On 27 December his place was taken by Lieutenant General Ridgway, the famous commander of the 82nd US Airborne Division in 1944–45.

On Christmas Day the Communists crossed the 38th Parallel and on 1 January, 1951, opened their new offensive, the UN forces withdrawing before them and evacuating Seoul on 4 January. Three days later, the enemy were in Wonju and all roads south were crammed with refugees.

Unable to hold the enemy's advance, by mid-January Ridgway had withdrawn to a firm defensive line stretching from Pyontaek on the west coast, some 75 miles south of the Parallel, across to a point on the east coast 40 miles south of it.

Meanwhile, General McArthur was pressing Washington for permission to bomb Manchuria and for Nationalist Chinese reinforcements. Both requests were refused and McArthur began to sulk, convinced that his President and fellow countrymen had lost the will to win, a view reinforced by the US Government's support in the UN for a cease-fire proposal put to the Chinese on 13 January and which they rejected on the 17th. President Truman had also declared that he was unwilling to consider any use of the atomic bomb, something that had clearly been mooted.

★　　　★　　　★

Full of thoughts of Christmas with their mates, the two prodigal sons finally reached the Battalion on 23 December and reported for duty, only to find that they were just one day too late. Because it had been suspected that the Chinese might take advantage of the Christmas celebrations and launch their new offensive, which was clearly on its way, Christmas had been brought forward by three days.

We found the Regiment in Corps Reserve just north of Seoul. The rest of the Brigade was forward in the line, the 27th Commonwealth Brigade being on our right.

We had arrived towards the end of the morning, at a borrowed American marquee, to find the whole camp flattened by a king-size hangover. Inside the marquee itself there were all the signs of one hell of a night. Half-emptied glasses adorned the top of a battered grand piano, which had been conjured up from God knows where, and even the elaborately decorated Christmas tree was hanging its head. All this was little to wonder at for, apart from the daily rum ration of about half a mug per platoon, alcohol had been off the menu virtually since we had arrived in Korea. For the occasion, our Colour Sergeant had apparently made a very potent rum punch from tins of diced fruit, rum and a couple of 'never you minds' – brake fluid, Brasso or meths? Tins of canned beer had been there for the taking since the previous day.

After gazing at the devastation, I made my way back to 9 Platoon which I found bivouacked, as usual, in an isolated spot. It was great to see Danny and Stan, who had lost none of their good humour and gave me a great welcome.

I gathered that, apart from reports of heavy troop concentrations, no actual contact with the Chinese had yet been made and that the hope was that they would halt at the 38th Parallel. However, that pious hope was to be shattered two days later, on Christmas Day. For the first time, even though in reserve, we were really 'up the sharp end' in real war – no more guerrilla hunting but tough fighting against an enemy that would fall upon us like a swarm of locusts. It was impossible not to have that feeling of apprehension which the prospect of a very tough scrap creates. Our attached 4.2" mortar battery, 170 Battery Royal Artillery, was soon to be in action quite often and I would wonder to myself just what it must be like for the Chinese to be on the receiving end. As our own shells whistled overhead, especially at night, I would be constantly reminded that the enemy were not far away and would suddenly realize that my stomach was tense and rigid. It took a lot of willpower to train oneself to relax. In reserve we might be, but we knew very well that if our mates in the line got into trouble, it would be our job to counter-attack to recover any ground lost or to act as rearguard in the event of a withdrawal. So we were waiting to bat!

New Year's Eve we celebrated by platoons with an extra rum ration, the aluminium mug being passed from hand to hand. The tinny twang of the first sip, with lips and teeth touching ice-cold metal, sent a shiver down your back.

Of course, being hogmanay, it was Jock's night, so we were upstanding, drinking a toast. A wee wet of the whistle!

During the Battalion's comparatively long occupation of our present location, which the lads had nicknamed 'Compo Valley', the platoon had rigged up quite a good lean-to shelter to protect us from the freezing winds. We had a ten-gallon drum, pierced with holes, as a brazier and as we gathered round it that evening, revelling in the welcome heat it was giving out, we sang a Scottish song in Jock's honour:

> *'I'm a decent railway porter*
> *And me name is Willy Gee.*
> *You can search all the stations*
> *From Dumbarton to Dundee*
> *But you never will set eyes on*
> *A more decent chap than me!*
> *And me duty is to tell ye*
> *Where to change fer.*
>
> *Chorus:*
>
> *Change for Ecklefechan an' Aberdeen*
> *An' all the stations in between,*
> *Unless yer goin' ter Tobermory.'*

Small wonder that I found it hard crawling out of my sleeping bag in the early hours of that New Year morning to do my 'stag'.*

We had had a heavy fall of snow, which now glistened in the light of the full moon. As I stood at the edge of a group of scattered, leafless trees, my rifle slung over my shoulder, I suddenly became aware of a large feline figure, nose to the ground, slinking towards me. I stood transfixed, undecided whether to unsling my rifle into the ready, though I realized that it was already a bit late for that. Still with its nose to the ground, the great beast veered slightly away as it passed only about fifteen yards from me, revealing itself as a very healthy and sleek mountain tiger.

The evidence flattened the cynics as we inspected the pad marks in the snow. 'What, tigers in Korea?'

'Yes, look at those pad marks, just feet away from where I was standing.'

On that New Years Day the Chinese opened their new offensive and

---

* Stag: Army slang for a spell on guard duty. In this case, I had to patrol the platoon area.

68

things began to hot up. They had begun with a full-scale attack in broad daylight, presumably to feel out the strength of the opposition but, either because of the weight of fire they encountered or because they had discovered what they wanted to know, they pulled back.

Their patrols were now being spotted on all fronts, which meant a fifty per cent stand to for us, by day and night. Shells began to whistle overhead non-stop, keeping us all very much on our toes.

On our left, the American 25th Division had withdrawn, leaving the road and our left flank exposed. Just as we had got ourselves all geared up for battle, orders arrived for us too to withdraw. We were becoming dab hands at this game by now and within half an hour we were ready to board the trucks waiting to take us off at full belt for Seoul.

As they had done earlier in the north, the Chinese had swept down in overwhelming numbers, across the hills and down the valleys, isolating whole divisions. In our brigade both the Ulsters and the Northumberlands were in trouble and needed tank support. A troop of Churchills from C Squadron 7th Royal Tanks went to help the Geordies, who managed to get things sorted out. However, the paddies had two companies isolated. A group of ten Cromwells was sent to them by the 8th Hussars.* During the night they took a terrible hiding from a massive attack and virtually all the tanks were knocked out by Chinese pole charges.

Abandoned Seoul, its once majestic buildings battered into mere shells, stood as a grim and silent witness to the passage of defeated armies.

As we crossed the Han River by such bridges as had survived, our sole desire in 9 Platoon was to keep going. This extraordinary war seemed to became increasingly pointless. As far as we were concerned, Communism was just a dirty word. What we were enduring was a nightmare and a long, long way from dear old England.

The refugees who had been sheltering in the city were now on the move once more, throwing dead or new-born babies into the freezing river as they left. Iced almost to its centre, that wide river brought instant and decisive relief from a burden that could not be buried in the iron hard frozen ground or which the poor mothers were unable to feed. The sight was heart-rending and unforgettable. Bill Cox and I had had our first experience of this tragedy when making the last part of our journey from Taegu with a beautifully dressed, doll-like baby, its peaceful, serene little face averted from a tragic world and its tiny nose stuffed

---

* The Cromwells came from the 8th Hussars Recce Troop and 45 Field Regiment RA. Korea was difficult country for tanks, which tended to slide on the frozen hillsides or in the muddy paddy.

with cotton wool. It had simply been abandoned on the seat of the railway carriage.

Ships were leaving Pusan daily, taking the civilian population to the islands off the south coast. Rumours of enemy penetration of these seemingly endless columns were rife. They all looked the same to us.

Yongdopo, with its tall industrial chimney stacks, was packed with humanity, the poor devils staggering to one side as we sloshed our way through their ranks. These people were not only a real hindrance to our movements but also a serious threat to our security. Nobody knew who or what was coming through with them.

We had passed through Anyang, Uiwang and Suwon, once again stopping at the last-named for a couple of days, enabling me to go off on one of my many lone explorations.

Looking back, I realize that it was a stupid and dangerous thing to do. However, I had acquired many souvenirs on these peregrinations of mine. Obsolete Korean bank notes, long-stemmed pipes, wire hats, which the Community Leaders wore, slippers with turned-up toes, photographs and much else of interest to me, all for the taking from the ruins.

It was a long time before I came to realize that the peculiar smell of Korean houses was due to the prominence of garlic in a mixture of pickled and salted turnips, tomatoes and red pepper paste, all preserved in very large clay pots in the rear quarters.

Those mud and wattle houses, with their thatched, rice-straw roofs were all built in a similar fashion. A kitchen, usually built lower than the rest of the house, would contain at least two large steel cauldrons, set in a mud bench-top with a fire underneath. The flues from these fires ran under the floors of the rest of the house, heating each room. At the opposite end of the kitchen, a wooden chimney emitted what was left of the smoke. Those wooden chimneys were the cause of the many fires that I saw on windy days, spreading from one thatched roof to the next. Ingenious as the system was and good in winter, in the summer it made the houses much too hot. The interior walls of each room were insulated with old newspaper, stuck on with rice paste.

I was beginning to enjoy this life, never staying anywhere too long, only washing occasionally – the cold deterring you from making too much of it, plus the element of danger. We eventually made our way back to the town of Pyongtaek. There we dug in on the southern end, close to the MSR.

On patrol one day, as we were marching in single file, a convoy of US trucks came tearing through. As we were unable to get right off the road, each truck, as it passed, threw a spray of muddy slush over us. Maddened by this, we hurled a good deal of abuse at them. Of course,

70

as foot soldiers, we had to put up with a good deal of this sort of thing, but I was so riled by this lot that I felt not the smallest twinge of conscience as I eased a 28mm carbine from its clip on the side of a truck belonging to two grinning cowboys who evidently found the drenching of the Limeys a bit of a joke. As soon as I had that carbine in my hands, I fell in love with it. It was as light as a feather and fired automatic or single shot. It became my constant companion and, from then on, I carried two rifles. What a weapon it was! I cleaned it diligently, often, I must admit, at the expense of the cumbersome Lee Enfield .303. I was lucky enough to be able to swap two bars of dark chocolate, for which some GI's had a passion, for six magazines, each of which held twenty-eight rounds, plus two boxes of refills. I paced out 200 yards and put down a cardboard box as a target. At that distance I found the carbine to be very accurate on both single shot and automatic and there was absolutely no kick.

Our main job at Pyongtaek was to keep the flood of refugees coming down the MSR on the move. It was a frustrating business and one could not but have a feeling of compassion for them and a wish to help, yet if you showed any compassion for them, they would pester you to death. So one was continuously shouting 'Currah! Currah!' (a Japanese term meaning 'Move! And move quickly!') It was a term they knew only too well from the days of the Japanese occupation of their homeland.

Each night, as darkness fell, thousands would camp at the northern end of the town and begin to wail en masse. It was an unearthly sound which echoed through the frozen valleys.

As I crawled into my sleeping bag, fully clothed, with my greatcoat on top, feet frozen from a day in wet boots, I lay listening to that pitiful cry, not in sorrow but in anger.

I would ask myself, 'What sort of a God could allow this to happen?' I cursed Him with every swear word in my fairly extensive vocabulary and challenged Him to strike me dead if He ever existed. How I would have loved to take a group of Bible punchers for a little walk to meet those poor devastated people.

About half a mile out of the town, a river crossed the MSR and every day someone from our platoon took it in turn to guard the bridge. There was a concrete bunker at the head of the bridge, a relic of the Japanese days. It had observation slits all the way round and you could sit in there out of the wind and still keep a good eye on the far bank of the river. So taken was I with the opportunity that that lonely vigil provided to escape from the woes and struggles that surrounded us in our main task, that I volunteered to take the job on as my own for the rest of our platoon's turn. 'What ya got out there, Dave? Some young peasant girl?', Stan would joke.

I found all sorts of things on the river bank to keep me occupied. On the far bank stood a dead tree whose branches I pruned, one by one, with a bullet from my carbine. One morning, a flight of wild duck, flying in their usual vee-formation and following the line of the river, came in sight, only to be thrown into disarray as the leader fell to the ice with a bullet from my carbine in his chest. He made a good supper for the family of the young refugee who quickly fished him out of the river.

Ever a day dreamer in such a situation, my thoughts would often stray back to my boyhood when I and my mates would go over the fields and through the woods to shoot rabbits and pigeons, armed with our trusty longbows with their deadly six inch heads, as described earlier. As I shot that mallard drake that morning, I was at once reminded how one of our number, Ron Carruthers, had won immortal fame by hitting a bolting rabbit. I wondered what the lads would have said if they'd seen young Dave hit that mallard on the wing! Sometimes, accompanied by a neighbour's dog, I would go off on my own, moving stealthily through the woods where I would wait, silently, for hours, for a roosting pigeon. In those woods and fields I found the peace and solace that I would gladly have found in my bunker, though my vigils there were the nearest thing to them that I could have hoped to find in our present circumstances, once the main body of the refugees had swept through, like a raging torrent, sweeping their misery along with them.

To my grief, they left one last reminder: a tiny baby, caught in mid-stream in the broken ice. Its beautifully shaped little head, which should have been nestling in its mother's arms, was wedged in the ice. With my carbine, I attempted to free it but to no avail. It drifted on and I was alone.

As that tiny scrap of humanity disappeared, my mind once again turned to the question of how it could be that God would allow so much suffering for innocent people. Surely, with all His power, He could stop it and bring peace once more? I wondered what my Dad's thoughts would be if he were out here to witness this terrible tragedy. Doubtless he would see it as a prime example of Man's innate wickedness.

Realizing that I was growing morbid, I tried to put all these thoughts to the back of my mind. They say that God helps those who help themselves. That was my selfish attitude. I knew for sure that if I did not look after myself, nobody else would.

A few days later we were on the move once more. A couple of days here and a couple there, sometimes sleeping in empty village huts, sometimes in the remoter areas where the inhabitants had stayed put.

In one such place, a woman brought me bowls of rice, which I had told her I liked – but not first thing in the morning without milk or sugar!

In another village I had slept the night with an old man and a middle-aged woman who had a young baby. She kept inviting me to have sex with her but I was still suffering from my legacy from that night out in Pusan and sex was about the last thing I wanted at that time, so all she got from me was a nice smile. Doubtless she thought I was a queer! Meanwhile, I took *mallaca* (rice wine), which is like milky cider, and salted turnips in ritual fashion with *Popasan*.

I spent that night comfortably enough on the floor, with a wooden block for a pillow and sharing a quilt with the family. The frustrated lady kept fumbling me with her foot – to which she got no response from me!

Whilst we were in the Osan area, it was decided that it would be good for our morale to visit a place in the hills adjoining our position, where the Turks had been involved in a battle with the Chinese. They had apparently declined any artillery support as they wanted the enemy to be in one piece when they met them. Possibly they had thoughts of revenge for the rough handling one of their units had suffered at Chinese hands soon after they had arrived in Korea and had gone straight into battle in the north. The idea was that we should inspect the scene and their handiwork, getting a first-hand look at the enemy and seeing that they were by no means invincible.

We found that the Chinese had held their ground. Some lay dead in their open dugouts. Each had a fatal wound of some description. Despite the fact that there were many corpses further down the hill, we found one man, cup and tooth brush in hand, who had clearly been taken completely by surprise. There he lay with his shirt pulled up and a massive bayonet wound in his stomach from which his intestines flowed onto the ground beside him. Another, his head like a crinkled mask, the bone structure having completely disintegrated, was still standing up in his dugout. Others, in larger bunkers, were sitting in groups of four or five, like waxwork figures from Madame Tussaud's. They looked as if they had never been disturbed. One man, who had attempted to flee, lay in the valley below with a bullet wound in his back.

The spur, on which the Chinese had been dug in, was some 300 yards long and, throughout its length, bodies lay in their dugouts as if they had been placed there. One might have thought that time had simply stopped for them. We came away pretty impressed with the power of the Turks as fighting men.

A few days later, we were redeployed and sent to a feature which, on arrival, we found to be covered with the partly buried bodies of North Korean soldiers, some still with their hats on, the red stars sticking out of the ground as if to claim that this was Communist territory. We moved on!

73

During those peripatetic days, I would often visit 8 Platoon, who were never far away. It was good to be with Pete for a bit and we would do the rounds of all our mates and go for little walks. I was glad to see Archie Coram, who was always good for a laugh, and MacIntyre, my old friend from Colchester days. Pete was the youngest in his section and Taffy Smith, a reservist, was his guiding light. He was a very pleasant and polite family man, for all his years in the Army, and I was glad to know that he kept Pete under his wing. For some reason, Pete was known as 'Farmer' but, although they knew that I, too, was a country boy, they didn't 'call I Buttercup Joe.' Pete was absolutely wrapped up with that Bren gun of his which he was forever cleaning.

Our wandering came to an end when we were moved back to our old stamping ground at Suwon. But we might have known it. No sooner had we settled ourselves, or rather begun to settle, in some empty houses with a welcome prospect of making ourselves warm and a bit more comfortable for a change, than the order came for an immediate move to the area of Inchon, south-east of the Han River and the scene of General MacArthur's brilliant amphibious landing in the previous September.

Truth to tell, my inveterate yearning to explore very nearly landed me in serious trouble that morning. Whilst the platoon was beginning to get organised in the new billets, I took myself off on one of my hunting trips. Returning three hours later, I was staggered to see the blokes all clambering into a truck, my own kitbags and large pack, clearly marked AWOL,* being stacked on one side. It had been thought that I had decided to go for a holiday! It was a close shave and one that taught me a lesson I long remembered.

Had this been peacetime, our new location might well have been a popular spot for tourists, the sheer beauty of the vista before our new trenches capable of being put into any itinerary.

Across the valley from our little hill, the smallest one that we had had to dig in on so far, was a formidable feature marked on the map as Hill 327, but it was more of a mountain than a hill. Meandering down the valley, a shallow river crossed our front, about 400 yards away and then turned towards the northern side. There had been something of a thaw and rain had cleared much of the snow. The river banks were still iced but the water ran freely, the whole producing a panorama which would have been any artist's dream. However, for the soldier, that dream could well become a nightmare, for that lovely vista was No Man's Land and those beautiful hills were held by the enemy, who might, at any time, renew his offensive.

* AWOL: Absent Without Leave. A very serious crime on active service. '

As was so often the case, Danny and I were completely on our own on a forward slope amongst thinly scattered little trees. The opposite side of the valley sloped more steeply and led down to a road directly to our front. Tucked in off that road was a small village but it was out of our sight behind a line of trees.

The rest of the Battalion was somewhere on our left, with elements of the ROK Army beyond them. On our right lay the 1st US Cavalry Division, dug-in on a spur running to the north-east.

Every day a young Gunner OP officer and his bombardier would arrive in their Centurion tank and take up their position on the road below us. Occasionally, perhaps because they were getting bored with nothing to do, they would take a pot shot with their 20pdr gun across the valley. That gun was extremely accurate and could pinpoint a target with the certainty that, if the first round did not hit, the second one certainly would.

Danny and I found those long hours of watching pretty boring too but, well aware of the possibility of enemy patrols, we kept very much on our toes at night. Now and again, after it got dark, the enemy would lay a barrage of airburst mortar shells right across the whole valley, making us more alert than ever.

Not long after we arrived in that position, we heard the shrill blast of a whistle, just after midnight. It was followed by a bugle call, which carried an unmistakeable message that something was afoot and brought us to full alert.

The Americans on our right were about to be attacked. A light machine-gun, sited on the far end of their spur on a high point, now opened up, its tracer bullets spraying their positions.

The nearest American positions were so close that we could hear the GIs waking up their mates. 'Hey Joe, we're being attacked!' Their defences ran parallel to ours and were about 100 yards from the road but on higher ground than us.

More light automatic and rifle fire had by now joined in the melée and an eerie 'Ha, ha, ha . . .' echoed across the valley from a Chinese attacker on the run, followed by '*Dola, dola, dola*'. They were in a state of high excitement and their panting voices carried quite clearly to our listening ears, as we strained our eyes into the darkness between ourselves and the road, in case we too were about to be attacked.

The enemy soon overran the forward foxholes. In a slight lull, we heard the smooth, calm voice of Major Walwyn speaking on the radio from the crest behind us. 'I say, old chap, it looks as if you are in a spot of bother over there. Do you need any assistance?' To which we responded quietly, 'What, get out of our dugouts for that lot? You must be joking.'

However, his American counterpart must have replied that, for the moment at least, he could handle it, for all we got was, 'Look to your front, chaps.'

Sporadic fire and the sound of exploding handgrenades moved down the spur and then all was quiet. We listened intently, watching every shadow in the half-light that shone through the canopy. Suddenly, we could hear the rattling sound of enemy equipment and the padding of running feet, but could see nothing. Then, right below us, came the chatter of Chinese voices. It sounded as if they were sharing out the spoils snatched from the well-endowed GI's. As we were unable to understand the excited chatter, it was hard to decipher their intentions. Nevertheless, even though we could not see them, had we opened up there and then, we would have been bound to inflict some damage. However, we waited for an easier target, fully expecting that they would attack us. As we waited, we came to realize that they had gone. The coming of dawn brought sighs of relief all round, though we were not best pleased to learn that the Americans had gone back 1,000 yards, leaving us stranded on our nice little hillock, which any well organised boy scout troop could have taken with ease.

Then followed one of those tragedies which, sadly, are so common-place in war but nonetheless distressing at the time. At about 10 o'clock, Danny and I spotted a figure crawling along the base of the spur which, until the previous night, had been American territory. The figure wore a hat with earflaps. We reported this sighting to Major Walwyn who agreed that, to all intents and purposes, the figure looked like a Chinese soldier. 'Take a shot at him, Green,' the major said.

Having adjusted my sights, I raised my rifle and fired. The round hit the ground just short of the prone figure and a second shot was just beyond it, ricocheting off into the distance. The figure showed some movement. Before I could fire again, two shots rang out from the area of 8 Platoon. As there was no further movement from the figure, Major Walwyn ordered Danny and I to go and check it. To my horror, when we got there, I saw that it was the body of a very dead US soldier. His dog tags, which I took from his neck, read, 'Pte. 1st Class Richard White, US 1st Cavalry.' His face had been completely shattered by the two shots from 8 Platoon.

As Danny and I stood beside the body, two of his comrades approached. The look of dejection on their faces reflected their feelings. They knew only too well that he had been responsible for his own death. One of them said in a scarcely audible voice, 'He's one of our boys. He came back hoping to retrieve some photos from his foxhole.'

I handed the dog tags over. Not a word was said. The four of us stood there, sick to the stomach, as we looked at the body. I imagined his poor mother reading the telegram informing her of his death.

With heads lowered, Danny and I parted company with the two GIs. When we were almost back on the road, Reg Coltman from 8 Platoon came running towards us. A Chinese soldier had been spotted about 50 yards uphill from the body of the dead American. It was probably from him that White had been hiding. Apparently this chap was wounded and was hopping around on one leg. We were to go and pick him up.

With Reg, we retraced our steps, climbing cautiously into a narrow ravine. As we came to a little clearing, we saw the Chinese, crouched in oriental fashion and holding the calf of his right leg. Two neat bullet holes through his padded trouser leg were seeping blood onto his well-worn canvas shoes. He was clearly a mature soldier, for his well-rounded, cropped head showed signs of greying at the temples. His friendly smile encouraged us to approach and it was clear that he was quite harmless. As Reg carried him on his back to our lines, he obviously realised that he was in good hands for he was grinning from ear to ear all the way.

That cheerful grin was all that Captain Mardell got from him too when he tried to interrogate him and waved his pistol at his head, pretending that he would shoot him.

'*Chingwade*?' (Are the Chinese over there?) brought absolutely no response. The question might just as well have been addressed to the wattle walls of the village hut in which he was being interrogated.

'He's as thick as two short planks', chuckled Whacker Walker, as our prisoner burst out laughing.

Captain Mardell gave up. 'Put a dressing on his leg,' he said, 'and get him back', giving the Chinese a playful cuff to his head.

At about this time, Lieutenant Waring, our Platoon Commander, had been moved to another company. We were sorry to see him go. His replacement was an equally young Lieutenant Haggerty. Another new arrival was one Bill Piggett, a reservist from London. He was a nice bloke and very helpful, but a pessimistic worry-guts, forever going on about our present predicament, which was the last thing we wanted to hear when we were battling inside ourselves to dismiss such thoughts. They did nothing to help our survival or our morale.

We soon realised that the Chinese had not occupied the American positions but had pulled back into the hills. We realised, too, that the Americans had not re-occupied them either, so we were still out on a limb, on our own.

As dusk came and the weak winter sun had disappeared behind the

77

distant hills, we prepared ourselves for another watchful night. Grenades and loaded rifle magazines were positioned within easy reach. As Danny and I busied ourselves with all this, a distressing call came from the valley below. It was clearly in Chinese and you did not have to be a linguist to realize that it was a call for help. The call echoed from a bend in the river, very close to the spur opposite us which the enemy had occupied during their attack on the Americans

As the calls continued and it was obvious that none of his mates were going to his aid, Stan, Danny and I volunteered to go and bring him in.

Night was drawing in fast as we scrambled down to the road, bayonets fixed and rifles at the ready. We made our way to the river, hoping that the Gunners would not decide to let loose one of their barrages. On the opposite bank of the river I could see a figure lying on his back and hear his moaning. With the others covering me, I waded across the river. As I approached the wounded man, fleeting thoughts of Japanese *kamikazes* went through my mind and I wondered if that was a grenade that he seemed to be holding. As I drew near to him I could see that he was as scared of me as I was apprehensive of him. We were both infantry soldiers, between whom a certain bond of comradeship and compassion always seems to exist, enemy or no. I made what I hoped were encouraging sounds and he seemed to relax. Danny and Stan now came over to give me a hand. The poor bloke had had the top half of his thigh blown away and recovery was not going to be easy. However, there was nothing for it but to do the best we could and get on with it whilst the going was good. He would be much better off in our hands, once we could get him back. Chinese medical resources in the line were minimal, thanks to the UN bombardment and could not begin to be compared with the quality of the US Medical Service hospital and its surgical teams.

Our prisoner was wearing two American jackets over his light Chinese uniform, so we decided to use one of these and our rifles with which to produce a makeshift seat. As we debated all this, I had an uncanny feeling that we were being watched, which could well have been the case. However, there was no time to be lost, so we lifted him, as gently as we could, although he was clearly in agony as we did so.

Stan and Danny were the stretcher-bearers whilst I acted as a sort of rearguard. The Chinese soldier was in agony as we traversed the rocky ground leading back to the road and screamed out but there was nothing we could do to make things any easier for him. When we got as far as the road we found that the Gunner OP tank had been brought down there and we handed the wounded man over to the young officer and his even younger bombardier. Months later, in very different circumstances, that young bombardier, Tommy Clough, was to become a very close friend. He told me that when the prisoner was interrogated, he proved to be an intelligence officer. Not surprisingly, his leg had to be amputated.

Meanwhile, we three had returned to the platoon and our daily and nightly vigil of the menacing feature which faced us, as thick with Chinese as a hedgehog is with fleas in mid-summer.

7

A Battle Honour Won : Hill 327

The Chinese rejection of the UN's Cease Fire proposal marked, oddly enough, the first signs of a turning point in the war. By mid-January the enemy had suffered massive casualties both from the fighting and the severe winter weather. Furthermore, just as the UN had suffered from an over-extended supply line when they were up near the Manchurian border, so now were the Chinese in a similar plight after they had crossed the Han River.

General Ridgway had done a magnificent job, not only in stabilising the UN's line but in restoring the morale of his army, which had begun to sag seriously as both commanders and their men were increasingly asking just what the UN was trying to achieve. He now began to probe forward to counter the Chinese offensive which, thanks chiefly to their overstretched supply lines, had come to something of a halt. Once more the balance of advantage began to swing towards the UN. By 9 February, Inchon and Suwon had been retaken and 1 Corps was pushing hard towards the Han River. On the 15th, the day before the next step in my own story, the Battle of Hill 327, the Americans won a fierce battle for Chipyang-ni which was to mark the next step forward in the UN's fortunes. Vast numbers of the enemy were being killed at relatively little cost to the UN. Just as, less than ten years earlier, General Slim and his XIVth Army had shattered the myth of Japanese invincibility in Burma, so was Ridgway beginning to demonstrate that the Chinese were most certainly not invincible, despite their overwhelming numbers in the forward areas. Morale began to soar although, in the minds of many of us, not excluding Ridgway himself, there remained a lingering doubt about the actual purpose of the war. Even in Washington, the politicians and the Chiefs of Staff had come to realize that all prospects of achieving a united Korea had gone and that their best hopes lay in exerting enough military pressure upon the Chinese and North Koreans to persuade them to negotiate a peace settlement based upon the former division of North and South Korea.

★   ★   ★

The time had come for Hill 327 to be dealt with and we were to be part of that process. Sabre jets strafed its reverse slopes and those of the adjoining hills as part of the softening-up operation.

The date upon which C and D Companies were to make a frontal assault upon that formidable feature was 16 February, one that will forever be engraved on my mind. Our attack was to go in on the western flank whilst the Americans, to the east, would attempt to take the lower hills that ran the length of the valley. Their attack would go in first in the hope that they would draw off some of the defenders of the No. 1 obstacle, our Hill 327.

As their attack formed up, the Centurion tanks of the 8th Hussars, which had moved up with them, opened fire, bombarding the lower slopes. This bombardment continued as the GIs, moving in waves of V-formations, crossed the open, grassy slopes in front of them and began their climb. We watched all this from our grandstand position and were much amused by the antics of a tall, lanky, coloured soldier who, despite being 1,000 yards from the action, ran doubled-up from one cover to the next, with long, intermittent pauses between dashes. He was clearly religiously practising what he had been taught in training but, at the time, twitched up as we were before our own part in the battle began, and glad to have anything to divert our thoughts, his extreme caution struck us all as being hilarious. I hasten to add that I tell this little story without intending any criticism of the courage or efficiency of the Americans, who lost many brave men and earned many honours, giving us as much support as we gave to them.

Now it was our turn. With a quick glance at his watch, Major Walwyn called out, 'Righto chaps. In we go!' Whilst we had been waiting, he had paced our front, looking at each of us in turn without speaking, his face doing the talking, as if to say 'Good luck.'

In single file we followed the road until it reached the river. Wading it, we fanned out to battle intervals between us, platoons being spread out equally. As so often happens with British soldiers going into battle, Stan obviously felt the need for a bit of light relief and kicked a frozen sod of mud to my feet. 'Here, Dave', he called quietly. I automatically passed it to Danny, calling 'Shoot!' However, this was no football match. We reached the spur which would, hopefully, take us to the summit, and probed forward, our platoons now in closer order, spanned across its crest. As we moved through the low scrub, we all scanned our front for the slightest sign of movement or enemy positions. As we did so, 170 Mortar Battery, which was deployed in the valley below, ready to support us when contact was established, sent over a couple of bombs, presumably to settle their base plates and check their sights.

We were now half way to the summit, having crossed a series of undulating ridges, with no sign of the enemy. Then, suddenly, bursts of automatic fire ripped through the scrub around us. These were the opening bars of a crescendo that was to follow and then subside after the initial shock of contact. Meanwhile, few of us had fired at anything which could be identified as a target. Now, bodies flat to the ground and hiding behind anything that might offer even a modicum of cover, we scanned our front whilst the bullets continued to fly overhead, as we tried desperately to see where they were coming from.

We had already had our first casualties. These included Sergeant Jock McKay, his sharp Scottish features wreathed in smiles – I'd never seen him happier. As he slid downhill on his backside, lovingly hugging his bullet-holed leg as if it was the FA Cup which he had just won single-handed, he was telling the world that 'I've got my Blighty one'!*

I felt a body come up beside me and, turning my head, I found it was Whacker Walker, who said quietly, 'You OK Dodger? Keep your head down mate. We'll get those bastards.'

To our immediate front the ground flattened out and had been cleared. It seemed plain that the Chinese bunkers were somewhere on the next rise but detecting them was extremely difficult. Another Jock, a corporal in 8 Platoon, was shot in the face and killed as he lobbed a grenade, his body falling back down the slope behind us. I was lying behind a small bush and cautiously raised my head, my natural hunting instinct together with my training 'shadow, shape, silhouette, movement' coming very much to the fore as I strained my eyes to spot the slightest clue of the whereabouts of the sniper, taking comfort in the presence of Whacker at my side, sharing my cover. 'No next of kin' Whacker. The Army was his life. What better bloke to be with in a scrap like this?

Ah! At last! I saw a movement. There, about 30 yards in front, was the opening of a dugout. Its Chinese occupants were just waiting for we sitting ducks. They had a clear view of anything that moved or raised its head from the rising ground. As we were deciding how to deal with them, Bill Pigget crawled up beside me with his Bren.

* Blighty one: Soldier's slang for a wound that would ensure his return to England (Blighty).

'I'll get the bastard. Where is ee?'

No sooner had he positioned himself, ready to fire a burst, than his body gave a violent jerk and he was thrown on top of me. Danny crawled up and pulled him off. We could see that he had had it. The bullet had hit him in the backside and travelled into his stomach, the contents of which had shot up into his throat, making him vomit and choke himself to death. Danny, with no thought of his own safety, had been exposing his own backside as we tried to help Bill, and was right in the sniper's line of fire but, thank God, had drawn no shot from that direction, which was pretty reassuring as far as my own exposure went. Whacker and I watched the dugout that I had spotted and in low tones discussed what we were going to do about it. Those Chinks were certainly pretty clever and if we were going to get them, we were going to have to move mighty smartly. The sniping was coming from the spur that was parallel to ours and, here too, the undergrowth had been cleared, giving them a clear field of fire.

Whacker signalled to me to throw a couple of grenades, something at which he knew I was pretty useful. As they exploded, he raised his arm and we charged forward, blasting the dugout and riddling it with bullets.

There is an old saying that one well-positioned soldier can hold up an army and it applied pretty well to the situation we were now tackling. On every rise and piece of flat ground there were just one or two bunkers, each giving complete coverage of its front, its Chinese occupants raking the whispy undergrowth with automatic fire.

My initial fear now turned to anger as we reached the top of one of these rises. Major Walwyn had been hit. His shattered arm hung by his side as he traversed the slope, fully exposed to withering fire, calling out in his familiar calm voice, 'Come on men. Don't be frightened of these people.'

His cool courage and inspiring reassurances gave me a great sense of pride in my officers, mates and regiment and I resolved that the enemy were going to pay dearly for what they had done to him.

Three stick grenades hurtled down the slope, one almost hitting my head. They landed further down the slope, giving two more of the lads early passages back to Blighty. As I raised my head again, I saw a Chinese scrambling up the hill and another halfway out of his bunker. Whacker and I opened up simultaneously. One of them fell back into the bunker and the other got half a magazine from Whacker's Sten gun. We then lobbed a grenade into the bunker for good measure.

As Whacker, Danny and I pushed on through the thickening vegetation, our bayonets glistening against the green of the vegetation, I found myself shouting, 'Come out and fight!', hoping against hope to come face to face with our enemy. As I slashed the undergrowth with my bayonet, my blood up and mad with rage, I shouted again, 'Come out, you slant-eyed bastards!'

We were going up that hill and nobody was going to stop us. It was sheer music to hear Major Walwyn's unmistakable voice, with its clear Oxford English accent, protesting vehemently, 'Bloody well leave me alone', as the medics dragged him, very much against his will, down to the RAP. What a man! And how we would miss him!

Then I heard a voice, loud in its protest, shouting out, 'Stupid sods. What am I going to tell them back home? Shot by my own mates. I'll never live it down.' Then I saw Terry, away to our right, with blood soaking the leg of his battle dress, as he hobbled along using a young sapling and his rifle to prop him up. As he bravely made his way downhill, he cursed and ranted through gasps of pain. An accidental discharge from the rifle of a fallen mate had put a bullet clean through his right thigh. On our left sat our radio operator, another recent arrival to our platoon. His left hand was still holding the headset to his ear and his eyes were wide open but he would never see his dear wife and children again. The cause of his death was a mystery. There wasn't a mark on him.

At last our sadly diminished numbers reached the summit. I shall always remember Sergeant Eames of 8 Platoon who stood like a conquering gladiator, silhouetted against the grey skyline for a few seconds.

From a nearby bunker a Chinese soldier emerged, hands on head. It seemed that he could not believe his luck when beckoned back through our ranks untouched. On the reverse slope some of his mates were attempting to make a run for it and were quickly dealt with. One young conscript, in his excitement, got up from his kneeling position and very nearly got his head shot off by a rifle discharged from immediately behind him.

Despite our sense of triumph at seizing the top of that great hill, we had in fact only captured the western end. D Company, who had cleared the left hand spur, now joined us and together we formed up to complete our task.

As we were sorting ourselves out, an unexploded Mills grenade became momentarily the centre of attraction as 'Mad' Captain Mardell, as he was known, was tossing it in the air like a tennis ball. Oddly enough, he quickly became very much alone! 'See', he said, as if talking to a bunch of school kids, 'There's nothing to be afraid of. Dead as a doornail!' Finally, his bit of fun over, he threw it away a safe distance, only to be transposed into a state of total shock as it exploded into a thousand pieces, along with his boisterous self-confidence, much to our amusement.

On the rear slope of the ridge we now began to clear, the Chinese had dug a series of shallow trenches in between their solidly-roofed, well-concealed bunkers. As we advanced along the top, a figure emerged from one of these open trenches. With his hands raised above his head, he stood, quite tall and robust, in his padded uniform, his head bare. I was disgusted when a reservist, one of a group who had gathered, fired a burst from his Sten gun at him. Luckily he missed. Another corporal, also a reservist, threw a phosphorous grenade into the shallow trench in which the man was standing. Fortunately, it was a dud and only smouldered. Both were cursing and swearing at him. Reaching out to him, I took his hand, shouting as I did so, 'What's the matter with you bastards? Can't you see he's harmless. Leave him alone!'

His cold, sweaty hand, grasped mine tightly, like a child on his first day at school, as I helped him over the rocky ground. As I handed him over to be taken back through the lines, his eyes searched mine for reassurance of his safety.

'OK. Englisho good man!' I said, pointing down the hill.

We met little opposition as we swarmed over the rest of the hill and within an hour we were settling into our newly acquired, well-made Chinese-roofed dugouts. Single berthed, they had a well-moulded mud opening, just big enough to crawl into. Although exposed, they were very hard to detect with one's bowed head and shoulders in the opening.

The previous occupant of the one allocated to me, obviously an officer, had clearly left in a hurry. His wooden pistol holster was still hanging from the roof. He hadn't travelled far. His body lay just ten feet away down the slope. His glazed eyes stared at me from his pale oriental face, surmounted by lank, jet-black hair. We were not long into the moonlit night when I decided that I had had enough of that stare. Crawling from my bunker, I gave the body a gentle shove with my foot, sending it down the hill.

We fully expected to be counter-attacked in some strength as Hill 327 was such an important feature but, after a few uneventful days, we came to realize that the Chinese had gone. It seemed that they had pulled right back to regroup, giving us a chance to relax.

I now felt I could set out on one of my lone reconnoitering expeditions and I took myself back down the spur which lay parallel with the one we had initially attacked. I couldn't help admiring the enemy's ingenuity. About half way down the spur I found a single dugout facing the line of our approach across the intervening valley. In my youthful ignorance, I gave no thought to the possibility of booby traps, even though I'd found some sort of tubular missile nearby, so I crawled inside. Pointing my rifle, I marvelled at the ease with which a sniper could have picked off targets on our spur, like poor Bill Pigget and at least half a dozen more chaps he had accounted for, one of whom could so easily have been me. You had to hand it to them. They were a mighty smart bunch. They had worked out just how we would be coming at them even though there had been a wide selection of possible approaches.

As I wandered over that spur, I could not help noticing the pattern of the many shallow trenches they had dug and, as I pondered about them, it suddenly dawned on me that, with their carefully shaven edges to eliminate any sharp outlines, a man crouched down in one, face down, wearing his padded uniform which matched the terrain to a T, would be virtually invisible from a fast-moving aircraft and by no means easy to detect from ground level, as we had found during the battle.

Not long after, I had the surprise of my life. We were still up on the hill and I suddenly saw a Korean porter struggling up the slope with the biggest parcel known to man perched on his 'A' frame. To my astonishment, that parcel was addressed to me! My sister Mary had been a GI bride and now lived in Florida. Like the rest of our family, she has a heart of gold and had packed up this enormous parcel with cartons of cigarettes, gum, Lifesavers, banana cakes and so on. The variety was unbelievable!

We were due to pull out from 'our hill' at any time so, after taking enough for my own needs and those of Pete, Danny and Stan, I handed the whole over to Captain Mardell to share out amongst the rest of the company. I shall always be so deeply grateful for that wonderful gift and never forget the joy it brought to us on that barren hillside, where 'goodies' had been in extremely short supply for a long time.

It was a magical ending to what had been a pretty hairy time from which, as Danny, Stan and I all agreed, we had been very lucky to emerge unscathed. To my joy and relief, Pete too had been untouched. He had put in some terrific work with that beloved Bren of his and his face was just one big grin from ear to ear for days after the show was over.

Later, I learned that General Ridgway had been watching our attack. Much later, I was to hear that we had been awarded a battle honour for Hill 327. For me, it had been an unforgettable experience for it had taught me that the tougher the fight, the greater the spirit of comradeship. It had also been my first experience of the power of leadership in battle. Who could ever forget the impact of Major Walwyn's calm voice encouraging us all and of his total disregard for the enemy's fire, despite the agony of his shattered arm, of which he showed no outward sign, protesting as he did when he was being taken away by medics. Then there was Whacker, his presence beside me and his leadership during that first charge against the Chinese bunkers having been a source of inspiration, as had the stalwart presence of Danny and Stan.

For some time after the battle, whenever I was alone and thinking about all these things, and about the good mates we had lost that day, a song which a Welsh boxer in the Regiment had once sung during one of our many singalongs, reflecting the price that the families of those fallen mates had had to pay, would come into my mind:

'Oh, I'll never raise my son to be a soldier.
I'll never teach him how to fire a gun,
Or lift a rifle to his shoulder,
To go and shoot some other mother's son.
Let the rulers of our empires
Fight their battles in dispute,
And let the others' mothers rest in peace.
There'd be no more wars today
If all the mothers did but say,
'I'll never raise my son
To be a soldier."

Such solemn thoughts apart, I had every reason to be feeling distinctly cheerful, for whilst we had been on and around Hill 327, my 'spot of bother' had begun to clear up and now was completely gone – for which I was profoundly relieved. Not until I had got rid of it did I realise quite how much I had been worrying about it. I'll never know just what the problem was or why it manifested itself in the way it did. What was important now was that it had indeed disappeared.

Until then I had kept the whole thing very much to myself, not even confiding in Pete. When I told him and his guiding light, Taffy Smith, the whole story, Taffy said there was no way that anything contagious would have manifested itself so quickly. His advice was that, in future, I should steer clear of girls like that and leave them to blokes like him! In his view the only damage I could have suffered that night was to my brain cells from that awful hooch that I had been drinking.

8

Heesoon

With Hill 327 behind us, we headed east, stopping at Anyang for a couple of days, which gave me a welcome opportunity to catch up with the washing of my well-worn underclothing.

I shared a water-hole there with a Korean woman and her daughter. Very soon I had them in fits of laughter as I wrestled with a shirt. Jokingly, I wrapped the wet shirt round the woman's neck, whereupon the young girl playfully held a gourd of ice-cold water over my head. We continued to lark about like this for a bit and I thoroughly enjoyed myself. It all ended with them showing me how to knock the living daylights out my washing with a flat stick.

I had been very attracted by the daughter so kept a watchful eye on the well next day. However, I was disappointed. In any case we were due to move on to Wonsan later that day so, as I then thought, all hope of getting to know them better was a non-starter.

Over the next two or three days we moved by fits and starts to a little village, virtually untouched by the war and with a number of its inhabitants still living and working there. However, there was plenty of room for us to install ourselves in the empty houses. We were then told that we would be staying there for some time. At last, a rest!

I described earlier how the Korean village houses were built and heated and the one in which my section was billeted was very much in that traditional pattern, with the kitchen, at the back, being the principal room and the source of the heating. Imagine my delight when I discovered my friends from the well were sharing our kitchen with us and had already got the fires burning. It transpired that this was their village, to which they had now returned.

The two gave me a great welcome which, needless to say I reciprocated. I just couldn't believe my good fortune. Needless to say, my usual wanderings in such situations were very much curtailed as I contrived to keep as close to the lovely young girl as I could. She was beautiful, upright and elegant. She walked like a gazelle and I like a panther.

Perhaps she and her mother were particularly pleased to feel that they had a friend amongst all these strange soldiers and one who they felt they could trust to look after them. We became firm friends and I soon learned that the woman's husband had been killed at Pyongyang. Within a few days, Heesoon, the daughter, was doing my washing. She had come to me and asked, 'Momosan speak. You washy-washy?' or words to that effect, accompanied by gesticulations and much happy laughter. In a flash I was fumbling in my kitbag for anything that would fit the bill. Just to stand so close to her sent a chill down my back and set my heart thumping. In the mornings that followed, getting out of bed at the crack of dawn was just too easy!

Our stay in that village was a happy one for us all. I don't think any of us realized how badly we had needed that rest. The Ulster Rifles were quite close and one day we were delighted to have a visit from two of our old Gloster mates, Marion and Johnstone, from Colchester days, who were now with the Paddies. Johnny had acquired a white streak in his black hair, the result of a headwound he had received soon after arriving in Korea. I remember him well for he had been a scrap metal dealer, totting the streets of Gloucester with a horse and cart. His exploits with the fair maidens there were legendary. We yarned together for some time needless to say; they wanted to know all about Hill 327 and in return told us about their own battles, some of which had been pretty tough. Both were looking forward to their first experience of St Patrick's Day, which is celebrated at about the same time as our regimental 'Back Badge Day'.

An American show had been staged in a big marquee for the troops in the area and our Regiment had been invited to send one company each night. When C Company's turn came, we all trooped over there to see the fun. To our intense amusement, by far the best turn came from a member of the audience, an extroverted black GI who got himself onto the stage and did a splendid song and dance act!

Meanwhile, back at home, home being where you hang your hat, the lads had unearthed an old gramophone and a number of records, which included some of the lesser known classics. We were now mixing quite freely with the locals and both sides were enjoying the experience.

Of course, I spent as much time as I could in the kitchen with Momosan and Heesoon. Fate took its hand one glorious night and placed it in mine – the slim, olive-skinned hand of the lovely Heesoon.

Momosan was elsewhere and, hopefully, busily engaged for a bit. For the first time, we were alone. As we sat together on the warm worktop of the kitchen, her long raven-black hair brushed my face. I kissed her heavenly lips, to which she responded with fervour, her brown eyes sparkling in the light of the fire. As we embraced, our two bodies trembled.

I discovered the secret of the peasants' baggy pantaloons. They have a split separating one leg from the other.

'You number one,' she said.

She was seventeen and I but nineteen. We were head over heels in love. Alas, our happiness was to be all too short-lived for, on the very next morning, we were given only half-an-hour to get ready to move and we were off. As we pulled out in the early morning light, I had a heartbreaking last glimpse of my love with her head buried in her hands.

★   ★   ★

As I sat in the truck, bumping over the ill-made Korean country roads, I felt as if the bottom had dropped out of my world. What chance was there that we would ever meet again? After a while and in response to Stan's ribbing, I began to cheer up a bit but my heart was like lead. At last we found ourselves in a ramshackle, shop-fronted warehouse built of rusty corrugated iron, in the town of Yongdongpo, once a thriving industrial centre and now an empty shambles. Like all the other towns we had seen in Korea, it would take a long time to put back on its feet. This go-down was our new billet.

No longer in reserve, we were now at an almost permanent state of instant readiness although, in theory, we were at one hour's notice to move.

The town lay on the MSR and, on the hills overlooking it, trenches had been dug along almost their entire length, presumably either for defence or shelter for, in the early days of the war, Yongdongpo must have been a major target. Away from the goodies of any American PX or supply point, we were now back on bully beef, powdered potato, known as 'Pom', and hard-tack biscuits which must have been salvaged from some ship sunk during the First World War. They were as tough as old boots. I had long sworn never to eat 'bully' again but 'needs must when the devil drives' and as we watched the Koreans in the rubbish pits licking out the empty cans, I philosophically decided to count my blessings.

With little to do except clean our arms and, where necessary, patch up our kit between spells of guard duty, my mind had plenty of time to wander. If I wasn't thinking miserably about Heesoon, I was pondering on the futility of war.

I'd had a few heartaches already in my young life but nothing approaching the one that was afflicting me now. My eyes would forever be scouring the road in from the south, hoping against hope that I might be granted another miracle but all to no avail. My beloved young peasant girl was gone forever.

As I looked at the ruined shambles around us it would often cross my mind that one day I might return to this Godforsaken land and do what I could to help rebuild the damage we had done. What in God's name was war all about? Some afflicted idiots in need of psychiatric care, throwing we indoctrinated peasants at each other's throats. And to what end? Politics had never interested me but I *did* believe in people power. There would be no Hitlers, Stalins or, come to that, Kim-Il-Sungs, if the people would only put them where they belonged, in a nice rest home, behind bars or, preferably, against a wall and shot!

Day followed dreary day. The boredom was broken a little by a spot of bullshit – I even got checked for needing a shave!

As was usual in these situations, despite the fact that much of the population of the town had fled, there were the inevitable gangs of kids forever hanging around us demanding *tab-tab* (food). A less usual visitor, who drifted, we thought harmlessly, from billet to billet, was a young girl in a Western-style frock, thick high-heeled black shoes and with a black silk scarf tied over her head. She gave the impression of being not quite right in the head and we could not understand a word she said. She certainly could not comprehend the few words of Korean that we had picked up. Even '*Currah!*' produced a blank stare. Like the rest of the kids, we fed her packet after packet of hard tack, of which there was no shortage.

One day her headscarf caught on a wooden shelf, revealing a well-cropped head of black hair, her oddity taking on a curiously boyish look. Boy or girl, to us she was just another victim of war. If her/his intentions were hostile and her/his mission amongst us was to seek information, it would soon have become obvious that the only information anyone was going to glean from us was that it was still bloody cold and that 'No, we would not be home for Christmas, 1951.' Furthermore, we were only interested in anything if you could love, drink or eat it, in that order or in any combination of the three!

I could just imagine some elderly former Chinese warrior, with a string of medals, reading this and saying to his grandchildren, 'That was me and this is the medal I got for it. Ha ha!'

March came and went in that desolate hole. There we sat, bored to tears and sick to death of the cold and the miserable rations. News filtered through from time to time of great things being done by the Eighth Army until, finally, we heard that they had crossed the Parallel and had been killing a lot of Chinese on the way. Then, at last, in early April, just after that good news had come through, we moved once more.

9

The Battle of the Imjin River

Five days after the battle on Hill 327, General Ridgway launched Operation KILLER. This took seven US divisions back to a line south of the Han River by 1 March. The losses inflicted upon the Chinese during this advance were very considerable, thanks mainly to the massive artillery and air support provided. A week later, Ridgway made a further advance on the central front with Operation RIPPER. This effectively enveloped Seoul, forcing the enemy to abandon the city, which was re-occupied by the UN on the 14th. Ridgway's intention was to establish the KANSAS Line in the general area of the Parallel. Meanwhile, the Chinese had decided to frustrate that intention and to drive the UN back south by launching a massive offensive in the latter half of April. Thanks to electronic intelligence, the UN were well aware of what was afoot.

Despite the American successes, the British Military Attaché in Korea wrote to London on 12 March, again expressing his concern over the problems of morale in a situation of intense warfare which still seemed to lack any clear-cut purpose. He observed that both officers and men, at all levels, were questioning what they were supposed to be achieving in Korea and for how long the war would continue against an enemy who possessed seemingly inexhaustible reserves of manpower.

A fierce battle of words was meanwhile being fought between MacArthur on one side and President Truman and the American Chiefs of Staff on the other. Truman had already made a public statement to the effect that he considered that the time had come to negotiate a peace. MacArthur, however, was pressing for an all-out war to eliminate Communism in Asia, a prospect that neither his own country nor the UN were prepared to contemplate. On 11 April 1951, Truman issued a formal statement removing MacArthur from his command. He was succeeded by Ridgway, who had himself already had more than enough of MacArthur's posturing and bombast. The appointment of UN Ground Forces Commander was given to General James Van Fleet, who was to take over command on 22 April.

On 3 April the UN had re-crossed the Parallel and work on the KANSAS Line was begun. Meanwhile, 29 Infantry Brigade had moved up and were occupying a position on the Imjin River on the western flank of the UN Forces, with 1 ROK Division on their left and 3 US Infantry Division on their right. The Brigade had a Belgian battalion under their command. Their frontage was 7½ miles. Deployed were two battalions, with the Northumberland Fusiliers on the right and the Glosters on the left, the Ulster Rifles being in Brigade Reserve. All were south of the river on a ridge of high hills. The Belgians were deployed north of the river on the right of the Northumberlands.

Some 30 miles north of Seoul, the position was potentially an impregnable one provided that it had been properly prepared with deep digging, mine-fields and wire, none of which had been done because it was thought that the enemy would be concentrating on the centre of the UN line and because it was assumed to be a temporary position, as the Brigade would be moving up to the KANSAS Line quite shortly. Patrolling to a depth of about eight miles had produced very little contact with the enemy. However, the scene changed dramatically on the morning of 22 April when both the Glosters' and the Northumberland Fusiliers' patrols reported that the enemy were moving towards the river in considerable strength.

★   ★   ★

In the early hours, our trucks filtered through another lost city, Ujongbu. Like Yongdongpo, it too had once been a thriving centre of light industry and was now derelict.

Seated on fixed wooden benches on either side of the vehicle, we had our windcheater hoods over our heads, the strings firmly tied under our chins. Each man sat silent. As dawn broke, there was just the flicker of an eye to acknowledge one another's gaze. A 'Good morning' was a bit much to men who were frozen to the bone and going to God alone knew where, like paratroopers about to drop on some dangerous mission.

Then, looming out of the grey morning mist, we saw the familiar, battered, sand-coloured buildings of Seoul. Well, at least we now knew where we were and in which direction we were headed.

Opposite me, I thought I saw a smile from the sullen-faced reservist who had fired that Sten gun burst at the Chinese soldier on Hill 327 and, by the grace of God, had missed him. Well, at least he was human.

Beside him sat Gravenell, his red nose more prominent than ever in his windcheater and, as usual, dripping its dewdrops. Next to him was Stan, like the rest of us, deep in thought, though his friendly, mischievous eyes were constantly scanning the horizon.

The convoy snaked its way round the chewed up mountainous roads with their deep drops alternating on either side as we changed direction. Abandoned military and civilian hardware was becoming increasingly common, a sight that snapped our turgid minds into thinking what we would do if the truck went over the edge.

Whacker was about to go on leave to Tokyo. He had been an acting Sergeant for some weeks now and I supposed that it was only fair that those who bore the most responsibility should get that privilege first. I, for one, certainly did not begrudge it him after all we had been through together on Hill 327.

At long last, the convoy halted and we found ourselves on a ridge of high hills, south of and overlooking what we soon learned was the Imjin River.

We Glosters were on the left of the 29 Infantry Brigade position with the Geordies on our right, still wearing their coloured feather hackles in their hats, and a bit closer to the river. Beyond them, just north of the river, in a U-shaped bend, was the Belgian battalion which had been put under command of our brigade. The Paddies were in reserve behind the Geordies. Behind us were our old friends 170 Mortar Battery, who had supported us so well on Hill 327. 45 Field Regiment, with their 25 pdrs, were deployed behind the Geordies. The 8th Hussars, in their Centurion tanks, were in support of the Brigade. Whoever got through that lot would have the 27th Commonwealth Brigade to contend with, some 30 miles back on the Kapyong River.

Within the Battalion, A Company was on the left on a feature known as Castle Hill; to their right were D and B Companies; and a road leading from the river crossing north of A and D Companies ran south-east through the Battalion position, forking eastwards across the front of D Company and thence across the Brigade front. We in C Company were on a high ridge which not only overlooked the river but gave us observation well to the north of it.

As the Brigade frontage was some 7½ miles, the battalions were pretty well spread out, giving plenty of gaps through which a typical Chinese attack could flow.

Battalion Headquarters and the cookhouse were just behind our Company position. Every day we went back down the hill for meals and to wash in a little pebbled stream which flowed past the abode of our Commanding Officer, Lieutenant Colonel Fred Carne.

We knew that the Chinese were expected to launch a new offensive very soon. However, it was thought, apparently, that the thrust would be against the centre of the UN line and that we were unlikely to be attacked.

We had, of course, dug in but in the light of that and the fact that it was believed that we would not be in the position for long, before moving forward to join the new UN line in the general area of the 38th Parallel, nothing elaborate had been prepared in the way of defences, obstacles, minefields or wire. I was surprised to learn that the river was fordable in most places, so it did not constitute a serious obstacle to any advance from the north.

Temperatures were beginning to rise, bringing with them the smell of new vegetation germinated by the thawing snow and the heat of the sun. As the day advanced, we would shed our shirts, revealing our *Windrush* tan.

Regular patrols were sent out by day and night. The 'winkling' group, based upon the Lifebuoy Flame Thrower, the weapon I had carried on that training scheme back in Suwong, was now resurrected. Its aim was to unearth the Chinese from their bunkers which were often like rabbit warrens. I was the mug who volunteered to carry this lethal contraption but no one was game to be my No. 2. The fuel tank, which was circular, like a lifebuoy, was full of napalm. It had a short hose and a cartridge gun. When fired, the napalm would ignite and shoot out a trail of fire some 30 yards long. I was still young and stupid and shrugged off such suggestions as, 'One bullet or piece of shrapnel hitting that thing and you're a pile of ashes, mucker!' Whacker, who was the leader of this group, was the only bloke who would come anywhere near me.

So, once again, here I was carrying the Lifebuoy on patrol but this time it was for real, as our Company patrolled across the Imjin River, looking for signs of the Chinese. In fact, the only living thing we saw was a beautiful stag! At least these reconnaissance patrols enabled us to relax a bit at night as, throughout the twenty-four hours, the Brigade was patrolling well north of the river and we would have had instant warning if any Chinese had been spotted. Nevertheless, we were in the line and so we maintained a permanent fifty per cent stand to.

Standing alone in one's trench on guard as the night closed in, gave one plenty of time for reminiscence. One night, as the sun set, the sound of a mouth-organ drifted across from a bivouac in 8 Platoon:

Mona Lisa, Mona Lisa, they have named you . . .

As I stood gazing out over the river, picturing my Mona Lisa, my heart ached for I knew that, though she was never out of my mind, I would never see her again. That memory will never die even though we had only known each other for two-and-a-half weeks.

The song changed:

Take me back to dear old Blighty . . .

As the words rang out, the singer was joined by the full-throated songsters of 8 Platoon. As the song neared its end, the voice of an even fuller-throated sergeant roared, 'Oy, where in the fucking hell do you lot think you are? This is the front line, you know. Pack it in for fuck's sake!'

I smiled quietly to myself. I had known those blokes for quite a while now. Like the lads in 9 Platoon, we were mates. I thought of the day when I had first met Pete, on the train at Gloucester, and how he had, only the other day, cut the curls from my lengthening hair; Reg Coltman, who had volunteered for Korea and had helped Danny and I when we rescued the wounded Chinese at the foot of Hill 327; Archie Coram, always good for a song and who had got caught on the little mound at Sibyoni with bullets buzzing around him like a swarm of bees! Great lads, we were muckers! And we all felt much the same about this seemingly endless war, which was causing so much suffering and bloodshed, not only to those involved in the fighting but to literally millions of unarmed men, women and children in both halves of Korea. Yet we had grown pretty philosophical about it, realizing that for soldiers it was a case of:

Theirs' not to reason why, theirs' but to do or die.

Somewhere about 20 April, intelligence reports came in that a swarm of about 24,000 Chinese were making their way to the Imjin. An ambush was laid on to cover the crossing just north of Castle Hill. 9 Platoon took its turn and we lay on the river bank throughout the night but we saw nothing of the enemy. On the next night, 22 April, it started in earnest, our mortars having been in action against parties of Chinese throughout the afternoon under the personal direction of Colonel Carne himself.

Like migrating wildebeest in Africa, the Chinese plunged into the river and began wading across under the furious fire of the ambush patrol commanded by Lieutenant Temple. Four times they were repulsed before the patrol withdrew into our company perimeter, all their ammunition expended. Meanwhile the Gunners took over the task. No matter how many Chinese fell and floated off down river, there were always more to replace them, herded by their officers, who were waving pistols and were said to be shooting those who tried to turn back.

A couple of hours later, our three forward companies took the brunt of a new assault. A company's position on Castle Hill, some three-quarters of a mile from us, took a tremendous hammering. Continuous DF* from the 4.2" mortars behind us whistled overhead and we could hear their commanders shouting 'Fire!', 'Fire!' whilst what felt like a seismic tremor made the very ground pulsate. A cacophony of battle noises, rifle and machine-gun fire, bugles and whistles and the almost ceaseless bursting of mortar bombs came to us down the wind out of a multi-coloured sky. Tracer bullets ricocheting off the rocks or dropping at the end of their spent trajectories, fell amongst us from time to time.

As the battle progressed throughout the night, we could tell from the flashes of the rifle fire that the Chinese were making ground. As the reserve company we could be called upon at any time to put in a counter-attack – a thought that did not appeal to me. However, that call never came, probably because the Chinese were so thick on the ground that we'd have had no chance against such numbers. As I learned later, a very gallant counter-attack had been put in by part of A Company, led by Lieutenant Curtis, in an attempt to regain control of Castle Hill but to no avail. They were too weak and the enemy far too strong. Lieutenant Curtis was killed but was awarded a posthumous Victoria Cross. He had led that attack despite being wounded earlier. I had great respect for our officers and he was one of the best.

By morning, what was left of A Company had been withdrawn. Amongst the survivors were three National Servicemen, Joe Collet, Roy Mills and Dave Gardener, all three members of our squad at Bulford. Joe had been wounded in the hand, Roy and Dave being the last two soldiers to come off Castle Hill. How proud Coxie would have been of them!

As the mingling clouds of mist and smoke began to clear, we kept a watchful eye open for the next attack. By this time 1 ROK Division had withdrawn from our left flank, creating a situation in which there was no way in which we could stop the Chinese encircling us. Meanwhile, B Company, who had stubbornly resisted a very heavy attack, had also been withdrawn.

That sleepless night was followed by a sleepless day as we prepared as best we could for what was bound to come. We were now, of course, up in the line. As night fell, columns of enemy infantry could be seen, like a lava spill, coming down the slopes of Castle Hill towards the road –

---

* DF: Defensive Fire. Pre-planned fire tasks for artillery, mortars and machine-guns.

and us. As I watched, it went through my mind that two hundred years earlier our forefathers would have opened the sluice gates of their reservoir and flooded the valley – no such luck here.

The bastards were coming and there was little we could do to stop that flood, except to take as many with us as we could. That thought had been bugging me all day and, although I was no hero, I would sooner have gone down to meet them than to wait like this.

Into the Valley of Death rode the six hundred. Yes, but we were only fifty odd. Better to wait.

The ridge that we were on rose upwards to our right. Then, after a slight dip it rose again to a little pinnacle which 8 Platoon was occupying. From their position a spur ran down to the road, for which the Chinese were making.

Throughout that day we had eaten very little. We had no appetite. However, the mugs of tea from the cooks' billies were life-savers.

My dugout was at the end of our ridge, overlooking the rising spur opposite. At about midnight I heard a metallic clink, sliding shale and voices. I could see figures moving upwards between the little trees silhouetted against the skyline of the spur leading up to Pete's 8 Platoon. I thought of him up there with his Bren poised and would have given a king's ransom to have had him, and it, alongside me at that moment. I wanted to alert the dugout next to mine but it seemed too far off – about twenty yards. Surely they could also see what I could? Perhaps I should shoot? The Chinese were about 200 yards away. I suppose my inexperience, rather than that I was scared (that was out of the question) stopped me from shattering that calm before the storm.

Then came the rat-tat-tat of a machine-gun. It had started! Almost before I knew it, my trigger finger had let off the first round and within seconds I had fired my first magazine. As I changed magazines, it dawned upon me that I had better watch my own immediate front as well.

Then all hell was let loose. 'There's bloody hundreds of 'em!' shouted Thomas from 8 Platoon.

Conserving my ammunition, taking pot shots at good targets on the spur, I was now more concerned with the slopes below me and 8 Platoon above, who were really in the thick of it – all ten of them. I could hear their Corporal Walker shouting, 'Look out! The bastards are everywhere. Watch them fuckin' grenades!' There's always danger in close combat of hitting one's own mates. With the Chinks swarming all over the spur, stuff was flying everywhere. I could hear them chanting '*Dola-dola*', out of breath and chattering, and doubtless swearing into the bargain. Lower down, whistles were blowing, no doubt ordering the rest of the Peking Wanderers to head our way.

There was a rustling in the undergrowth coming my way and I swung round with my rifle poised. Just in time, I heard Thommo's voice: 'This way. Come on Reg. Watch that bloody rock!' They were carrying a wounded mate, whose groans I could hear.

The shooting had died away as suddenly as it had begun, apart from an occasional burst of machine-gun fire. I could hear what was left of 8 Platoon sliding down into the valley behind us to where Battalion Headquarters was set up. Still feeling pretty tense, despite the lull, I wondered just who those 8 Platoon survivors were and whether dear old Pete was among them. It was some time before I found out.

With the Chinese now sitting right above us, we were fully exposed and were well and truly in the shit. Come daylight, our chances wouldn't be worth a busted flush. I could hear the Chinks up there, settling in and getting reorganised – something they would badly need, for they had taken a hell of a lot of casualties. I was quite alone in my dugout and seeing the blokes in the next one climbing out was all I needed to make me follow suit.

Things were a bit shambolic as we moved back. The Chinese had opened up with machine-guns and bullets were flying everywhere. Williams was frozen in his dugout and had to be dragged out. Captain Mitchell, our new Company Commander, ordered us all to kneel and form a straight line. 'Mac' MacIntyre and I were lying side by side in the rubbish pit, on top of a pile of empty cans, at the end of that line. At least it offered some sort of cover. Neither of us was too keen to obey that order to kneel, not given directly to us. So we didn't!

Then came orders to withdraw. We did! In double-quick time, scrambling down to join Battalion Headquarters and 170 Mortar Battery, who by this time had virtually no protection in the open valley.

That was the last I saw of our Company Commander or Lieutenant Haggerty who, I was told, had been wounded. We got on with helping the Gunners to carry their 4.2" mortars up the other side. It had been decided that what was left of the Battalion would regroup on Hill 235, a westerly ridge running parallel to the southern side of the road. For most of the rest of the day, the survivors of the various companies were sorted out and reorganised whilst such officers as remained took stock.

I well remember trying to dig myself a dugout, having only my bayonet with which to do so, all the picks and shovels having been left behind. It was soon quite obvious that I was wasting my time; the job was impossible. In any case, we were not going to be in that spot for long. As I sweated, I saw Regimental Sergeant Major Jack Hobbs sitting on a slope some thirty yards away and watching my frustrated efforts with a look on his face as if to say, 'Don't bother, son. It's a waste of time and energy.' The Jack Hobbs I knew was the very model of all that a soldier should be. Now, even he was looking dejected as he propped himself on one elbow, obviously coming to terms with the situation which could, at best, only hold out the hope of survival in a Chinese prison camp. It was only about six years since he had been released from captivity in Germany, so he'd done it all before. I sat up from my labours and faced him like a naughty schoolboy. By now, all the hills to the south were swarming with Chinese infantry. Thanks to the disappearance of 1 ROK Division, we were completely surrounded. So, like every other member of the Battalion, we were in the shit together.

The sick and wounded had been gathered together in a makeshift RAP on a ridge just above us. As I looked up there I could see the Chaplain giving the last rites to 8 Platoon's Sergeant Eames, who had been shot in the chest. As I saw him lying there, my mind flashed back to that moment on Hill 327 when I had seen him silhouetted against the evening sky, full of the pride that comes with success in battle and looking, as I put it then, 'like a conquering gladiator'. He was a fine bloke and it came as no surprise to me later to learn that he had died with a calm dignity.

By now we were out of everything – ammunition, food and, perhaps most important of all, water. We then heard that an airlift was on its way. At last we saw the Dakotas in the far distance, headed our way. Their side doors were opened as they approached and the parachutes began to tumble out. To our anger and great disappointment, they drifted like dandelion seeds in the wind and fell outside our perimeter. The aircrews must have been on their first mission, utterly clueless and lacking any sort of common sense. All we could do was to shake our fists impotently at them, shouting all the names we could lay our tongues to. Without that resupply we were in dead trouble.

As the day wore on, it was decided to move to the upper ridge that ran parallel to the road, taking the wounded up with us. Our platoon took the rear flank yet again, though, in all truth, since we were in a position of all round defence, every platoon position was a forward one. The Chinese had followed up as we left the lower base and we could now hear them digging in. Throughout that night, I and two others lay protecting this rear flank whilst the rest of the platoon dug weapon pits with tools salvaged by the Battalion and passed around to the now greatly reduced companies.

The night passed without incident and, come the dawn, I was given a dugout nearest to the closest Chinese which I shared with another National Serviceman, Parkinson. As I had remarked to Danny at

101

Sinan-jui all those weeks ago, I reckoned the regulars thought that we National Servicemen could run faster than them!

We could now feel the net closing in. Right opposite our dugout, just about where I had tried to dig on the previous day, a Chinese soldier stood up and began to scan our ridge. He must have been about 600 yards away. However, we took a couple of shots at him, which seemed to leave him quite unmoved. Either he was stupid or just scoffing at us. His survey over, he just dropped down into his hole behind a little bush. A good mortar man could have got him with his second shot, if he had been worth the precious bombs. As we now knew only too well, one dead man would be replaced by many more, some of whom we could hear only 50 yards away.

Suddenly, we heard a helicopter approaching, greeted by sporadic rifle fire. It headed for the far end of our ridge where Colonel Carne had his headquarters. I was told that this was Brigadier Brodie, our Brigade Commander, come to weigh up the position and discuss possible action for escape. As the machine swept past our dugout, I imagined myself clinging on to its undercarriage and heading for freedom.

That day passed quietly enough for us, but at the northern end of the ridge our blokes were kept hard at it repulsing Chinese attempts to overrun us.

Despite the grimness of our situation, there was one incident which had us all in fits of laughter. Unbelievably, coming down the road from the river crossing, which we now overlooked, came a group of Chinese cyclist troops, pedalling in single file as if on a Sunday morning outing. They were heading south and so getting ever closer to our position. Even though they were as yet some distance away, we could tell from the turning of their heads in conversation and the lifting of their feet, that they were enjoying themselves.

One of our surviving Vickers machine-guns was soon getting a fix on the road at its nearest point to us, with plenty of advice from the dugouts along the ridge, whose occupants were relaying the action to one another. All eyes were fixed on the group as they came closer. When they were about 3,000 yards away, the music of the Vickers sent a chorus of cheers from all along the ridge, followed by gales of laughter as the Chinks spilled over one another in a huge pile-up! One man stood up for a second or two in shock and then ran like a hare across the paddy, with bullets kicking up the earth around his ankles, just to help him on his way!

The pile gradually got disentangled and figures could be seen scuttling like rabbits into the sparse cover each side of the road. Whether any of them had been hit was of no importance; it had been a fine show of defiance and welcome light relief for we seemingly doomed, and certainly tired, hungry and thirsty, survivors. As had our Drum Major Buss's superb rendering of a medley of bugle calls, from Reveille to Last Post, as he stood, fully exposed, contemptuously answering the cacophany of sound from the Chinese bugles.

Snatches of information filtered down the line of dugouts throughout the day and we learned that a Filipino tank squadron and a battalion of infantry were supposed to be coming to reinforce us, if they could break through. However, we realized only too well that any bird brain who had seen the volume of Chinese infantry, who must by then have been 10 miles south of us, would have known that their chances of success were zero.

At about midday a squadron of Mustang fighters came roaring in over the treetops, giving a brilliant display of precision strafing no more than 50 yards from us. We had a front seat and were cheering like men possessed until the napalm started to fall. Our admiration changed to disgust and pity, if you can believe it, for our Chinese counterparts, front-line soldiers like us. The look Parkinson gave me echoed my feelings. However, it was a lucky break for us, as the impact of that airstrike gave us another uneventful night whilst the enemy licked their wounds although, of course, it brought no sleep, for they were only just below us, knocking on our front door.

In the morning, much to our relief, the message was relayed to us to pull back. We were going to attempt to break out.

As I climbed out of our trench, a bullet cracked past my ear and thudded into the loose soil at the top, inches from my hand. The effect upon me was magical. Despite my cramped legs and dulled brain, I was out of that foxhole like a greyhound out of a trap, with only one thought in my mind: to get over the crest and join the Company. Bullets skipped around me all the way, but I made it!

Seeing what the reaction had been to my quick dash gave my mate Parkinson little comfort, but he knew only too well that he too had got to run that gauntlet. He came flying over the crest, not knowing whether to laugh or cry. 'Jesus Christ!', he gasped, panting his heart out and hitting the ground with his open palm. 'Fuckin' 'ell, we made it!', he said. 'When I watched you go, I thought that it was a bloody miracle that you weren't hit.'

'Only the good die young', I replied with a laugh.

It was now going to be a case of 'every man for himself'. Our last orders came from Colonel Carne, to go in groups or singly to the south. 'Make your way back as best you can and good luck!' The Medical Officer, Bob Hickey, and the Padre, Sam Davies, were going to stay with the wounded. What a decision to have to make! I have the greatest admiration for those men. There was no possibility of 'every man for himself'

103

for them. In accordance with the finest traditions of the Army, they knew where their duty lay.

For the rest of us, 'every man for himself' was the logical answer. We had virtually no ammunition left. One burst from a Russian sub-machine-gun, and just about every other Chink seemed to have one, could wipe out six men as quickly as one. By now my own instincts for self-preservation were uppermost in my mind. Whether I would stop to help a wounded mate with disregard for my own safety, had yet to be put to the test.

There was only one way for us to go: down to the valley below. The Chinese had been seen to occupy all the surrounding hills. 'Where there's hope, there's life', they say, and we had not given up yet. There was only one way down to the valley, as the hills on both sides of it were fairly steep. A footpath led to the bottom, and very soon there were about 100 men scattered along this stretch, some of whom were wounded, with blood-stained dressings on their head or limbs. It was hoped that the valley would open out on the far side of a ridge that stretched across it. Meanwhile, we all dismantled our weapons. Bolts and pins were thrown in opposite directions and, finally, rifle stocks were smashed on the rocks which littered the hillside.

As the leading group approached the ridge, we came under fire from the hills to the north. This had the effect of charging our weary bodies with sufficient energy to enable us to get to the cover of the ridge, hoping that we were not just 'sitting ducks' in their sights. We all realized full well that if one of us were wounded he would have to be left to the mercy of the Gods, or a good mate.

Our hopes for a widening of the valley on the far side of the ridge were dashed. It just continued in much the same way and we had not gone far before we were under heavy fire from both sides. That was it! We had reached the end of the road. Unarmed as we now were, there was nothing for it but surrender. I could see figures, fanned out and firing into our midst, coming down the hills on both sides.

I was desperate with thirst, for no water had passed my lips for three days and the sight of a pebbled stream, full of beautifully clear water, made me decide that at least I would have a good drink before I died. I dropped into the stream and, as the clear, running water rippled past, I lay face down in its shallow depths. I could hear sporadic shooting and mused, 'Maybe I'll lie here and pretend I'm dead.' Then the thought of a bayonet in my back passed through my mind. Revived by that life-saving drink, I was seized by a wave of anger and, grabbing a rock in one hand, I determined that I would not die like a coward. I stood up and an amazing sight met my eyes. A horde of armed, lightly leather-belted men in sand-coloured uniforms were hugging and shaking hands with our blokes who, like me, were in a state of shock. Who the hell were these men? South Korean or North Korean guerrillas? On their feet were tattered gym shoes. The Chinese we had seen to date had all been wearing padded uniforms. The burst of hope that had sprung up in my mind changed to resignation when I realized that they were Chinese soldiers in their summer uniform.

We were prisoners-of-war!

Gathered together we were led to a clearing . . . to be shot? No. But that thought *did* enter our minds.

Still undecided about their friendly behaviour, we sat with 'burp gunned' Chinese on all sides. Now, for the first time, I noticed the congealed blood on my socks. Pulling up my trousers, I found that I had small pieces of shrapnel, some three-quarters of an inch long, jagged into my flesh and also a sliver of rock. Fortunately, I had no difficulty in removing them all.

Close to me was a deep open dugout, occupied by a cowering Chink who went half out of his mind whenever an aircraft was heard. Was it fear or shellshock? Who knows? Had he not been there, I might have had other ideas about the use of that dugout.

A squadron of fighters came screaming over and we were ordered to stand out in the open and wave. This we did. Fortunately, they got the message and the leader did a victory roll to let us know. Good lad!

Two hours had passed and units of Chinese infantry were passing through the valley on foot, each carrying a small branch for camouflage. Those caught in the open when aircraft came over simply went to ground, blending in completely with the terrain. I could not help pondering on what we were seeing at close quarters and thinking how many lessons there were for us to learn about this form of warfare, for which we had been so ill-equipped, from our cumbersome .303 rifles down to the soles of our hob-nailed boots.

An authoritative-looking character came along with two hangers-on, one of whom carried a camera. He told us that we were now prisoners of the Peoples' Republic of China and, being working-class people, were their friends. Here in Korea we had just been cannon fodder for the American warmongers. Luckily for us, they had now saved us! Having what they called a 'lenient policy', we would be well treated and taken to a prisoner of war camp in a safe zone.

'Mac' MacIntyre, who was sitting next to me, murmured, 'How about some chop chop then, mush?'

Earlier in the day, we had had little appetite but now, having eaten nothing for three days, we were ravenous, in fact starving. We spent that night in the open. Huddled together in groups, our close proximity to one another ensured that we did not waste bodily warmth, all turning in unison like good soldiers. Although we had no idea of what exactly was in store for us and hence most of us were feeling a bit apprehensive, the cold, like the danger in which we had lived for the past week, ensured that our thoughts were concerned with the immediate future – like how we would get through the night and when we were going to get something to eat? Fortunately, I was still wearing my heavy duty pullover, cap comforter and the camouflage net that we wore as a scarf.

Thank God it was spring!

*   *   *

The quality of the Glosters' stand on the Imjin is succinctly described by Max Hastings in his The Korean War:*

> 'The serene conviction of most officers and men that they could cope, even as their casualties mounted, their perimeter shrank, and their ammunition dwindled.'

Of some 600 men in the forward area, 63 were killed and nearly 200 wounded. The bulk of the survivors were taken prisoner apart from 39 men from D Company, who were led by Captain Mike Harvey on a circuitous escape route.

The Northumberland Fusiliers, the Ulster Rifles and the Belgian battalion, together with the supporting arms, the Gunners of 45 Field Regiment and 170 Mortar Battery and the cavalrymen of the 8th Hussars, had all fought magnificently and paid a very heavy price in casualties. The Brigade had suffered some 1,000 casualties, which represented some 25 per cent of its total strength.

Brigadier Tom Brodie had twice asked the Americans for permission to withdraw. Both requests were refused by Corps Headquarters. That as much of the Brigade survived as was the case was little short of a miracle; they had been fighting two full-strength Chinese divisions, upon whom they inflicted extremely heavy punishment despite the fact that their supporting medium artillery had been withdrawn just before the battle; and they had had virtually no close air support, apart from one or two isolated sorties. As Hastings records:

> 'In the Korean campaign, from the beginning of 1951 to the end, there was no other instance of the UN Command permitting a substantial force to be isolated and destroyed piecemeal over a period of days.'

---

* *The Korean War*: Max Hastings (Michael Joseph, 1987).

The Chinese offensive foundered completely and, despite the cost, 29 Infantry Brigade's contribution to that defeat had been considerable, for the attacks put in by the Chinese on the western flank were, in fact, the main effort of their offensive. As Hastings tells us, never again could they launch another major offensive with the slightest prospect of strategic success.

Lieutenant Colonel Fred Carne was later awarded the Victoria Cross for his magnificent leadership in the battle and, uniquely for a British regiment, the President of the United States awarded the Glosters a Presidential Citation for valour.

10

The March

Eight days later, on the verge of starvation, we found ourselves wading back to the wrong side of the Imjin River, with dead Chinese bodies everywhere. The only thing that had passed our lips since we were captured was boiled water. Even to walk for a *shobean* (toilet) made you feel dizzy. We now shacked up in a large brush-fenced farmhouse. Mac and I had cast around for anything edible and had managed to find some little grains of rice around the grinding stone in the middle of the farm-yard. To these we added bits of root that we had dug out and some tiny edible-looking green vegetation around the fence.

All the next day we watched a Korean peasant planting rows of seed potatoes about 35 yards away. Just about three or four feet from the brush fence were some slightly raised rows of earth and we realized that these must be where he had heeled up some potatoes which he had planted a few days earlier. We were absolutely desperate for food and, whatever the risk, we determined to see if we could not raid those rows as soon as it got dark. So, in the meanwhile, we very carefully made a narrow gap in the hedge through which I could wriggle in order to get my hands into those rows.

With Mac watching the guard who patrolled that side of the yard, I quietly eased myself out as darkness was falling. At full stretch, taking care not to disturb the surface too much, I scratched into the stony soil, taking out anything that felt damp. My 'catch' was five pieces of potato. In our waterbottle mug we made a sort of 'brew' with our bits and pieces and, fortunately, survived!

The Chinese were almost as short of food as we were, thanks to the activities of the UN air forces, known to them as the *Figgee Fongala*.

Their supplies came in by porter, mule cart or donkey and the system, thanks to the aerial harassment, was stretched to its limits.

When all was going well as far as their logistic support went, the Chinese soldier in the field carried his own rations, consisting of crushed and powdered soya bean and peanuts carried in a stocking bandolier. This powder was mixed with water in the bowl which every man carried and he would live on that dreary but substantial and nutritious diet for weeks on end.

All eyes became fixed on a shack on the far side of the potato field, for we had learned that this had become a cookhouse and that our first meal was being prepared there.

At last it arrived, in a massive steel cauldron, steaming-hot. It was placed out in the open and left. Despite the strength of the urge to grab some of its contents, Mac and I held back, watching in disgust as a group of about ten men ran like hyenas to the cauldron, groping and squabbling, trying to snatch all they could. One even dipped his dirty hat into the mixture and got badly burned for his pains.

When it was clear that their efforts would be to no avail, they just stood as if some giant hand had smitten them. Our disgust was as great as their embarrassment, as our Chinese captors watched this shameful exhibition. One could almost hear the Chinese thinking, 'What sort of people are these?' The Chinese cooks then appeared and dished out the contents of the great pot fairly to us all, supervised by their officers.

That pot was all of three and a half feet high and contained a very watery mixture of grain, even when well stirred. The problem for most of us was the finding of a container to put our share in. Fortunately, I had found a hardened gourd in the eaves of the farmhouse, which Mac and I had been using for washing. Though rather big, I was able to use that. Mac had the cup of his water bottle. Greatly cheered by even this watery mess, he and I entered into the spirit of the situation and made chopsticks out of twigs broken from the bush fence.

A couple of wise former prisoners of the Japanese cleaned out the bottom of the cauldron, scraping off the lightly burned skin from the rice grains which lined it. This delicacy soon became in great demand after future meals, for it could be kept like a packed lunch to satisfy a hungry stomach.

Our stomachs had shrunk so much that even that apology for a meal had gone quite a long way towards satisfying us, but it had made our craving for a smoke even more acute. On the following day, we were given a more wholesome meal in the form of crushed soya beans. Rather like thick brown semolina, it was not too bad tasting and was rich in vitamins. To our delight, there was enough left over to give us second helpings, although some poor blokes, though hungry, could not face it as dysentery had already hit them. My old mate Stan Lee, like several others, was beginning to look pretty gaunt.

That night we were to start marching north once more, which may explain the appearance of some nourishing food for, without it, many of us would have been in no state to undertake long marches. Travel by day was avoided, at least for the early part of our trek, because of the continuous threat from American air surveillance. We were told that we were heading for a camp where food would be plentiful – though that prospect was something we would have to see for ourselves before we believed it! It was not just food we wanted but also the chance of a smoke.

It was good to be on the move once more, even though we were northbound. We were still more or less grouped in our old platoons. Danny led our group and I brought up the rear, which was also the tail of the column. Two Chinese guards marched behind me, the older of whom was a cheerful, friendly fellow. The younger one was a miserable little bastard. Soon, getting into the rhythm of our march, the old fellow fell into step with us. He loved the sound of our boots and, during our first rest, he inspected my tipped and studded soles. '*Dinghoe*' (good), he said.

Sitting there in the dark at the side of the road, sharing our 'packed lunch' of a sticky wodge of cold, crushed soya beans with Mac, I thought to myself, 'If my Mum could see me now!'

A Chinese unit came through on foot. Like us, they moved in single file, some carrying heavy loads hanging from poles across their shoulders. Where broken-down trucks were blocking the road, they moved on with a stoical sort of shuffle, pushing past us.

To my amazement, from the middle of that column a voice asked in a loud whisper 'What regiment, mate?' It had been said with a strong Geordie accent. I could hardly believe my ears but replied, 'Glosters.'

That voice belonged to Kinne of the Northumberland Fusiliers, who would join our own march a bit later. I well remember him pulling a Korean peasant halfway through a brush fence when he was supposedly swapping a watch for a few leaves of tobacco. That watch became his tobacco ration ticket. He never, ever let go of it! He was a real rough diamond and gave the Chinks trouble from day one. Apparently, his brother had been killed in Korea. Whatever the reason, his vehement hatred of all things Chinese, his pig-headed stubbornness or whatever, he got himself into one hell of a lot of trouble and spent long periods away from his mates. He was probably lucky not to have been shot.

Whilst I was still musing about that voice, the cry of '*Figgee Fongola*' was relayed down the column as an American fighter shot over our heads like a single rifle shot, followed by a rolling thunderclap, its sound echoing amongst the distant hills until it became inaudible. Until then

110

we had had mixed feelings about these aerial visitations, which were incessant, but then we got the taste of one. Rockets were skidding off the road and ploughing into the bank behind which we lay. It was only when we saw the smoking wrecks of burning trucks and other hardware that we remembered that they were on our side.

Every night we marched between 20 and 25 miles, resting during the day. Apart from my blistered feet, which were a continual problem, I was feeling pretty fit, believe it or not. During those long slogs, I lived in a world of fantasy, imagining that I was walking down the streets of Cheltenham, looking to see what was on at the Regal cinema or hoping to bump into some of my mates. I was lucky to have escaped the scourge of dysentery. For blokes like Stan, those marches were absolute murder. It was a miracle to me that they survived.

Tobacco was still an awful need. During the twilight hours of each march, with Danny up front acting as spotter, we got pretty good at collecting the stray butt ends, much to the amusement of our old Chinese guard who twice slipped me little packs which he had scrounged for us. In absolute contrast to our old friend was a guard who was pig-faced and pock-scarred, with tiny eyes. I had mentally christened him 'Pock-face'. He was not only disliked by us but also by his fellow guards. One day, in an argument, he pointed his burp gun threateningly at one of them, who replied by grabbing two stick grenades from his belt and challenging him to shoot. Luckily for him, he didn't.

We very nearly had a tragedy on our hands when quick-tempered Tug Wilson stupidly shook his fist at Pock-face who came within an ace of shooting him. It certainly wasn't funny and he undoubtedly tucked Tug's tail between his legs.

Considering the extremely tough life we were living and the demands it made upon even the fittest of us, the irrepressible British soldier's spirit was well to the fore, although that spirit was sometimes dampened when we found that we had been marching half the night in a complete circle. We even wondered whether the Chinks were doing it on purpose, in the hope that we would drop dead from exhaustion. However, we soon put a stop to that by finding our north-pointing star and bringing any deviation from our northbound progress to the attention of the Chinese with cries of '*Bahoodie*' (no good) and singing our song which went:

> '*We are poor little lambs who have lost our way.*
> *Baa, baa, baa.*'

That one was high on the repertoire of the songs we sang. Even my old Chinese mate behind me would join in the chorus, grinning all over his jolly old face.

One could not but recognize that our captors fared little better than we did, despite being admittedly on the right side of the fence. We were soldiers who had been taken prisoner in battle, but we were still being paid. Their only pay was the sustenance they were given to keep them alive for another day. Yet, night after night, rain or shine, they would be foraging amongst the Korean peasantry to provide the essentials for our daily meals, which depended mainly upon their success or failure in their searches.

We could never get away from those ceaselessly patrolling Sabre jets of the US Air Force. One night, as we were crossing a river, barefoot, with our boots hanging by their laces round our necks, a patrol of Sabre jets came screaming in, shooting up our crossing place, the tracer hosing from their wings and spraying the surface of the river. Mac and I were caught in mid-stream. Despite the extreme unpleasantness of our situation, we could not help laughing at each other as we shook our fists at the pilots, calling them all 'sons of bitches' and any other epithet which came to mind. Although the empty cartridges from their canons were dropping all around us, hissing in the cold water, there were, mercifully, no casualties. 'Whose fucking side are you on?' shouted Mac.

One night Mac and I were both taken short and dropped out to relieve ourselves, squatting in the pitch black just off the road. A young guard was escorting us. As the sounds of the column began to fade, I could tell that he was getting nervous, a fact that became only too obvious when he upsticked and left us. So there we were, free as air to go which way we chose, north or south. Knowing full well, from our own experience, the folly of trying to slip through the huge concentrations of enemy in the south, we found ourselves running to catch up the column!

We came to what was known as the 'Halfway House' where we were to rest our weary selves for a few days. This gave us a chance to see our mates who had been marching ahead of us in the column and gave me the opportunity to ask for news of Pete from my mates in 8 Platoon. I was very sad to learn that he had been killed. Reg Coltman told me that Pete had got out of his trench with his beloved Bren gun fully loaded and stood there pumping bullets into the Chinese until he himself had been cut down, badly wounded in the stomach. Reg and Thommo had then managed to get him back to the RAP – so the wounded man I had heard them dragging through the undergrowth that night had been Pete. There had been no hope for him. When they overran the position, the Chinese mercifully shot him to put him out of his misery. Thommo was also at Halfway House, with a neat bullet hole through his arm, which by then was healing fast.

What Reg had told me had really only confirmed my worst fears for

Pete and I did not allow myself to dwell on the thought of his death. It is one of the curious things about war that soldiers quickly learn to accept death, even the death of one's best friend, with a philosophical calm, any sense of loss perhaps coming much later. In all truth, each of us was primarily concerned with his own survival. I had survived and for that I was grateful.

The diet upon which we had been subsisting on the march, and for which our guards had to scour the countryside, consisted chiefly of crushed soya beans, rough unskinned rice and, on one occasion, black beans as well. The best had been a top quality rice with a delicious nutty taste which had come from a little village at which we had been sheltering one day, located in a rich agricultural area.

As we were enjoying this meal, we were watched by a group of well-educated, friendly Koreans who called me over to the kitchen where they were boiling sugar cane. They spoke English with an American accent and asked me to tell them who we were.

We stood watching the contents of the can boiling and one asked me, 'Do you like?' Now, that was a silly question, but a kind one.

'Very much', I replied. What I also liked was the two-pound tin in which a generous helping was being ladled.

'Can I keep?' I asked, holding the hot tin in my jersey.

'OK, you keep.'

That night we shared the best meal we had had to date – steaming-hot best quality white rice with sugar cane syrup, christening my precious new billy. To add to our good fortune, we had managed to trade a fountain pen for tobacco with a small Korean boy. Little luxuries which one normally takes for granted, such as having a full stomach and a smoke, were becoming very significant.

Escape hardly entered our minds. To where? We looked nothing like Orientals and it was too early in the year to attempt to live off the land. At least with the column we had security, the importance of which was brought home to us when we stopped over in a town that had just been bombed. We were lucky to escape with our lives. As we arrived, the casualties were still being recovered from the ruins. The town was pretty well to the north of the war zone and, by the look of the people who lived there, they had been enjoying a fairly peaceful existence. As soon as we were seen, a very hostile crowd of North Koreans gathered, some of whom were baying for our blood. We had every reason to be grateful for the firm stand taken by our guards to protect us, especially as amongst the crowd was a unit of particularly aggressive North Korean soldiers who certainly wanted to shoot us all and argued fiercely with the Chinese, who finally cocked their weapons and dispersed them in no uncertain manner. They continued to hang around like a flock of

113

vultures and I wouldn't have given much for the chances of any prisoner who had fallen into their hands.

As the trek had progressed, the guards had relaxed. Their main concern was to make it to the next stopover, for they were finding the going as tough as we did. Because of the diminished danger, we had begun to march by day rather than by night. We spent the night after the near riot in a row of empty shops, feeling distinctly uneasy and only too glad to shake the dust of that town from off our worn ammunition boots on the following morning.

It was good to get out into open country again, though our guards' habit of taking what they thought was a good short cut would all too often lead to our going round in circles. On reaching a village or an isolated farmhouse, they would go off to get directions, returning with much babbling and chatter and to be greeted by us with our '*Poor Little Lambs*' song.

Marching by day, we no longer had our guiding star and the guards had no map (they probably could not have read one anyway), with no food either, so that we indeed looked a sorry sight. Luckily, the sick and more seriously wounded had been left at Halfway House, although there were still some blokes with wounds needing urgent medical treatment. Our guards were changed and I was sorry to say goodbye to my cheerful, fat friend who had tramped behind me for so many miles.

It seemed clear that we had not much further to go. It had been a very tough experience. We thanked God that it was not winter, for the cold of North Korea might well have proved the last straw and put paid to those who were ill, or had wounds to make life even more difficult for them. Even our guards were clearly impressed with our British spirit and our ability to lift ourselves out of our depression with our songs and various antics, which made them laugh.

At long last, we came to the village of Chongsong and what was obviously some form of camp. Then we saw 'Welcome to Chongsong POW Camp No. 1'. Our bedraggled, footsore, bootworn lot had arrived! Two stone lighter than when we had started out as well. Little did we realize that this was to be our home for some two and a half years.

We had no means of knowing just how far we had tramped but, allowing for all those circles we made and the questionable 'short cuts', the distance cannot possibly have been less than 400–500 miles. With the skimpy rations we had had to survive on, to have reached the end of the road still singing and marching was some achievement, even for those of us who were relatively fit and well. For the sick and wounded it was beyond all praise.

11

A Prisoner in Chongsong

To most people, the words 'Prisoner of War Camp' conjure up visions of barbed wire, watch towers and searchlights, surrounding a large group of huts or an ancient German castle converted into a prison. The camp at Chongsong, in which we now found ourselves, was entirely different. Not a coil of barbed wire or a single watch tower were to be seen, although armed guards could be seen on patrol. Situated as it was in the wilds of North Korea, the Chinese had recognized that the chances of making a successful escape were remote.

Uniquely, the camp was based upon the village of Chongsong, which we always called Chongsong Town, and which lay in a picturesque valley not far from the borders of what was then Manchuria. Along its western side flowed a tributary of the Yalu River, which formed the border between North Korea and Manchuria. A main road ran through the middle of the village and was used by the few locals still living in what might be termed the 'town centre' and the farmers who worked the surrounding countryside, so the traffic consisted of a few bullock carts and an occasional truck passing through.

The camp itself was divided into sectors based upon the empty housing lining the edges of the road. An American sector, housing prisoners who had been taken in the earliest days of the war, lay in the northern end of the town. Anything but picturesque, its occupants, looking grey and gaunt, shuffled around aimlessly, having clearly abandoned all hope. Their sick lay at the roadside by day, being gathered up by their mates at sunset and dragged into their houses. Several of the Yanks seemed no longer to be quite right in the head. One of these approached a young Chinese guard, who took fright and shot him in the head.

115

Every day we would see their burial squad, shovels in hand, making two or even three trips up the little hill to the cemetery, which was known as 'Boot Hill'. These Americans had just survived a Korean winter. On their way up from the south by train, about 100 of them had nearly choked to death as the train sheltered in a tunnel to escape the attention of marauding Sabre jets. The carbon monoxide fumes had made the tunnel a virtual death trap. It was also plain that the Yanks were not embraced by the 'lenient policy' that we had been promised and had a much tougher time than we did. The very sight of those tragic, hopeless figures had reinforced the determination of us all that we would never throw in the towel.*

We British were divided into four companies, two in the northern end of the town and two in the south. I found myself in the northern sector opposite the Americans. Our two British sections were separated by the Camp administrative blocks and we were housed in empty Korean housing that ran like ribbon development along the central road. Crops of cotton, black bean and maize grew in fields which ran right up to the edge of the housing. Across the road from the administrative blocks was a large sports area with a hard, stony, clay surface.

Within the companies we were grouped in squads of ten, based mainly upon our original regimental platoons but later we would be switched around and I would then find myself in a squad mostly from 170 Mortar Battery. Those early days in the camp were no picnic. To build us up after our long trek, we were put on a 'special diet' consisting of 2 lbs of hard cracked corn and, if we were lucky, three mouthfuls of greens. You needed a good set of teeth to eat that stuff but you had plenty of time to do so – all day!

The poor Yanks had apparently decided that if they took any exercise they would burn up any energy which that diet gave them. This, to us, was a counsel of despair and we were all determined not to fall into such a hopeless way of thinking. We were a hardy lot and once we had settled into our new surroundings we determined to make the best of the circumstances in which we found ourselves and to take all the exercise we could. Within our perimeter we had a stretch of the river in which we could wash and swim – a real Godsend. One of our first projects was to build a dam across the shallow rock stream which the river became in summer, turning into a raging torrent in September and frozen solid in the winter, weaving its way and running parallel to the main road.

---

* Dupuy's *Encyclopedia of Military History* reveals that of some 10,000 American prisoners, less than 4,000 returned home. The rest, apart from 21 who refused repatriation, either died or were murdered.

We did what we could to keep our tattered uniforms clean and patched up; from our well-worn boots we fashioned razors from the slivers of steel supporting the soles; from corn cobs we made pipes and scrubbing brushes.

Our day would start with the blast of a whistle calling us to assembly, where, as in all POW camps, the guards checked our numbers. In a relaxed military fashion, our own corporals called the roll of each squad. This was always done with a bit of humour, which completely floored the Chinese, who could understand neither our language nor our sense of fun. The roll having been called, Ginger Nawley, one of our regimental Physical Training instructors, who had been limbering up on the road, would yell, 'Come on, lads! Get a shift on!', in return for which he got a lot of good humoured flak from the blokes.

'Get stuffed!', 'You still playing soldiers?', Can't play today!' and so on. It was all good fun and we would be out there to a man, on the road doing our exercises. 'Bend that back, palms down on the deck, uuuup sloooowly, breathing in'. 'Corporal Griffin, can you smell that shithouse? Get it emptied tomorrow'. 'Sir', the corporal replied. 'Breathe in deeply, lads, it will be gone tomorrow.'

That latrine was all too well known to us all. Dysentery was rampant and most blokes spent time up there day and night.

After we had been doing our PT for a couple of days, we suddenly saw that one of the Americans, a bit of a nut case, with red hair, was copying us. Next day he was joined by two others and then, on the day after that, by the whole company.

This was great and we gave them the thumbs up sign. Even the guard patrolling the dividing road was smiling.

Ginger shouted 'Good on yer, mates!' and gave them a silent hand-clap.

Within a week, an air of renewed activity could be seen in the American sector, though, sadly, those trips to Boot Hill went on.

Thanks to our combined efforts to keep fit and as tidy as conditions would allow, that wonderful Glosters spirit ran right through the companies and even the scourge of the summer heat, the lice and the flies, could not dampen it for long. Lice were an unending trial and one had to devote a good hour each day to delousing. Flies seemed to flourish under the conditions in which we lived and were a bloody pest as we tried to eat our tins of hard cracked corn, with one hand covering the tin and the other making a continuous strafing of our faces.

An invaluable contribution to the maintenance of our morale were the typical Glosters sing-songs that we often held in the evenings. We would sit in a big circle in a large open space in the middle of our company area. Corporal Mick Richards, known to us all as 'Spike', was our

Master of Ceremonies. He would open the proceedings with something like this:

'OK lads, you've all had a good day, a nice swim, got rid of those creepy, crawly things, and you've got a bellyful of hard tack, so let's hear those lovely voices.'

And off we would go with a long list of songs of every variety – humorous, sentimental, traditional and, inevitably, bawdy barrack favourites.

It would not be long before we heard Archie Coram's melifluous tenor strike up with 'The Blackbird', followed by 'Buttercup Joe' and a string of splendid West Country songs. Archie just lived to sing and we all loved to sing with him, lifting the roof of the starlit Korean sky. We always finished with two great favourites, 'I'm a Fine Musician', presenting the Chongsong Philharmonic Orchestra, in which each singer in turn introduced a different instrument, ending with a five-foot-nothing Jock being lifted by his mate, so that he could reach the top notes on the double bass! This always sent the guards into paroxysms of laughter. Finally, giving it all we'd got, we delivered a rousing 'Land of Hope and Glory' which would go echoing round the valleys.

Those sing-songs were enjoyed by everyone, prisoners, guards and the Korean peasants, who we could often see sitting in rows along the edge of the footpath that crossed the hills behind the camp, a vantage point from where they would also watch us playing football. The Americans, who also looked forward to those evenings, dubbed us 'The Singing Bloke Regiment'.

The PT, swimming, football and sing-songs played a very important part in our lives, going a long way to countering the inescapable depression which hits every prisoner of war from time to time. They also rubbed off on our American neighbours although we could get no closer to them than that at that stage, thanks to the patrolling armed guards whose job it was to keep us apart. For us, they did so much to keep alive the spirit of comradeship which had always been so strong in the Regiment and reinforced our determination not to be got down by the trials of prison life and the uncertainties of the future. How long our incarceration would last was anyone's guess, for we got little or no news of the progress of the war.

Our billets were in rows with areas in between where we could play football or any other game we could organize. We also had a well, as in all Korean villages. From it we drew our water for cooking and drinking, which we boiled, enjoying the nearest and only substitute we would get for tea throughout our captivity.

Every time I passed that well, my mind would take me back to those magical days when I had first met Heesoon and her mother. I had long tried to put those memories out of my mind for I knew, only too well, that we would never meet again but memory is a fickle jade and mine would not be denied.

As the year moved on and the level of the river rose, I would pit my strength against the tide each day, for I had always loved to swim. There were small catfish in the river but short of the rather ineffectual Korean method of fishing, which involved stunning the fish by smashing one heavy rock against another, there was no way we could catch them.

Our maize diet was replaced by sorghum, a round pink-looking grain which is fed to cattle in England. Although it had a high protein content, it had an indescribable taste to which one had to get acclimatized and some blokes simply could not stomach it. Fortunately, I *could* eat it. The stuff was either boiled or made into mauve-coloured bread, which was a bit more palatable, but we all felt that almost any change of diet would be an improvement. Then, to our delight, manna came from Heaven in the shape of a wild black pig which had been knocked down on the main road. As a special treat, we were to have him for dinner, with rice too, which to us was a luxury in itself. That poor pig would never know the adrenaline he aroused in some 150 men. Picked up by one of our Chinese instructors, he was to be shared by all in our sector.

On the morning of the feast, we watched the Chinese prepare him, an education in itself. Laid out on a makeshift table outside the cookhouse, the skin of all four trotters was cut. Into these incisions a long half-inch steel rod was inserted, separating the skin of the pig from its flesh. Two front legs and one rear leg were then bound above the cuts, the fourth cut being used by the Chinese cook to blow air into the carcase from his powerful lungs. His audience cheered his every blow as the pig began to swell like a balloon until the last leg was finally tied and he (the pig!) lay on the table with his four legs pointing skywards. He was then suspended over a large wooden tub of boiling water and every vestige of his hair was either shaved or scraped off, making him ready for the pot.

The aroma that drifted from the cooking pot was to us like the bouquet of a fragrant wine, stirring our taste buds to dripping as we eagerly awaited the call of 'Connor up!'*

We had nearly all, by now, mastered the art of using chopsticks, which we had whittled from suitable pieces of wood. Our 2lb tins of corn had provided us with '*chop chop*' tins. In order to get the last drop of blood from the stone, most of us had beaten the bottom of our tins to make them dish-shaped. They were presented to the 'disher-outer' in the palms of both hands, our caps held beneath for protection from the heat

* Connor: Army slang for food.

119

or overspills. The cookhouse was run by the Chinese with the help of a few prisoners, who were definitely onto a good thing! A much coveted job.

At last the meal was ready. Each man was given a 2lb tin of first grade white rice and half a one pound tin of delicious stock together with two small pieces of pork, the size of Oxo cubes. We revelled in it as we dipped the rice into the stock, our lean bodies extracting all its goodness. After all those months of hard cracked corn and sorghum, it was nothing short of bliss.

Not long after that feast, the Chinese began to get better organised and to subject us to indoctrination, which was, frankly, a complete waste of their time, though we weren't so stupid as to make that obvious to them. They also put us into a dark blue uniform made of light cotton material with wide-bottomed trousers, a white collarless shirt and a soft cap. In fact, it was identical with their own uniform, except that that was khaki.

★   ★   ★

Whilst we had been on our long march north and during the trying summer months, in which we had gradually adapted ourselves to prison life, there had been some important developments in the war, of which we, of course, knew nothing.

By 1 May, the first phase of the Communist offensive, which had landed us in Chongsong, had petered out. On the 15th they had launched the second phase which proved even shorter-lived than the first. Eight days after they had attacked, General Van Fleet launched his own counter-offensive, designed to exploit the exhaustion of the Chinese. In three weeks the Eighth Army had occupied the area south of Pyongyang known as the 'Iron Triangle', the heart of the enemy's supply and communications organisation.

Chinese morale was by now in tatters, to the extent that by 1 July Kim Il Sung and Peng Teh-huai, the commander of the Chinese 'volunteers', had agreed to an approach from Ridgway for armistice talks. These began at Kaesong ten days later. This new situation had its roots in the expression by the American Secretary of State of America's readiness to discuss a cease-fire and armistice, followed by a call from the soviet Ambassador to the UN for a ceasefire and a similar call on the Chinese radio.

It soon became clear that the Communists would use the talks as a massive propaganda exercise —something that came as no surprise to the UN team. When they realized that the UN was not going to give them what they wanted, they trumped up an excuse, that the US Air Force had violated Kaesong's neutrality, to break off the talks. Fierce fighting followed but by

October the Chinese, who had suffered massive casualties, were back at the
table. Meanwhile they had begun and now continued work on a vast defen-
sive system, burrowing into the hills like moles. It ranged from 15 to 25 miles
deep. At the same time, their forces were being steadily built up again.

It was, perhaps, as well that we were in blissful ignorance of what was
happening, for our hopes of an early release would certainly have been
raised. In the event, it would be almost another two years before we would
be released, thanks to the intransigence of the Communists.

★   ★   ★

The decision to begin our 're-education' brought with it a shuffle of the
squadding and I found myself as a squad leader of a group drawn largely
from 170 Mortar Battery. Apparently, it was Chinese policy for
the young indoctrinated, pure, or not so pure, virgins, like me, to be the
leaders of the New World.

In my new squad was a young, curly-haired bombardier called
Tommy Clough. He had joined the Army on Boys Service at fifteen and
became what was then known as a 'Badgee'.* He it was who I had seen
on many occasions in the OP tank that used to come into our company
position before the Battle of Hill 327, though I had not really got to know
him then, although we could not help noticing his invariable cheerful-
ness. He hailed from Blackpool where his Mum had worked on the
'Golden Mile' but not, I hasten to add, as a girl of the night. He was a
bright lad and read anything he could get his hands on, before we
smoked it! His Dad, a coal merchant, had been a prisoner in Japanese
hands, hence Tommy's hatred of anything with slant eyes, though even
he had to admit that the treatment we got from the Chinese made our
camp seem like Butlins, when compared with the living hell of imprisonment under the Japs.

Essentially, we two were complete opposites. He was more of a spec-
tator than a player when it came to sports and, politically, a true blue
blood for King and Country, though neither of us really knew anything
about politics. Although Communism was a dirty word to us all, deep
down I had a certain respect for equality and a sharing of wealth
according to ability and needs. Tom and I had many a discussion on
that issue. I would tell him he had tunnel vision, for he just didn't

* 'Badgee' (pronounced 'Budgie'): The nickname given to boy trumpeters in
the Royal Artillery. The word means 'time' in Hindi and trumpet calls being
sounded at fixed times during the Army's day led to the boys getting this nickname many, many years ago.

want to hear – an attitude which, quietly, I respected – British to the core.

As for the smoking of books and papers, this was due to the fact that although the Chinese had begun to give us a ration of quite good tobacco, there were no papers on which to roll it. A Gideon's bible which lasted us for some time had proved ideal but then we were driven to use 'The People's Daily', a communist paper published in English, which we were supposed to study but was sent up in smoke by us to enlighten some other more appreciative souls.

To enlighten us on that very subject of equality and the sharing of wealth, we were to start compulsory study periods and were confined to our billets for two hours at a time for this purpose. For my sins, I was to become the monitor as well as the leader of our squad. This entailed a daily visit to the 'office' on the main road to collect the questions for the day which we were supposed to discuss. Typical questions were, 'Who started the war in Korea?', 'Capitalist society needs a war every two years. Why?'

To me, the whole business was way above my head, like looking at a car engine! My mind was an impenetrable void. Yet I was the bloke who had to run the discussions and take notes which I then had to go through with a girl we had christened 'Myrtle', who was an instructor working in the office.

My new squad were all North Countrymen from the real working class areas of Newcastle, Oldham and the like. Although the questions were no more than a big joke to us all, our enforced confinement used to generate heated arguments on football, such as who won the FA Cup in a particular year. The Chinese instructors making impromptu visits, who only spoke limited English, hadn't a cat's chance in hell of understanding what was going on!

'Manchester United stood as much hope of winning that game as that slant-eyed bastard at the door! Isn't that right?' a Geordie would ask, turning to the instructor with a sweet smile to add, 'You go and make love to that Myrtle you've got up there', expressed in army terminology. 'OK' replied the Chink and disappeared, leaving us all in fits of laughter.

Myrtle could have been attractive were it not for her collarless tunic and fringed, short haircut. All of four foot nine, she had a shy, pleasant air about her. Her real name was Liu.

We were all getting into the state in which we could fancy anything and I fancied Myrtle. My vivid imagination told me that she fancied me, like all the other young monitors who had to take the notes of their 'meetings' for discussion with her. Completely clueless, I always found it extremely hard to produce anything that even remotely offered an opportunity for discussion, I just had to bluff my way out of it, like all the others. All we could do was to gaze into her eyes with an air of innocence, which I suspect she rather enjoyed.

A welcome break from our daily routine in camp was a weekly expedition to collect dead wood for the cookhouse stockpile from the surrounding hills. It was a job we all enjoyed even though the Chinese expected us to bring back the heaviest load we could manage. There was even some competition between some of the blokes, for which they would get praise from the Chinks. Always something of a loner in such situations, I would often sit out on the hillside enjoying the view and doing my best to forget that I was a prisoner and the dismal living conditions of our existence, though I grudgingly admitted to myself that as prisoners of war we were enjoying more freedom than we would ever have expected and finding the Chinese surprisingly ready to smile and leave us to do our own things, always provided that we played the game by their rules and didn't try to pull a fast one over them. The few blokes who were foolish enough to do such a thing very soon found that there was a heavy price to pay.

The valley in which the camp lay was beautiful, with the river following the line of hills to the west and the rich, fertile soil, which was already bearing the signs of the spring sowing of the Koreans' crops. Inevitably, I compared it with the lovely valley in which Cheltenham lay, on the edge of the Cotswolds and the scene of all my boyish adventures with my mates and our longbows . . . but, of course, that was different.

We were now reshuffled into new squads, Tom and I remaining together, in a squad of our own age group. I was glad of this for he and I, despite the disparity in our natures, or perhaps because of it, had become firm friends and did most things together, as I had with Pete in the old days. As the year drew on, thoughts of escape came into our minds. In about a couple of months it might be a bit more feasible. We often heard the sounds of heavy bombing at night now and decided that it must be the port of Sinuiju, at the mouth of the Yalu River, that was getting pasted. So, clearly, it seemed to us, the war was still very much on. Of course, we hadn't a clue how near the UN forces would by now be to us and, truth to tell, we were not all that sure just exactly where Chongsong was, except that our river ran into the Yalu, so we could not be far from the Manchurian border. But which way could we go? All the old factors emerged again. For example, any thought of going south was a non-starter. So it had to be into Manchuria or heading for the west or east coasts. As we had known from the outset, Chongsong was a natural prison, needing no walls. From the hills around it anything moving could be seen for miles. The difficulty of living off the land posed a real problem, particularly if we could only move during the hours of darkness – the colour of our skin and my hair made daylight movement extremely dangerous. It seemed that everything was against us. And, of course, we had first to get through the patrolling guards who encircled the camp. In any emergency, those security rings would be extended immediately.

Our confidence was not enhanced by the knowledge that every one of the few attempts to escape already made had led to the blokes being caught within a few days, brought back and charged with countless offences against the Chinese and Korean peoples. Some were in the Korean prison. In the light of the stories told about the brutality of the Korean guards in the Japanese POW camps, this hardly bore thinking about. Others were in solitary confinement, about which all sorts of rumours abounded. As we had already come to realize from our own experience, it was one thing to be a prisoner under the Chinese 'lenient policy' and quite another to be confined as a criminal. So far we had had no confirmation of the treatment meted out to such prisoners but clearly we could expect the worst. So, the whole idea went on the back burner.

Meanwhile we had been put to building a stage in the main square. This was to be used for lectures by our Chinese instructors and for variety shows that we were allowed to put on.

Those lectures were a compulsory bore. All were held outside, sometimes in company lines and at others in the main square. We all made personal stools out of 4" slats nailed to small logs for this purpose. They were very necessary, for the lectures would go on for hours, though sometimes there were touches of humour about the whole proceedings, which helped. At others, the programme would include 'self-criticism' speeches which were intended to redeem those who had spent a spell in solitary confinement. The simplest and easiest thing to do was to write out a full and frank confession. In true soldiers' fashion, the penitents would weave a few twisted words into their speeches to give the lads a laugh. For instance, 'I have been a very naughty boy and I have to tell you men, including the Marines out there that . . .' which, of course, to any serviceman meant 'This is a load of gash'! Ad libbing in a broad country accent had the Chinese absolutely baffled and looking at each other in bewilderment! Then, perhaps the speaker would end 'Oh, I am naughty. Who's naughty?' to which the whole camp shouted 'You are!'

Sincerity being the key to freedom, we all had to play along with this nonsense, stifling our mirth until later. As every soldier knows, once humour has gone out of the window, the outlook is grim indeed.

Our variety shows were something to which we all looked forward, to lighten the dreariness of our days. An ugly scene developed at one of them when Sergeant Sykes cracked a joke, if you could call it that, which ended 'Will he be shot or will he be hung, that great elusive Mao Tse Tung?'

All the material for these shows was censored but, in this case, Sergeant Sykes must have kept his script back, for any reference to Chairman Mao was absolutely out, particularly if it was as offensive as this one. The Chinese were, of course, always present during a show, though much of it was completely lost on them, but they picked up this one alright for, in a flash, our mate was being escorted off stage, to a chorus of 'Boos' from all of us. We decided, as one man, that if they were taking him off, that was the end of the show! In what had almost become a riot, the Chinese panicked. As we broke ranks and started to make our way back to our quarters, armed guards, with rifles cocked and pointing at us, tried to stop the flow, shouting at us. But we were in a maddened mood and called their bluff, just keeping going and ignoring their threats. Fortunately no trigger fingers slipped; had anyone been shot, there would have been a disaster.

It took us some time to persuade the Chinese that in our democratic, free society, free speech was a way of life and that all our political leaders were fair game for any comedian's barbs. It says something for our powers of persuasion that Sergeant Sykes was let off with a severe bollocking and all was forgiven.

In addition to our sing songs and variety shows, we gradually acquired the means of other entertainment or exercise; for instance, a dartboard and a set of darts suddenly appeared from goodness knows where and teams, with names based upon English pubs, were formed. I played for the Barley Mow which was made up of blokes from Cheltenham and district. Of course, it was all very light-hearted stuff; how could it be otherwise with 'Nutter' Roberts as our captain? He was a bit of a character and the instigator of many a ruse to baffle our guards, such as an imaginary ball being passed between a group of the lads or an invisible dog on a lead being taken from post to post, and so on. Groups of us would stand pointing at an invisible object in the sky, making exclamatory remarks and gestures and bewildering the Chinese who began searching the sky in vain! In fact we did occasionally see real dogfights between Sabres and Chinese MiGs.

We even had dancing classes! These, as you might imagine, were a bit of a laugh. Of course we had no ladies as partners. Polly Perkins, who, believe me, was no queer, used to have me in fits as he taught me the Palais Glide, taking the lady's part himself. It was all good clean fun and helped to fill our empty hours between our study periods and the lectures.

Study had become a prime time for card playing, with one of the squad on the door keeping an eye open for wandering Chinese who would drop in unannounced from time to time. They were really no problem as the snoopers mostly had very little English and any mention of Rockefeller or American Imperialists would send them away convinced that we were hard at work! By far the worst aspect of study was the preparation of the notes on our discussions which I then had to go through with Myrtle. Needless to say, everything we wrote in those notes was designed to be acceptable to our instructors.

We were proud of the success we had with our efforts to convert the run-of-the-mill, uneducated guards, some of whom actually became close mates of ours. Even amongst the instructors there were one or two who were pretty well liked by us. These were 'Maggot' and 'Smiler'. Maggot was a tall, broad-shouldered, square headed fellow with quite a fair skin. Like Smiler, he stood apart from the more ardently indoctrinated messengers of the faith. He spoke reasonably good English but, like most Chinese, had problems over getting his tongue around the letter R. Like the rest of his kind, he called me 'Glin'. With a good sense of humour, his main interest in life was to improve his English. With his notebook in hand, he would solemnly take down slang expressions that I had either invented or rearranged. He gave us many a good laugh as he tried them out on us. I confess that, at times, I felt a bit mean about this and gave him some genuine ones. When our tobacco ration was running low, Maggot was my best source of resupply. Once, when we had been out of stocks for over a week, he called me over to his office and handed me a neatly folded little package with genuine pleasure. There was no need for me to open it for the smell told me at once what it contained – a badly needed resupply of tobacco. Later he walked gleefully by as I was sharing a smoke with my mates, sitting in the evening sun outside our billet.

One day, not long before Christmas, we got our first inkling that something was afoot down south which might affect us. We were assembled on the company square to be told that a mug-shot would be taken of each prisoner, with an identifying number. These were to be exchanged with the UN for their prisoners' records. A bit later we were summoned for this to be done. Each man sat there with a piece of cardboard carrying his allotted number. We were not at all fussed about this, for it could only mean that the two sides in the war were talking. That must surely mean at least a glimmer of light down the long, dark tunnel for us.

After Christmas 1951, at which the Chinese made some effort to give us some extra fare, there was a gradual improvement all round. The soya bean must surely be the most versatile, nutritious vegetable that exists. We had it in every shape and form – crushed, boiled, in curds or in milk. Although the quantity of our 'side dish', as we called it, did not vary, the quality sometimes did. We had large white radishes boiled in water with soya bean oil, potatoes cooked in the same way, greens or peanuts. Very

126

often we would get the same side dish day after day with awful monotony. The grades of rice fluctuated, the worst being pretty awful, the best very good. At times we were fed millet, which was worse than sorghum.

Then, luxury, things really looked up with the arrival of a large round three-tier steamer. You have to hand it to the Chinese, they certainly know how to cook. Apparently, cooking is mens' business in China. The steamed bread the Chinese cooks now began to produce was delicious when hot. Cooked in little bricks, or 'cobs' as we called them, it was a major step forward as far as our diet went. But the rest was still virtually chicken-feed. Today, as I feed *my* chickens, I often look at their ration and say to myself, 'What wouldn't I have given for that in the dark old days.' Grub was usually better in the summer months but, come the winter, we were back to square one.

As is normal throughout the Far East, the principal fertiliser on the surrounding paddy fields was night soil, and with the arrival of our camp the local farmers had profited substantially in that respect, for the output of our cesspit was considerable. One day, one of the lads fell into that twenty by ten foot pool of unmentionables, poor bloke, much, I am sorry to say, to the amusement of some of his mates. The incident guaranteed him a few lonely hours until he had been able to make himself presentable once more, thanks to the presence of the river!

Some months after we had first arrived in the camp, all the officers and senior NCOs had been moved and I often wondered now how things were going for them. From the start, Colonel Carne had been in solitary confinement at our end of the Chinese administrative block and we had been able to see him, sitting out, some 150 yards away from us. It was while he was there that he carved the stone cross which is now in Gloucester Cathedral. One of the instructors told me that they had all gone to a camp near the Yalu River and, later, when we heard more heavy bombing in that direction, we were all anxious for their safety.

As the food improved, so too did other aspects of our life. For example, we were provided with the wherewithal to set up volleyball and football pitches on the big sports area across the road from our billets and these were all marked out and brought into use just as quickly as we could manage. Teams and leagues were formed and we all began to benefit from the additional exercise.

As we began to approach our second summer in the camp, the Chinese showed us how to make fly swatters to help us cope with the inevitable swarms that would soon be pestering us again. Each squad was expected to swat fifty flies a day. As the pests began to thin, so the quotas were diminished. Although we joked about it, we all took this task pretty seriously and squad leaders took the bodies to the office

127

where they were scrupulously counted by our captors. We were told that by this means the fly problem in China had been almost eradicated.

Although at times rather like overgrown schoolboys or peasants, the Chinese were absolutely sincere in what they set out to achieve and many of their methods were basically good. Individuals who excelled in any of the tasks given to them were duly praised at the assemblies.

Odd and even childish though the system of self-criticism may have seemed to our Western minds, these sessions were carried out with great sincerity on the part of the Chinks, any unpleasantness committed during the previous week being discussed, each party having its say, so that all views had been aired and we were ready to start a new day or week afresh.

However, as I had long realized, anyone who committed what they saw as a serious crime was in for a thin time. Sergeant Sykes had been extremely lucky. I was one of a number ordered to attend the trial of an American who had been stupid enough to insult Myrtle, calling her a 'Shanghai whore'.

The court was set up like a court martial but all real similarity ended when we came to find that the accused was not allowed to speak. It was patently obvious that the case had been cut and dried beforehand. The Yank got three years imprisonment. My immediate reaction to the sentence was 'God, how long do they think we are going to be here? And three years just for that!' As we were led back to our company, my mind was full of depressing thoughts.

Of course it was inevitable, Dave being Dave, that I should also be in severe trouble ere long. After a restless night's sleep, I was taking a nap but was woken by an instructor who had only recently arrived. In a miserable mood, I told him to 'Fuck off!' He was furious – and so was I! 'Offica!' he shouted. 'Offica!' I followed the miserable so and so to the office. Once inside, he began shrieking almost hysterically.

There were three other instructors in the room and a Gunner called O'Neill who was looking even more scared than I was. However, I was still in an aggressive mood and was calling my man every name under the sun. Unfortunately, his English was much better than that of his colleagues and he understood everything I was saying. He reached up and grabbed a pistol from one of three holsters hanging on the wall. The other instructors dived at him and wrested the pistol from his hand. It all happened so quickly. O'Neill looked amazed and I was almost laughing at him – not that I was playing the hero but probably still only half awake.

An armed guard was summoned and I was whisked away to be locked up in a kitchen of the Chinese administrative block, opposite the main square. There I was left cooling my heels for two days with no food and

128

only the clothes I stood up in. From there I was taken to a small rice storage shed which I shared with a bunch of very friendly furry, creepy-crawlies, who I did my best to ignore. They only came out at night and, apart from uttering a screeching 'Aaaaah!', which frightened me far more than it upset them, there was nothing I could do to get them to go away.

I was fed intermittently, mostly on millet. At times I wondered whether I had simply been forgotten. Then a guard would come along, peek through the top half of the open-slatted door, grunt and walk away. Many of the guards were absolute peasants, plucked from the remotest corners of China. I well remember how one was eating a large slice of watermelon, making the most disgusting noise as he did so. They were all illiterate and few had ever seen a Westerner in their lives before, especially one with fair hair and blue eyes. Some would stand motion-less, gazing at this strange creature – like so many monkeys in a zoo, except that, this time it was I who was behind bars!

Ten days had passed before I was taken out for interrogation and had to listen to a load of rubbish about reactionaries. I was then given a piece of paper and told to write down my thoughts. Needless to say, I wrote what I knew they wanted to read. My many afternoons of discussion with Myrtle had taught me all I needed to know about that! Had they been able to read what had been in my mind, they would have found that what was really occupying it was thoughts of the fair sex, as I sat alone on my rice sacks, longing to conjure up images of my beloved Heesoon, but that experience had now become just a dream and Myrtle tended to take her place.

Two days later I was taken back to my company and my squad, for the inevitable self-criticism. I felt that I had been locked in my room for a few days, like a naughty boy! When I thought back to what had happened to that wretched American who had insulted Myrtle, I re-alized that I had been extremely lucky. What I had hurled at my hysterical Chinese was infinitely more offensive than what the Yank had said! I then learned that it had been decided that there was no place for hysteria at Chongsong and that the fellow was clearly not cut out for instructional work. So he had disappeared from the scene.

Up to the time of that incident, I had got on quite well with the Chinese although they had always seemed a bit suspicious of me. They found it hard to understand how a working class boy could write so well. 'Mac' MacIntyre had once told me that, but for my West Country accent and speech, I could have passed for the Colonel's son. I had often been summoned to the office for what was called a 'free talk' with 'Hedgehog', who was the company's political commandant. He spoke English with an American accent, quite well too, and would ask me such things as, 'If you could order a meal, what would it be?' Now, I could not tell the difference between a lamb- and a pork chop. It was just meat to me, so I said 'One of my Mum's Irish stews and apple pie.'

'No!' he said, 'in a restaurant.'

'I've never been in a restaurant of any note', I replied, 'only cafés.'

The free talks I had really enjoyed were with Myrtle. She always sat very close to me, her little face framed in her fur-lined, hooded winter jacket, her soft voice purring in my ear. Any one with an ounce of common sense could see through any talk bordering on 'information' and such awkward questions were quite easily played to leg but, with her, those sessions were more personal; they were as if I was talking to a girlfriend, except that she asked all the questions. It was nice.

Now however, thanks to my fall from grace and spell in the rice store, I sensed a change in attitude towards me. No more nice smiles from Myrtle and, apart from Maggot, the other instructors ignored me. All of which made me realize that they had, quite wrongly, thought I would be a soft touch and had clearly believed all the garbage I had been spilling for their benefit!

12

A Failed Escape :
The Cages and Slave Labour

At Panmunjom both sides had agreed that operations would continue until satisfactory armistice terms had been established. An attempt by the UN in November 1951 to get a cease-fire line, based upon the current line of contact, provided that all outstanding issues were resolved in thirty days, was a failure. It soon became obvious that the enemy had no intention of calling a halt whilst they were rebuilding their strength and creating a massive defence line, burrowing into the hills like moles. They knew perfectly well that the Western Nations had had more than enough of the war and they believed, therefore, that the UN were unlikely to do anything that was going to involve them in further heavy casualties. They also knew that an increasing number of UN officers and soldiers were becoming utterly disenchanted with the brutal regime of the Syngman Rhee government in South Korea, not least with their treatment of those refugees who were believed to have communist leanings. They were simply shot out of hand –men, women and children, making their UN allies wonder what on earth they were supposed to be fighting for. Furthermore, both Syngman Rhee himself and many of the South Koreans well outside the battle area were openly declaring the presence of UN troops in their country to be unwelcome.

Early in 1952, when the screening of the prisoners on both sides was put in hand, disorder broke out in the camps run by the Americans, where a considerable number of enemy prisoners declared themselves unwilling to be repatriated. In April the UN delegation at Panmunjom informed the Communists that out of 132,000 prisoners in their hands, no less than 70,000 were declining to go home. All attempts to settle the question of repatriation failed and, in May, both sides declared a deadlock.

On 12 May 1952, General Mark Clark succeeded General Ridgway as C-in-C. Less than a month later, in June, the US Air Force bombed the Yalu River power stations in the hope of persuading the enemy to develop a more co-operative line at Panmunjom. It was this bombing that we heard in the camp and which had raised such fears in our minds over the safety of our officers and senior NCOs. That bombing was followed in August by heavy raids on Pyongyang. However, by October the whole question of the future of the prisoners had once more become gridlocked and all talks were suspended yet again.

In November of that year, General Eisenhower was elected President of the United States and it at once became clear that he intended to take a close personal interest and a tough line on the Korean War.

By this time, the UN had gone some way in following the enemy's example over the fortification of their defence line and a near-First World War situation had been established.

★   ★   ★

Although it had little to do with the actual conduct of the war, something of immense importance had occurred on 31 July, 1951. Determined that the sorry story of the fate of 29 Brigade in April should never be repeated, the Commonwealth Heads of Government decided that an independent Commonwealth presence, with strong links to the higher echelons of the UN command structure, should be created. A Commonwealth Division, under the command of the deeply-respected and popular Major General Jim Cassels came into being on that July day. It had three brigades, 27 (Commonwealth), 29 Infantry and a Canadian brigade. A high proportion of the senior members of all its units had fought with distinction in the Second World War and it was small wonder that under Jim Cassels it soon became an outstanding formation. So outstanding was it that newly appointed American divisional commanders would be taken to see it in the field before they assumed their new commands. Within the British units there was a high proportion of National Service officers and men. All would fight magnificently during the months ahead, though, sadly, at a heavy price in brave young lives.

★   ★   ★

In the Spring of 1952, Tom and I decided to make a break for it. We had had more than enough of the Korean winter and, as the weeks and months rolled by, had become increasingly frustrated by a situation to which we could see no end. Tom, ever the good soldier, was deeply conscious that it was his duty to escape if it was humanly possible. As

132

for me, the itch to get off my backside and really do something, the challenge posed by the fact that a successful escape had yet to be achieved and my inborn love of adventure, were what drove me. To be honest, neither of us had really thought the thing through.

There was an escape committee in the camp but we had resolved to do this one on our own – for a start, the committee might not let us go and, in any case, we did not want to put the responsibility for our attempt on anybody else's shoulders.

Young and foolish as we were, we had decided to make our way right across North Korea to the east coast. There we fondly imagined that we would be able to steal a boat. There were now plenty of ripening crops, such as maize and beans, in the fields across the countryside and having survived on them for a year, we knew we could survive on them for a bit longer. One of Tom's friends, a Geordie who worked in the cookhouse, had got a few rations together for us and we had both made ourselves a backpack for the trip.

The night for our departure had arrived. We had spent the evening playing cards with our mates by the light of our flickering soya-bean oil lantern. The lads all knew. As we prepared for *sweejo* (sleep), a hand on the shoulder or a 'Have a good night Dave' was their 'Goodbye'.

Throughout the night, the guards would check each squad from time to time, shining their torches and counting heads, ten to a unit. About ten minutes after the second count we made our move as planned, quietly easing ourselves out into the shadow of the overhanging eaves. The two guards on the road were talking together. We were hoping that as there had been no attempts at escape for some time, and most of those had been from wood-gathering, security might have slipped a bit.

Slipping past those two guards, we made our way towards the Chinese quarters and a path through a field of maize which would lead us down to the river. Keeping close to the edge of the maize, for to walk through it would have made too much noise, there being not even the slightest breeze to stifle the sound of a breaking stem, we suddenly saw a shadowy figure ahead of us and heard the bolt action of a rifle being loaded. Simultaneously, whistles began to blow in all directions. The game was up! We sheepishly raised our hands. The thought passed through my mind that we must have made an all-time record; we were hardly out of the company compound!

Lights now appeared from the alerted Chinese quarters and two more guards appeared from the direction of the river. We were taken to the Camp Commandant who questioned us briefly and then took us to the rear, or river-end of the administrative block. They first put me in what smelled like a stable, twisting wire tightly round my wrists. Tom was led off elsewhere. The door of my 'cell' was locked and I was left to my own devices. After I had felt my way round the small stable, which had a four foot dividing wall down the middle, to create two bays, I settled down in the straw and slept.

When I awoke in the early morning, I at once saw that my guess had been right and that I was indeed in a low-roofed stable, divided into two bays. On one side, thick interwoven wattle filled what had originally been an opening giving access to further bays. On the other side, a door had been made a permanent fixture. The outer door was slatted, allowing anyone to see in or out. The back wall was solid, that is as solid as any wall in a Korean wattle and daub building can be. The roof was, of course, the traditional Korean thatched affair. When compared with a solid brick building, it would have been a comparatively easy matter to bore a way out – but that thought hardly entered my mind.

I soon found that I was not alone. From behind the fixed door, I heard a powerful American voice demanding to be let out to the latrine: '*Shobein!*' accompanied by typical GI terms of abuse, the meaning of which was quite lost on the guard, although the tone probably was not.

I moved across to the point from which the sound seemed to have come, peering through a crack into what had once been a kitchen. There, on all sides, standing upon what had originally been the work-tops, were wooden cages, each containing a prisoner, who could just sit up in it. I could hear the voice of a REME Corporal called Masters, who I knew had attempted to escape a few months earlier. The GI whose voice I had heard abusing the guard was continuing to do so, urging him to let him out, which he did. Whilst they were away, I whispered through the hole in the wall, 'Hi, you in there. Who are you?'

I learned that they had all been in those cages for months, the Mexican-looking GI, who had been abusing the guard in such round terms having been there for over a year. They told me that there were more cages and boxes round the back. Godwin was in one of the boxes. They had convicted him on some trumped-up charge of being a re-actionary and he had been there for some months. I found that there was another GI on the other side of my cell, nicknamed 'Moose'.

I got to know this interesting bloke. He was married to a Japanese girl. As we communicated through the wall, he taught me a Japanese song called '*Kom, Kom, Musume*' which, I believe, was about a girl walking down Ginzano Street in Tokyo, swinging her hips tantalizingly from side to side. I wondered if he had got his nickname from the title of his favourite ditty. He had lived in Japan and I learned a lot about the Japanese from him.

Over the next two or three weeks, I got to learn quite a bit about my new surroundings. The place was known as the 'Kennel Club'. The

Mexican, Tom Cabello, when escaping had got within rifle shot of the front line, covering over 200 miles.

Throughout the day, we were made to sit upright away from any support, although the severity with which this routine was applied depended very much upon the character of the guard on duty. I soon found that it was easy enough to tell when a guard was about to poke his head in: they were as noisy as a bunch of barnyard fowls. When I knew one was coming, I would sit bolt upright in the correct position but in between such visitations I would stretch out my legs. The sanitary arrangements were extremely primitive. On request, I would be conducted round the back to a hole in the ground in a little hut but if no one answered my call and I was hard-pressed, I would urinate where I could. The smell of urine soon became overpowering, reminding me of a boyhood friend's ferret's cage.

Despite pretty strict security, we still managed to get messages through to each other. It seemed to me that the Chinese were trying to demonstrate their understanding of Karl Marx's famous dictum:

'You can keep some of the people down some of the time but you can't keep all of the people down all of the time.'

As I sat in my cell I would often marvel at my good fortune to be in that stable and not in a cage or a box. How those poor blokes stuck being cooped up like that I'll never understand.

When in prison in England, I had been able to split an 'England's Glory' match into four but Chinese and Korean matches were already very thin. Most Chinese like a smoke and we could sniff out the guards' fags a mile away. The great hope was that they would drop their butt ends outside my door so that I could retrieve them with a stick pulled out of the wattle walls of my cell.

I was taken for interrogation several times and whilst outside had usually managed to nick a butt end or two and even some matches. Time seemed to be of no importance on these occasions and they would often leave me in a room to think a bit and indulge in their favourite pastime of self-analysis, in the hope that I would understand and correct my wrong doing. What a hope! Then they would come back again and bore me to death with the same dreary questions over and over again.

The wire with which my wrists had been bound when I was first arrested had been replaced with handcuffs, done up to the last notch. They cut into my wrists which soon turned septic, the consequent swelling making things even worse. I asked a guard to loosen them. He told his superior, who came to see for himself, took the cuffs off and then replaced them exactly how and where they had been before.

One of the guards, clearly a real peasant, would stand endlessly staring into my cell – just gawping. I suppose he had never seen blond hair before. Perhaps he was a 'queer', I just wouldn't know. To my surprise, we had a visit one day from a barber. My hair was now very long and I was lousy – both my head and my clothes, so despite his reluctance to acquiesce to my request, I got him to cut it all off.

When he next appeared on duty, the gormless guard was very upset by the sight that met his eyes and pointing to my head, said, '*Nidi bougho*!' meaning 'You no good'.

To go with the haircut, I was taken down to the river for my first wash for weeks. They refused to take off my cuffs and I found it both difficult and painful to cup my hand and rub my head in the scooped water. Back in my cell, I began to itch like hell as the disturbed lice started to dig in once more.

I shall never forget seeing poor Godwin being lifted out of his box, which was windowless with a hole just big enough to pass through a bowl of sorghum. His brown hair and beard were long and matted. Adjusting his eyes to the light, he moved unsteadily in the direction pointed. Whatever they wanted from him was going to take some time as he was a solid type, and as stubborn as a mule.

They say that every man has his limit and it is my belief that there's not a man who cannot, in the end, be broken. The Chinese were accusing us of the most outrageous crimes and they had to be made to believe what was the truth. Godwin was a man who stuck to his guns through thick and thin, some might say stupidly, but that was the sort of man he was and I, for one, admired him for his guts and integrity. It is a soldier's duty to give the enemy as much trouble as he possibly can. But where do you draw the line? I have often wondered about that. Perhaps it is when the trouble we are creating affects us all, in terms of retribution, more than it harasses the enemy?

Back in the main camp we had our fair share of romancers, who would do anything to attract attention to themselves. In contrast there was a bunch of hooligans who specialized in bullying so-called 'Reds'. In some cases their victims were blokes who were admittedly creeps or 'yes men' and certainly not known for fisticuffs – had they been, they would never have received the treatment they did. I most certainly did not go along with that and despised the bullies who never made any worthwhile contribution to the life of the camp.

*   *   *

My cell offered no creature comforts except the precious freedom of movement denied to the poor blokes in the cages and boxes, but I *did* have a straw mat on the floor to sleep on. On one particular cold night I rolled myself up in it for a scrap of warmth, only to be woken by a bunch of screaming guards and to find the door was open. As I pulled myself up on one elbow, three guards came through the door, all shining their torches on me. When they saw me looking at them, they let out a long drawn-out 'Aaah! followed by what I imagine was the Chinese for 'There he is! He hasn't escaped!'

One of them was so pleased to see me that he gave me a big hug, pointing to me rolled up in the mat and laughing with relief. I do not know what his punishment would have been for losing a prisoner but it would probably have been pretty draconian.

Although I have never been one to stick to the rules, I have always accepted that, if caught, you have to accept the consequences. From what we could see of it, the Chinese soldier faired only a little better than we did and that applied to punishment also.

Moose had been taken away from the cell beside me and his place filled by a Chinese soldier who was visited every day by a correction officer trying to convince him of the error of his ways. Ever the gambler, I called through to him one day, asking for a match. His only response was to summon a guard. To my surprise, the guard held my arm sympathetically saying '*Bohoodee*', or 'No good', as if he were honoured that I had sought help from one of his own comrades. We never could understand their logic!

As, in consequence, I stood in front of the interrogating officer's table for the umpteenth time, I was reminded of my days on probation as a boy. The probation officer would just sit there staring at me and then would ask 'What have you been doing?'

'Oh, I've been down at the Youth Club', which was always a good answer despite the fact that I'd never been near the place.

Now this Chinese bloke was staring at me in just the same way and his question, when at last it came, was just about as fatuous:

'What are you thinking?'

In a fit of temper, I replied:

'What am I supposed to be fucking well thinking?'

I suppose that this outburst was just the consequence of sitting in one place for weeks on end trying to occupy my mind. Whatever the reason, it had a remarkable effect upon my interrogator. Looking quite shocked and also frightened, he got up and left the room. Why I should have had that effect upon him I cannot guess, as I was still in handcuffs. The moment he was through the door, I cleared out his ashtray, before the guard came in to take me back to my cell. Clearly it was the best reply I could have given, for I was never called for interrogation again.

Like every prisoner since the beginning of time, I kept a daily scratch count on the mud wall of my cell. At long last, in my fourteenth week, I was taken out of that ferret hutch, my handcuffs were removed to my intense relief, and I was transferred to the Slave Labour Unit or SLU. This was an organisation for the further punishment of prisoners labelled as reactionaries, escapees and so on. It was housed in a large former farmhouse about a mile from the main camp. What you might call the principal dormitory was in a long storehouse with a wooden floor, standing on stilts and with a verandah outside. Next to it was a wash-house. At the opposite end were two single rooms with open doors, facing a central courtyard. Each housed an American prisoner in solitary confinement. A guard was so positioned outside that he could see both men. The predominant character was a handsome Mexican called Mandosa. Those Mexican Americans were pretty tough fellows. The food was no problem for them. They looked, or could look, even more Korean than the guards. Tom Cabello, in the cage at the 'Kennel Club', had got 200 miles in his bid for freedom, further than any other prisoner to date. As it turned out, that distance was never surpassed. Not a single prisoner ever escaped from the camps in Korea.

There were some great characters in that unit. I would say that they were the cream of the prison's population. There were no bullshitters, no romancers but all were blokes with strong personalities and a privilege to work with, as I quickly found out.

There were almost as many Chinese as prisoners in the SLU. The buildings which housed them formed the walls of what might almost be described as a Mexican *hacienda*. A courtyard in the centre divided the 'sheep' from the 'goats'. A gateway with a thatched roof and built of pine poles formed the entrance to the unit. There was a well of similar construction outside.

When I arrived at the SLU the prisoners were all out working, with the exception of the two GIs in the single rooms and, to my surprise, Floyd, the GI whose trial I had witnessed after he had insulted Myrtle for which, the reader will remember, he got three years. I had thought it an excessively harsh sentence at the time so was glad to find him there helping the cooks, free to walk anywhere within the confines of the unit and even to visit the well outside where he drew water, carrying heavy cauldrons on a yoke. A real country boy, strong and handsome, with dark curly hair and a pale complexion, he looked pretty fit and seemed to recognize that he had fallen on his feet. Had he been sent to a Korean jail, as he might well have been, things would have been very different for him.

The Chinese Commandant of the SLU gave me a rundown on the place, telling me that our work consisted of cutting down and trimming trees for timber. A massive log pile, which I had noticed when I was first brought through the gate, represented the result of the prisoners' labours. I was then taken and shown my bed space in the long room and left to my own devices until the blokes came in at about five o'clock. Fit and muscular, they welcomed me and then went for a wash in bowls out on the verandah. I could see that I was going to enjoy this. I didn't mind hard work in the fresh air and these were just the sort of mates that I would like to be with. They were clearly in much better shape than the prisoners in the main camp. One good reason for this was that the food, by camp standards, was excellent. We got as many cobs of bread as we could eat, with a type of runner bean and diced cucumber as the side dish.

I quickly decided that this prison within a prison was going to suit me down to the ground.

After three months cooped up sitting on my butt doing nothing but ponder about the futility of life, I had put on weight, despite the fact that our rations had been so basic – millet, sorghum, third-grade unhusked rice and so on. I well remember on my first day out on the hills, as I was lopping a felled tree, one of the guards was concerned about my scratching my by now yellowed and tanned skin, which did not look much different to his own. I guessed that he must be a queer. I wasn't a bad-looking bloke and had been fancied, in fun, by other lads many times. When all you can see around you is men, for month after month, you might be forgiven for thinking 'Why not?' Back in the main camp we had had a few poofters, some surprisingly open about it. Our dance nights were a real laugh. I often wondered whether these Chinks were the same. It was commonplace to see them walking hand-in-hand and even with their arms round one another. My old dad used to say 'Dave, there's nowt so queer as folk and I have my doubts of thee and me!' One thing was quite certain, Dave Green was no queer and would never allow himself to become one. I was all man!

The Chinese encouraged hard work and we enjoyed the competitive spirit that had grown up on the hillsides from which we cut down marked trees. Each of us would then carry as large a log as our bodies could handle. We were healthy, no longer hungry and even happy, always enjoying a joke. In such circumstances, the spirit of comradeship which built up was tremendous.

In the main camp, the British and the Americans were kept firmly apart. Here we were about equally divided and very much integrated. A couple of the GIs were real hillbilly types, one of whom, from Oregon, was a bit strange. For some misdemeanour, the Chinese had put him in a cage out in the middle of the courtyard. Overnight, he had unlashed the whole structure and got out. Nevertheless, he was adamant that he would show his captors how to build one from which no one could escape. They realized that he was a few cents short in the dollar and let him off.

There were a couple of Americans who were younger than me. One was an epileptic and prone to the occasional fit, the other, Dick Sneider, was something of a comedian and used to take off radio and television commercials – things that were unknown to us in Britain at that time. To my delight, a week after I had joined the SLU, Tommy Clough had arrived. He had been locked up in a cage and had had a rougher time than me. As we talked together about our experiences, I realized how lucky I had been. I had at least been able to stretch my legs and move around my cell when the guards weren't looking. Why I had been so lucky I will never know; whether it had been by design or simply that, by the luck of the Gods, there had been a shortage of cages and boxes, it was impossible to say. I was certainly treated to a great deal of interrogation until the day on which I blew my top, after which it all stopped. Perhaps Myrtle had suggested that I was worth working on and my easier treatment had all been part of a plot to that end. If so, they finally realized that they were wasting their time. Whatever the reason, I had no cause to complain. Tom was pretty tough and, as I have said, was no lover of the Chinese. He was no fool either and had kept a low profile, sticking to the straight and narrow as far as they were concerned. We were both clear on two points: we had only ourselves to blame and had dropped no one in the shit.

One day, during a random inspection, a cob of bread was found hidden in my cap, which hung on a nail over my bedspace. Along with three other prisoners, I found myself paraded in front of a desk in the Chinese quarters where I was tried for this minor offence. The officer in charge, who was obviously well educated, thinking that I might be embarrassed, standing there hatless with a shaven head, instructed the escort to give me back my cap. In truth, I was not in the least embarrassed, but I appreciated the gesture.

Every prisoner will have had his own views on the conduct of the Chinese and their treatment of us. My own view was that, although they were sometimes difficult to understand, yet in the light of their background and national culture you received the treatment which your experience should have led you to expect.

I feel sure that there were many men who would have disagreed with that view, men like Kinne for example. He was, frankly, impossible to deal with and, at one time, the Chinese had him trussed up like a chicken. In the struggle, one of their officers accidentally wounded himself fatally with his own rifle. God knows what political motive got Kinne out of that one, but he survived! That man would break out of anything they put him in, collect a few luxuries, and get himself back into his cage or box and the Chinks never knew he had been on the loose. One simply could not imagine Kinne doing anything to please anyone if he did not agree with what was being asked of him.

Knowing what I have since learned about the other Chinese camps, I have come to appreciate how lucky we were to be in Chongsong. Our early imprisonment was certainly rough and, even after things improved, we were still living on chickenfeed but, in Chongsong, a man could survive if he kept his nose clean. Break the rules and they would try to break you. That was their way, even for their soldiers, and fair enough.

For all that the bonds of comradeship meant to us, each prisoner was at heart his own man and chose his own path to follow. As for me, I never became a red or informer, queer or politically bent in any way. There are those who would say that that was abnormal, but that was the path that both Tom and I trod, each for his own good reasons, and we had no grounds to regret it.

During the summer, we went on what Tom and I called our 'hollies'. We were taken up to some woods overlooking the Yalu River to cut trees and bring them down river on barges. We concluded that wood must be one of the few power sources available in North Korea. Even such trucks as they had ran on charcoal. Their power stations on the Yalu had by this time been destroyed by the US Air Force. In any case, that was all by the way as far as we were concerned. We had a job of work to do in pleasant surroundings and the trips down river were a breeze. Once loaded, we could lie on the deck of the barge in between swims over the side. All that was missing were some nice girls.

We did, in fact, see one girl when the boat stopped for water and we were able to get off and go walkabout. There seemed to be nobody about so we opened the door of a homestead near the river. There we saw a poor girl with a totally vacant look on her face. It was clear that she was completely out of her mind.

All good things come to an end and all too soon our work on the Yalu was completed and we returned to the SLU.

First recognized by one of the Mexican Americans, marijuana was found to be growing all over the countryside. It came to be known to us as 'the weed' and a new era in the life of the camp, and in my own life too, had begun. At that stage in my life, I was game for any new experience, within limits, and this came within them. My introduction to the weed came from a joint shared between four of us, sitting on the floor of the long room. My first few drags, not knowing what to expect, were, perhaps, taken with a little more caution and less enthusiasm than was shown by the others. However, if they were going anywhere, I would follow. For a start, the floor began to develop waves, persuading me that surely I should have been a sailor. Standing up, I found that I could hardly keep my balance. 'I joined the Navy to see the sea, and what did I see, I saw the sea!' 'Whee', I thought, 'this is great!'

By now, Dick Sneider was standing on his head, making up some commercial for the local weed. Gruer, another American, with a voice like a prime bull, was hanging on the doorframe, clearly convinced that he had become a gorilla. The rest of the blokes were getting apprehensive. 'Cool it you guys', shouted Floyd, who was busy trying to pull Gruer back into the room. He was too late. A guard burst into the room shouting '*Kia Sima*?' or 'What are you doing?', in English. We all sat down rather sheepishly, Dick Sneider giving a bit of a giggle. As for me, everything had gone into slow motion and voices echoed.

Another guard was summoned and the two of them began to search our kits, such as they were, throwing everything into heaps. Finding nothing, they finally left, coming back later with the Commandant. 'What is going on here?', he asked. Floyd, who had by now mastered quite a bit of Chinese, assured him that all was 'OK, Sir' and added a bit which, of course, we could not understand. Whatever it was, it seemed to have calmed the situation.

The Commandant's gaze traversed the hut. 'OK, *sweejo sleepo*', he said and they all strutted out and we settled down.

That was our first and only 'smoke' in the SLU.

Unbeknown to anyone else, that had been my twenty-first birthday. I said to myself, 'I'll always remember that one'. Incredibly, something even more memorable occurred that night. A guard came to our room with a letter for me, the first I had had in captivity. The incredulous look I gave him produced a pat on the shoulder. '*Dingho*', meaning 'Very good', he said. '*Momasan*'. And indeed it was from my dear old Mum. Almost eighteen months after receiving a telegram telling her that I was 'Missing In Action', she had had a letter from me. I really treasured that letter. The best birthday present ever!

13

Back to the Main Camp :
The Chongsong 'Olympics'

Throughout the winter of 1952 and the first seven months of 1953, as the two sides faced one another from their heavily defended positions, fighting continued sporadically, often at very heavy cost in casualties to both sides, the Communists being by far the heavier losers, though this did not deter them from launching major attacks at intervals. The Chinese had been heavily reinforced and casualties did not seem to concern them.

Within the UN force there was a marked difference in approach between the US formations and the Commonwealth Division. The former seemed to be driven more by politics than military reality and suffered heavily in casualties although they inflicted far more on the enemy than they actually suffered themselves. In contrast, the experienced and battle-hardened Commonwealth formations played the game strictly by the tactical needs of the moment, wasting no lives whilst making the enemy pay heavily for his temerity and refusing to be driven by the Americans into undertaking operations which seemed militarily pointless and would not have justified the casualties they would inevitably have incurred. General Mike West, another great fighting infantryman, succeeded Jim Cassels in command of the division where his robust approach and great sense of humour made him greatly admired and respected. In October 1952, the Division took over a feature known as 'The Hook' from the US 7th Marines, who had just administered a severe thrashing to the Chinese when they attacked them. Hardly had the Division settled in than the Chinese attacked again. The Black Watch, who were holding The Hook, saw them off in style although not without suffering heavy casualties themselves. Not until the end of the following May did the enemy venture to attack The Hook again. On this

143

occasion, the defending battalion was The Duke of Wellington's Regiment. This was a more prolonged affair and a very tough fight indeed, so tough that before they finally drove the Chinese off the feature, leaving swathes of dead behind them, the Dukes had been driven to bring down heavy DF on their own stoutly constructed defences from which many men had later to be dug out. Their own casualties amounted to 149 of whom 29 were killed.

It is a notable fact that both battalions had a large number of National Servicemen on strength. In the case of the Dukes, these amounted to almost three quarters of the Battalion. Once again, the value of the National Serviceman had been proven to the hilt.

In February 1953, General Van Fleet, furious that he had not been allowed to mount a massive offensive to drive the Chinese right out of Korea, retired and was succeeded as Commanding General 8th Army by General Maxwell Taylor. In the same month, General Mark Clark proposed an exchange of sick and wounded prisoners. This was agreed to by the Communists in March and exchanges began at Panmunjom in April. Armistice negotiations were also resumed at that time.

★   ★   ★

Just before Christmas 1952, they released Tom from the SLU. I followed him a few days later.

The sight that met our eyes back in the main camp was depressing. Thanks to our spell in the SLU, Tom and I were both pretty fit but the blokes in the camp looked what we called 'down the pan'. Marijuana had found its way there and they were dabbling.

I was put in a squad that was housed in what might have been a village sick house or granny flat. Standing on its own between two rows, it was barely big enough for ten men, let alone ten large men, for none of us was small. Lofty Large – his name endorsing his nickname – was all of 6 foot 3. He came from Guiting Power near Cheltenham. He had a withered arm, the hand of which he covered with an army glove. Two bullets were still lodged in his body, something that I would most certainly not have wished on myself, yet I never heard Lofty complain. He had joined the Army as a boy, as a drummer in the Wiltshire Regiment. Somehow he had found his way to Korea, joining us on the Imjin. Within a couple of weeks, he had been wounded and had become a prisoner. Slim Birch and Tom Surtees both came from Southampton. Sid (or Geordie) Bartell was a Northumberland Fusilier and had been a miner in civil life. He came from Sunderland and had the unmistakable accent to prove it. Cyril Warren, from Dorset, had a laid back personality that took everything in its stride with a shrug of his shoulders. Bill (or Nobby) Clark was from Reading, a great lad whose smiling face conveyed confidence and optimism. Our different backgrounds made for interesting conversations. One evening, as we were having a laugh and a joke before we got our heads down, I kidded Tom that I knew Southampton. In truth, the only time I had been there was when boarding the *Windrush*. Tom, an RAOC driver, said he had driven through Cheltenham and that it was a 'hick town'. In response, I said that Southampton was full of 'poofters'.

'Come off it,' he said, 'you've never been there!'

'I have', I said.

'OK, then. What's the name of the cinema?' he asked.

'Was it the Odeon?' I answered. 'There's a pub just opposite and a fish and chip shop down the road.'

In point of fact, there are not many towns that couldn't match that set-up and Tom took the bait hook, line and sinker!

Re-naming the pub, which I had pretended not quite to remember, he added, 'That used to be a good pub'.

'You bought that one, Tom. I've never been there in my life!', I chuckled. He and Sid Birch both set on me and, with Lofty propped up in one corner, protecting his arm, the wrestling soon spread to the rest of the squad. That night we slept the sleep of the just, where we lay, exhausted, in a heap.

There was no need for blankets in that little hole. I believe the cooks used the kitchen at the side for heating water for washing up. Thanks to the traditional Korean underfloor heating system, the floor seemed hot enough to roast us, even though the winter was setting in and temperatures were falling below freezing.

With our little soya bean oil lanterns, we'd sit up playing cards. In really bad weather, we'd play for most of the day and night. Peanuts, which had become the usual side dish, were used as counters. Our favourite games were nine card brag, pontoon and nap. We became so preoccupied with them that they even filled our dreams. Lofty described how he had heard Nobby Clark call out 'A prile of Queens' in his sleep, to which several of us answered! Lofty was a great asset to our squad, as he very soon became able to write out the minutes of our so-called 'study periods', leaving the rest of us to more serious occupations, like marking the aces in the pack.

When winter came, the rations started to get low. We all had sore tongues due to some form of vitamin deficiency. As our own flour supply had run out, the Chinese got hold of some large loaves, probably from local sources. Wherever it came from, it was terrible stuff, stale and frozen. Despite being given half a loaf each, it was murder to eat. Even to break a piece off was nearly impossible. I found that the only thing to do was to suck it, like a baby with a rusk. Sorghum usually took care of

145

this particular deficiency but there were many other much more serious problems due to a lack of proper vitamins. One of these was beri beri, due in the main to lack of Vitamin B.

Waking one morning, I found that Lofty, who was sleeping next to me, was saturated in sweat, as though he had just got out of a hot shower. His clothes were literally clinging to his body. We realized that these were the early signs of beri beri. In this disease, fluid builds up from the lower body, creeping its way upwards until it floods the lungs and the patient dies from drowning. Cholera, on the other hand, does just the opposite and you die of dehydration. Both these diseases were prevalent in Korea and a constant source of apprehension in our camp, for medical resources were virtually non-existent. Dysentery was rampant, sometimes amoebic, and seemed to stay around throughout our whole imprisonment.

We were all deeply concerned about Lofty but, with little fuss or ado, he simply took off his sodden clothes and dried himself.

By now the outside temperature must have been at least some 40 degrees below freezing and the Siberian wind was unrelenting. However, in our little chicken coop, with its heated floor, the heat of ten bodies and the door tightly shut, we made our own little world. Furthermore, the Chinese had issued us with winter clothing – padded kapok uniforms like their own but blue, thick, padded soft boots and large quilts. Apart from the food, our only real hardship was the quick dash to the latrine. This was a large rectangular pit with long poles on each side upon which one sat, hoping devoutly that you would not get frost bitten.

In our little den of iniquity, we had acquired some of the noxious weed. That evening, sitting in a close circle, we passed the joint around.

'Tell us a story Dave.'

'I can't tell stories', I retorted, laughing. Then, as the conversation drifted, from somewhere deep down inside me, that challenge, 'Tell us a story' registered in my brain.

'Hey, you blokes, do you really want to hear a story?'

'Yeah!', was the eager response.

To my own amazement, words were coming from my lips, 'Hansel and Gretel'.

Tommy Surtees repeated, 'Hansel and Gretel?' and the whole squad then repeated the words again and we were in fits of laughter.

I went on to tell the story of how the two children got lost in the woods, each sentence being examined by them all, rearranged and given a pornographic slant.

'Dirty little bastard that Hansel, making out that they were lost in the woods', said someone.

146

By this time even words had become significant.

'Woods', said Nobby, spelling the word out 'W.O.O.D.S. woods!' Then, half-closing his eyes, he wandered off into some little wood of his own. Meanwhile, the wave of extroversion had temporarily left my body, only to return, as if working in cycles.

After some hours of hilarious laughter, we were exhausted and sat there just gazing at one another. The front of our clothing was soaked with the tears of that laughter. To we youngsters, that first real experience of the power of the weed was a night never to be forgotten and certainly something to be repeated.

Fortunately, the weed was not readily available at that time. It was a bleak winter, but we got through it, greatly assisted by our collective sense of humour. In his book *The Korean War*, Max Hastings describes how the Americans tended to suffer from what he calls 'give up-itis', a condition that greatly assisted their deaths in thousands. Of course, like all prisoners, we British had our ups and downs, but the strength of our comradeship and that infectious British sense of humour kept us going, under even the worst of the winter's trials.

The Chinese loved to celebrate and so did we if it meant a few extras coming our way, as they did on May Day which was such a special source of celebration for them, though its significance was completely lost on most of us at that time. Nor was I, for one, particularly interested in finding out. What we all appreciated was that chicken, pork and bean shoots – admittedly in minute quantities – were added to the menu. There's no such thing as a free lunch, they say and, of course, there was a price to be paid – sitting for an extra lecture or two.

The dreary, bitter winter behind us, things really began to look up in the spring as far as our living accommodation went. In some smaller units there were now even bunk beds. This entailed some rearrangement of squads. I was lucky enough to be moved to one which boasted this new-found luxury. There were six of us but our house often contained twice that number as blokes were attracted by the characters that lived there.

The squad was made up of Ron Hall (Glosters), Alan (or Geordie) Hogg (a Sapper), P.J. Coates and Sam Sears (8th Hussars), Andy Allcock (who was blessed with the unattractive but well-deserved nickname of Wanker) and myself (both Glosters).

Ron came from Poole. To us he was not outstandingly handsome, yet wherever we had been in Korea, we were led to believe that he was some sort of celebrity and would be pointed out for special attention. Perhaps he looked like some well-known character. He was always ready for an argument with the Chinese on any issue, no matter how trivial. He could argue that black was blue, at times being right off the track, with the

147

Chinese almost pleading with him to believe them. 'Not 'avin' that' was his usual comment.

Geordie Hogg had made love to so many women. He was a great story-teller, the tales getting more and more improbable as the night wore on. I'm sure he convinced himself that they were gospel true even if none of us believed them! However, the bedtime hours of pleasure he gave us in our wonder at his vivid imagination and all the contradictory fibs he came up with were immense. For that alone, he should be proud.

On many a night we were taken to the hotspots of Newcastle-on-Tyne, his stamping ground.

'Did ya 'ave 'er, Geordie?'

Of course he did. Geordie always 'ad em'! Some he had to abandon later for health reasons! One look from Geordie and those poor girls were fallen women, much to the delight of the five sex-starved hunters of the night who hung on his every word.

Despite the way in which we contrived to keep up each other's spirits, we all suffered from bouts of depression for thoughts of home were, inevitably, negative and depressing. It was the fearful uncertainty of not knowing when it was all going to end. Were we going to be here for another five or even ten years? If only someone could tell us and rid us of those nagging thoughts (if we allowed them to be so). It used to bring to mind that song we so often sang in our evening sing-songs:

> *'Oh, get your coat and get your hat,*
> *Leave your worries on the doorstep,*
> *Then direct your feet*
> *To the sunny side of the street.'*

When you had mates who, by now, knew you better than your own mother, you couldn't hide a thing. They always knew when something was wrong.

'Come on, mucker. Out with it!'

A very popular visitor, who often brightened our billet by his presence when dropping in to see his best mate Sam Sears, was Jim 'Be-Bop' Bissell. Jim was a Gloster who came from Richmond in Surrey. Sam was a well built Lewisham lad who, in addition to having a liking for intelligent conversation, loved to sing rock and roll. His accomplice on stage was Jim. Who could forget their rendition of 'Hey! Barbaree Bear'. Sam, in his deep bass voice, was the daddy bear, playing the straight man role – the still, solid and steady one – whilst Jim, with his tall, slim build, gave it some rhythmical bite as he played the little bear and mother. Although Jim was not officially a member of our squad, he spent so much time with us that you could have been forgiven for thinking that he was.

148

Jim was by no means so loose-limbed when Sam, who had become the Company dentist, pulled out two of his teeth on successive days without, of course, anaesthetic!

This business of extractions was extremely painful and we had all experimented with what we called the 'psychological knockout'. The patient would bend down to touch his toes and then rise, with arms outstretched, towards the ceiling. On the third rising, he would be bearhugged. The immediate effect of this was that he would become unconscious for a few seconds, hopefully recovering to find that his tooth had been pulled! The dentist's only tool was a pair of rusty pliers with padded handles. In most cases the business of extraction took all of an hour. A smoke of the weed was helpful in allaying the agonising pain a bit but God alone knows what all this did to our brain cells.

Andy Allcock, who had his bunk above mine, lived up to his nickname. To give him some additional stimulation, he had made a window in the back wall which enabled him to watch a Korean girl on the far bank of the river who came down there occasionally to do her washing. Oddly enough, bedtime activity did not seem to sap his energies in any way or to impair his acrobatic feats on the parallel bars we had built out at the back of our billet.

One early spring day, Andy and I were sunning ourselves against the wall of the latrine of all places, discussing our early encounters with the law. I mentioned a Welsh boy who had been our centre-forward at the Padcroft Boys' Home. Oddly enough, Andy had known him. They had met in the Borstal at Portland; Padcroft had clearly not cured him!

Our Andy was anti-authoritarian, anti-Communist and, in fact, anti-anything that attempted to stop him from doing what he wanted to do. He had a deep interest in wildlife and would share his last cigarette with a mate. Last, but by no means least, P.J. Coates, or P.J. as we called him, came from a middle-class background and was pretty articulate. Nevertheless, he was a bit of a lad and had served in the 8th Hussars with Sam.

The sheer boredom of prison life often led to our experimenting with various ideas, one of which was the possibility of tattooing. My claim to fame was that I have on my arm the first tattoo ever performed in Chongsong. Its simple message is just DAVE, scratched on with a pin. The ink was made from the dye of our new issue blue padded suits plus a bit of soot. For that I can thank Ernie McAlone, a Paddy, who was another adopted squad member like Jim. He was a friend of P.J.'s. P.J. and others held me down, half-protesting, for the experiment. It turned out so well that the idea caught on and Geordie and Jim became the Company tattooists, adding to my DAVE a butterfly, at my request, and, on my other arm, a Japanese girl, complete with parasol and waving a

handkerchief. I never cease to be amazed that I never got blood poisoning from these crude operations.

Dreary though life was in the Camp, there were days when things happened which brightened things up a bit, such as the day on which we acquired proof positive that there were Soviet air defence troops operating in North Korea, much to the embarrassment of our Chinese captors.

It was like this:

As the winter went on, dead wood was becoming increasingly hard to find on our usual local excursions to the hills overlooking the camp. By chance, two American trucks, which had been captured and reconditioned, together with their Chinese drivers, had stopped for a couple of days in the town. Our own Chinese decided that this was too good an opportunity to miss and we were packed off northwards in the trucks, looking for pastures new.

As we stood in the back of the open trucks, we noticed the unmistakable leaves of marijuana growing wild at the roadside about five miles out of Chongsong. Leaving these behind us, the trucks pulled into a clearing a few miles further on at the end of a track leading from the main road. There we saw what we at first took to be a loggers' hut. However, as we looked around, it quickly became apparent that it was no such thing, for, some 50 yards away from the hut, stood what we recognized as a Russian anti-aircraft gun, the camouflaged barrel being in full view of our inquisitive eyes. A Russian soldier, in what was obviously a guard dugout, was nearer to us still and was vainly trying to hide his face. On the verandah of the hut stood a row of jackboots and items of Soviet uniform were hanging out on a washing line to dry. A white-faced soldier in uniform appeared at the door of the hut. When he saw us, he shot back inside and reappeared at the window, waving his arms wildly and obviously telling us to 'push off', which we did in a rather erratic fashion; our driver, attempting to do a U turn in a bushy area, knocked down several small trees in the process! Through all this we had remained silent and it was only as we drove away that the significance of what we had just seen dawned on us. We of course knew that Russian MiG fighters, flown by supposedly volunteer Chinese pilots, were operating in Korea but the presence of Soviet troops on the ground was something altogether new. The trucks had pulled off the road and Ding, an instructor with limited English who was supervising us, and the two Chinese drivers, began discussing the situation, their gesticulations clearly indicating to us the seriousness of what we had seen.

After some time, we continued our way back towards Chongsong and came to the little bridge where we had seen the marijuana. In a clearing just off the track was a stockpile of wood, presumably collected by the

local peasantry, one of whom appeared with a bundle on an 'A' frame which he dropped onto the pile. All that remained for us to do was to load all the wood onto our trucks and our mission was achieved, despite the drama! As we passed the patches of marijuana, I lowered a branch which Andy had snaffled and hooked up a few handfuls of the weed – enough to give us a few smokes anyway.

As part of the various 'improvements' made to the camp, a tannoy system had been installed in place of the usual whistles with which our attention had until then been drawn. Over the tannoy we began to get news reports. Though obviously biased, anything was better than the long and dreary months and months we had endured without news of any sort, except what we could pick up on the 'bush telegraph', which had been very little and of doubtful veracity. It soon began to get on our nerves to hear, day after day, how the Yanks had done this or that, thereby causing a stalemate in the peace talks down at Panmunjom. At times, our hatred was evenly divided between the two sides.

Summer came and with it the heat. Much of our time was now spent down by the river, where we bathed in our birthday suits. In total contrast, the Chinese seemed to keep out of the sun. The hotter it got the more clothes they seemed to wear. It was quite usual to see one shuffling down the road on a scorching day wearing his quilted jacket and overcoat, topped by a padded hat with the earflaps down! Our only respite from the heat was a beautiful mug of boiling water – the only beverage we had ever known since being captured and which we enjoyed as much as we would have a cup of tea before that sorry day.

We now had a permanent barber's shop, run by a bearded guru of a Royal Artilleryman. Apart from being a good barber, the bloke could turn his hand to anything. He had started a Company newsletter and his billet was smothered, inside and out, with *objets d'art* which he had produced, whittled from old tree roots or bits of scrap metal and so on.

We had always put on shows, originally on the square in the middle of our Company area, but by now they had moved up market to the cinema. The ingenuity of the talented men who ran them would have won them many Oscars. Some of the 'leading ladies' had to watch their step in camp, vehemently denying any feminine tendencies – they were only playing a part. However, there were a couple who seemed to enjoy the attention paid to them!

Musical instruments, such as saxophones, guitars and harmonicas were provided by the Chinese who also gave us an old and fairly large store house for use as a Company club, complete with a table tennis table and a stage. Despite our anxieties about the future, life was beginning to look up a bit. I began to enjoy the guitar pickings of the American hillbillies, especially the performances of a tall red-haired Texan. His

151

songs and those of his mates soon became part of our repertoire: 'Filipino Rose', 'Shotgun Boogie', 'From Old Montana Down to Alabam . . .' and many others. Fortunately, those early days, in which we and the Yanks were kept apart, were a dead duck.

Talent guest nights were very popular. They invariably ended with a rousing sing-song and were often quite hilarious. I remember one lovely warm summer's night out on the main square particularly well. I and my mates were seated or sprawled with a front seat view of the stage above us, our heads propped on our stools. Myrtle, who was accompanied by two other attractive women of the administrative staff, stood at the side of the stage. Some pretty bawdy songs had been sung, with all our usual energy, accompanied by a quartet of harmonising mouth organs. Myrtle, whose English was pretty good, was interpreting for her companions. With their hands to their mouths, they pretended to be embarrassed but, in truth, they enjoyed every minute of it.

Towards the end of the evening, as 'Blue Moon' echoed across the valley, I looked up and saw that our usual audience of Korean peasants were sitting along the footpath that ran across the hills overlooking the camp. As I did so, Myrtle, romantically prettier than ever, caught my eye and gave me a smile that would indeed have 'launched a thousand ships', sending me up to Cloud 9. Clearly my misdemeanour was now either forgiven or forgotten! Little did she know, or perhaps she did, that a piece of the clothing that had once clung to her body was now caressing my neck, in the form of a collar. It was one of eleven that had been painstakingly made from a pair of her knickers, stolen one moonlit night from her washing line. The horrible thief, who was very well known to me, had overnight become the most popular boy in the Company! He hired his ill-gotten gains out to various perverted, sex-starved layabouts, finally sharing them with his best mates to adorn their collarless prison shirts.

Hardships were the only ships we saw as that winter drew in. One I will long remember was sitting out in the freezing open air for no less than six hours, watching an opera entitled 'The White-haired Girl' and put on by a touring Chinese company. Doubtless based upon an actual episode in the days of the warlords and ruling landowners, it was the story of a landowner's lust and greed, in which a young girl was subjected to all sorts of sexual brutality to save her family, who owed him money, from eviction.

Two or three hours of clanging cymbals drove us to joining in the choruses from sheer desperation at the boredom. Every time that the poor girl got raped we cheered, and when her hair eventually turned white from the appalling treatment she had had to endure, we cheered again because, hopefully, it signified the end of the story and so of our own frozen misery! I can only think that this opera was part of the brain-washing we were supposed to be succumbing to and meant to show the evils of capitalism and the private ownership of property! What a hope!

At about that time, we had a visit from a Marine Commando called Andrew Condron. He had been taken prisoner during the fighting round the Chosin Reservoir at which 41 Commando so distinguished them-selves. He was an obvious convert to the Chinese political faith but his talk did nothing to enlighten those who bothered to listen. After the war, Condron elected to go to China, where he lived for some years and married a Chinese girl. He later returned to Britain where no charges were ever laid against him.

As a welcome change from the dreary routine of prison life, we were taken out to dig storage pits at the foot of the hills near the Chinese block, and also an air raid shelter, which we talked of sabotaging though not very seriously. In any case, the Chinese put the roof on themselves. We used to joke with the guard who was assigned to our work squad and fill him up with grossly exaggerated stories of the delights of the Geisha girls in Tokyo – which made his day!

Christmas brought welcome luxuries. On such occasions the Chinese really went to great lengths to try to make us happy. I think they worked on the basis of 'A good ship is a happy ship, with few problems.' It was always hard to really understand their policies and attitudes but they always seemed quite genuine about what they were doing. Their study programme had been a total waste of time. Certainly no man that I knew in that camp had been changed one iota. Nevertheless, they never ceased to try to get through to us. Our own attitude to them was the same as to anyone else in authority; we could still laugh and joke with them.

Each man was given a present of a red notebook with a dove of peace on it and the words 'Happy Christmas 1952' embossed on the cover. Varied but minute portions of tasty dishes were on the menu. For what-ever reason they were given, those little goodies were most welcome.

The reader might be forgiven for thinking sometimes that what I have described was more like a holiday camp than a prison. Believe me, it was no holiday camp. If you could have seen our daily diet, you would never have believed that a man could live on it . . . a barnyard fowl maybe, but not a man. Despite the arrival of the bread oven, our basic diet had not changed since we arrived – a one pound tin of sorghum or millet twice daily plus the side dish, as we called it, of about one third of a baked bean tin of turnip tops or peanuts, a very watery edition of these being issued at about noon.

I was talking one day to one of the reservists who had been a Japanese prisoner in the Second World War. He told me that the diet we were living on in Chongsong was worse than what they had received from the

153

Japs. Their biggest worries had been tropical ulcers and cholera. What had made life intolerable was their captors' total disregard for human life. In complete contrast, most of the Chinese I met were not aggressive but hard-working, happy people who were content with their lot in life and, unless we chose to break the rules, were mostly easy to get on with. If, on the other hand, a bloke thought he could give them the run around – then watch out!

The toughest thing about prison life was the mental stress of captivity. This became worse as the months rolled by and the aura of uncertainty persisted. We knew, thanks to the tannoy broadcasts, that our freedom lay in the hands of the players at the table in Panmunjom, who had reached stalemate.

The weather in January 1953 was atrocious and we were pretty well confined to our billets, which did nothing to improve our morale. One day, as I ventured out to relieve myself in the paddy field out at the back of our lines, I was momentarily siezed with a sense of claustrophobia. The ground was iron-hard and covered in frozen snow. My urine froze into a pinnacle as it fell and, as I looked around the grey skies, the bleak hills seemed to close in on me. Fortunately, my better senses pulled me together. 'Get a grip on yourself, mate', I muttered, as I made my way back to our billet, my thoughts still as depressing as the scenery. 'God, how long? Another winter here and we will go off our rockers.'

The whole squad was feeling like this and for sixteen days on end we had smoked the weed until it became obvious that we were behaving in a very odd manner, so we decided to give it a miss. A bunch of the more intellectual blokes, two of whom, unbeknownst to us, were in the Intelligence Corps, began talking in double Dutch, reversing their words. We simply could not understand a single word of it, so the Chinese had no chance – which may have been just as well.

Day by day our diet deteriorated. Potatoes, frozen in their winter storage, became less and less edible at every meal. Finally, all that could be eaten had gone. Peanuts, greens or turnip tops became our only form of nourishment of any substance.

A table tennis league had been formed in our clubhouse and individual and doubles championships were organised. We were watching Geordie Hogg playing in the singles final when we heard a bit of a commotion outside on the road. A tall, bushy-haired, dishevelled American had gone beserk. Running down the road pursued by a host of Chinese and one other prisoner, his path was finally blocked by the guard at our end and he was restrained.

The game had been stopped as we witnessed this tragic little scene. Poor devil. It had just all become too much for him and he had gone off his head. 'There but for the grace of God . . .' A claustrophobic cloud seemed to descend on us all in that natural prison. Once again we had been reminded that we were caught like flies in a spider's web.

The game was re-started and Geordie won, watched by a dampened and deeply depressed audience.

At that time I always tried to make my letters home sound as 'rosy' as I could, for I so well remembered hearing my Mum crying for my brother during the war, when he was at sea in the Mediterranean in his destroyer. One letter, in which I had described the Christmas fare, was published in the local newspaper. Dad had written to me enclosing the cutting which, needless to say, was snaffled by the Chinese. The first I knew about it was hearing it read out over the tannoy system. The Chinese were determined to make the most of it as propaganda for their lenient policy, but it backfired really, as it was also good propaganda for our freedom of speech in the Western world. I had no repercussions from my fellow prisoners.

No matter where you are in the world, the coming of spring is always welcome, but in countries like Korea, where the winters are so punishing, spring is especially welcomed. The thawing of all that snow and ice gives a lift to the heart and, in our case, a boost to our morale. At last, supplies began to become more plentiful and our rations to improve.

Day after day, the tannoy ground out its news, good today, grim tomorrow. Its broadcasts were interspersed with music: Paul Robeson singing 'Old Man River', '*Dung, fung, hung*', the Communist anthem which began, 'The east is red from the blood of our dead' and a variety of Russian pieces. To all of these we put our own words, like in the International, 'Arise you prisoners of salvation [starvation]' and so on.

An Australian journalist from *The Daily Worker* visited the camp. With the help of a bottle of hooch, he tried to persuade us that we 'had it pretty good'. Even a short stay would have changed his mind for him.

To be honest, things were improving and no doubt, when compared to the sufferings of prisoners or the victims of famine in some other parts of the world, maybe we were lucky. The most important thing to us was that the Peace Talks, at last, were making some ground, the first tangible sign of this being the signing of an agreement to repatriate sick and wounded prisoners who were no longer fit for active service. Our Lofty came under this category. It was a good thing the Chinese did not know him as well as we did. He could take care of most things and most people with one hand.

In a last ditch effort, they sent Lofty to the hospital we knew as the 'Death House'. A former temple on a hill not far from the camp, it had a 'real' doctor and a couple of nurses but if ever a hospital deserved the slogan 'Abandon hope all ye who enter here', this was it. Few who went there ever came out. However, there are, I suppose exceptions to every rule. We heard on the grapevine that a bullet had been extracted from Lofty's rib-cage. I recorded this is my little red book with its dove of peace logo on 12 April, 1953. On the very next day, he was on a truck which passed through the camp, heading home. On 21 April I recorded 'Lofty exchanged'.

That little red book was put to good use in many ways, chiefly as a diary and as a place in which to record the words of the songs we learned.

Inter-camp sports were programmed and were at once dubbed as our own 'Olympics'. I entered for the boxing and was chosen as trainer for our Company team, a job that primarily entailed rigging up a punch bag and disengaging newcomers to the sport who were unfamiliar with the word 'Break!' and thought 'Spar' was a roof truss.

We had some useful boxers in the Company; some, like Patrick O'Laughlin, were well-built, strong fighters who would go in like a tank, throwing left and right punches which really hurt. But the one I will always remember was another Irishman, Patrick Maher, who was an entirely different kettle of fish. Fair-haired and skinny, he was a fast lightweight, his footwork being a joy to watch – an Irish Jimmy Wilde.

In addition to the boxing, I was selected for the gymnastic team, which included four members of our squad.

Despite the wretchedness of our diet, we British had done all we could to keep as physically fit as possible and, to that end, with the help of the Chinese, had done a lot of work on our main square which by now was divided into two, with a football pitch in one half and a stage, basketball and volleyball pitches in the other. With these 'Olympics' coming up, further improvements were made. A covered gallery with poled seating had been built beside the football pitch, with raised seats at the road end, also made of long pine poles. Working as we did with extremely limited resources and the crudest of tools, we were proud of the final result which would have graced any small town's football club.

Of course, the fact that, as the tannoy had told us, the peace talks down on the 38th Parallel were beginning to get somewhere, despite intermittent walkouts, which made our chances of release look pretty good on one day, only to be shattered on the next, was a driving force behind our efforts. At long last, something positive did seem to be happening, as the exchange of sick and wounded prisoners had demonstrated. Needless to say, the Chinese would bend the news to suit their own ends, but they could not conceal the fact that the talks were going ahead and, on that, we pinned our faith and hopes.

Another good sign was a distinct improvement in our living conditions and the easing of the rules, giving us more freedom and the ability to visit and mix with American friends. Before this fraternisation with the

Yanks had become the norm, Tom and I had sneaked our way into the American lines one dark night by scuffling down the road between the two companies, like the Chinese, who were still not used to the calf-length leather boots which they had been given. The guard in his sentry post at the American sector challenged us to which we had responded with a hearty spit, as we had often seen the Chinese do. He acknowledged our response and we shuffled on our way.

Tom and I were always on the lookout for some excitement. With the coming of the summer rains, the river had become a raging torrent. As we walked down to it one day to inspect this impressive scene, to my surprise Tom suddenly said, 'Let's jump in!' Now, like so many blokes who live on the coast, he could hardly swim – a phenomenon I have never been able to understand. In fact, his first encounter with water had been in this very river.

'Are you sure?' I asked.

Holding out his hand, he replied, 'As long as you hold on to me and we jump together.' The look on his face clearly showed that he meant it.

'OK', I said. 'Fair enough.'

Together we climbed out onto a branch of a small tree which over-hung the swirling water. With the noise of the raging flood below us, I had to shout to make myself heard.

'I'll count three and then jump.'

'OK!' and, gripping my hand, he nodded approval.

'One, two, three, jump!'

As we hit the water, the initial shock of the freezing cold took our breath away and the force of the current swept our feet from under us. Under we went, temporarily entangled but, as I emerged, gasping for breath, I saw Tom's head about 30 yards in front of me, bobbing up and down as we were both swept along. Very soon we were dumped on the bank at a bend in the river, some 150 yards downstream and in the American sector.

We were both trying to get some air into our lungs. Thoroughly exhilarated, we shouted out in triumph, 'That was great!'

As we made our way back upstream, it crossed my mind that that would be one way of escaping out of the camp up to the Yalu River. We'd have to wait until the river quietened down a bit and make use of a small branch or a floating log. I chuckled to myself, 'With my luck, some poor peasant would want that log for his woodpile or I'd get sucked to death by those elusive catfish!'

Our little adventure over, we resumed the prison routine once more. With the Olympics coming up, there was plenty to do both in the way of training and preparing the equipment we were going to need.

The Glosters had always had a first-rate track team, most of whom were in camp with us. Just to watch them was sheer delight. Meanwhile Ginger Nawley, our enthusiastic PT Instructor, who had done so much to keep us all fit, had our squad of gymnasts going through our paces. Our only piece of equipment was a box horse and springboard which we made from offcuts of the planking supplied for building the boxing ring. As with everything else we had built on the square, the only tools we had with which to make these were a small handsaw, which only cut on the back stroke and a simple but efficient hand pick-cum-nail-puller. The pick was sharpened at one end. I had earlier watched with awe as two Koreans had been working on the conversion of our clubhouse, using just the same tools. With the sharp end of the pick they had cut square holes to accept the squared ends of poles. Very few nails were used and those that were had been straightened from a bag of recycled ones. Watching those simple but highly skilled peasants at work had brought home to me the appalling waste in the Western world and the marvel of the simple efficiency of Korean housebuilding, with their wattle and daub walls and ingenious under-floor heating without which life in the Korean winter would have been unbearable.

At last the games got under way. It was marvellous to watch Tony Eagles on the last leg of the relay around the football pitch, his athletic figure streaking away from the opposition like a gazelle and winning with ease.

When it came to football, the game with the Americans was a friendly affair, with moments of high humour for, by this time, many of them were good mates of ours. Football may have been our game but the tide turned in the basketball in which the GIs dominated the scene, although our top team had reached a point at which they could give the Yanks a good game. Two of the American players will always remain in my mind. One was a tall, slender, tobacco-chewing, drawling Southerner and the other an equally tall and loose-limbed coloured lad – both were absolute masters of the art. However, the tide turned yet again in the walk, in which Reg Coltman and Dodger Green, my two old C Company mates, had it to themselves, winning by a distance.

Different areas around the football pitch, which was not grass but stony compacted mud, had been allocated for field sports. In the centre was an area for various displays. We kicked off with our gymnastics which ended with Geordie Hogg, our 'fairy' story teller, perched on the top of the pyramid. This was followed by a demonstration of precision marching by the GIs. What little I saw of that made me thankful that it had not been a part of our recruit training programme at Bulford. I very much doubt if it would have been old Coxy's cup of tea either.

Even the Chinese participated in the games. Some, who had had university education were very athletic and competitive. Unfortunately, their taller members were not into basketball but, to some extent this was off-set by their agility. Playing a very different game to the calm, dribbling US 'Globe Trotters', the situation was sometimes comical as the ball passed from one seven footer to another. Nevertheless, it was a friendly affair, our differences lost in the name of sport.

A first-class boxing ring had been built, as good as any I ever fought in. My first fight was against a Mexican. His muscular build made up for my advantage in height. He was tough but, happily, I beat him, earning the compliment of 'a gentleman boxer'. Little did they know that I had only stood back when he was on the ropes because I was exhausted!

My next encounter was of a very different order. My opponent was a mate who, during his days in the Guards, had trained with Jack Gardner, then the British and European champion. His name was Charlie Brierly. Normally a cruiserweight, he had dropped down to welterweight, either through lack of opposition or loss of weight in prison. When captured, he had been serving as a Royal Marine Commando. I shall never forget him, for he gave me the hiding of my life, although I am glad to say that he did not escape unscathed!

I had Ernie Ross in my corner, a first rate boxer who could have been in with a good chance had he entered the competition but, for reasons best known to themselves, a number of useful boxers, like the referee, Dave Crawford, had declined. I decided afterwards that they had shown good sense.

After the referee had been through all the usual preliminaries and had invited us to 'Come out fighting', as we touched gloves Charlie said 'No hard feelings, Dave', and I very soon understood his meaning when I saw the businesslike look on his face at the gong.

Much the same build, we were a good match, but he had learned a few useful tricks. A devastating right which followed a left feint had me on the canvas within a minute. That same punch got me time and time again so that I lost count of the number of times I'd been down there. At the end of the second round, I was exhausted and quite ready to throw in the towel but Ernie Ross, with whom I would gladly have exchanged places, was saying, 'Look at 'im! He's knackered! Watch that right and you'll nail 'im!' as he pushed me out for the last round.

The crowd went wild. Charlie was getting tired and, in a clinch, I saw his bare midriff. Mustering all the strength I had left, I thought to myself, 'One good punch.' Wham! To my delight, I'd really hurt him. His 'Ooh!' was music to my ears as he doubled up. However, my follow-up punches lacked any sort of real power and did him little damage.

We stood in the centre of the ring, both near exhaustion. Amidst the roar of the crowd, I heard 'Get him, Dave. He's had it!'

With arms that felt as if they were attached to ten-ton trucks, we battled on, exchanging punches to the end. Then that heavenly gong went and we supported one another to the robust cheers of the crowd.

As I dropped onto my stool in my corner, Ernie said, 'One more round and you would have had him', to which I gasped, 'You must be joking mate.'

Charlie won on points. A better man than I but I had nothing of which to be ashamed. It was no little consolation to me that he was unable to continue into the final. Charlie confided to Tommy Clough later that it had been his hardest fight to date. Good on you, Charlie!

Charlie had had a taste of the cages and a Korean prison. His mate was one of the caged men next door to my cell, Corporal Matthews of the REME, with whom he had attempted to escape. Charlie himself had been in a cage just round the corner.

After the fight, it transpired that one of my biggest fans was 'Maggot'. He congratulated me and said I would have a good future as a professional when I got back to England. I thought, 'Not me, I'll be a lover not a fighter!'

The winner of our division, a good-looking Mexican American, shook my hand, saying that it was a pity I'd not fought him in the final – just my thoughts!

Throughout that whole week of the Olympics, a holiday atmosphere prevailed and we were able to come and go at will. I think the athletic prowess shown by many, the intricate marching display and the all-round ability shown in the ball games, had shaken the Chinese a bit. The majority of them were peasants who had never enjoyed any education or had any experience of sport as we knew it. Some of them even threw a ball under arm, like little girls.

With the games behind us, an unsettled air now disrupted our acceptance of prison life. The return to normal routine after that splendid week was a dampener and our thoughts were continually on the talks at Panmunjom and the prospects. That the size of the national flags being flown there should have become a major issue was depressing. Nevertheless whilst the two sides were talking there was hope.

Even at that stage, we were all suffering from a mild form of dysentery which, in itself, was something of a trial. Even though the food had improved, our appetites had not. In an uncertain, stagnant manner, we roamed around the camp. The rumours and the raucous blaring of the news broadcasts on the tannoy, which usually came on whilst we were eating, were sometimes encouraging and sometimes quite the reverse.

Like many others, I was finding it hard to sleep and my nerves had become so taut that I began to think, 'I'll go round the twist, like that poor American.' I developed a constant fear that I might do something wrong again and get locked up. Little worries, molehills, had all become mountains. My faith in God was long gone. My faith now lay in my mates; my muckers were now my means of survival.

I made regular visits to my guru, the barber. Always busy, his squad's spacious accommodation was filled with his handiwork. But, busy or not, even *his* face showed signs of strain.

Not wanting, or able, to get involved in anything that would keep me committed for too long, my only source of relaxation was the river. There I met up with two GIs to whom I had talked previously and whose homes in the States were close to that of my sister Mary in Lakeland, Florida. Dear Mary, who had sent me that unforgettable parcel on Hill 327.

As we sat one night on what had been the start of a wooden bridge, which was to have been built across the river at that point, but for some reason had been abandoned, to our surprise, a Chinese, who was quite unknown to us, approached and asked if he could take our photograph, which he then did, no doubt to add to others he had taken of our now reasonable conditions.

It was then just four months since the exchange of the sick and wounded had taken place and, at last, it seemed as if things were coming to a head. Just a few preliminaries remained to be ironed out.

One very welcome development was the improvement in the arrival of our mail from home. Even my Mum, who found writing really hard, sent me a regular letter every month. On 14 July, I got one from Lofty. He was now at home but feeling very guilty about having left his mates. The doctors had told him that, had he not been captured, his arm would certainly have been amputated. His continual exercising of it in the camp had kept some life in it but, they said, it would never again be as it was. Once again, my old mucker proved them wrong, finishing his service in the Army some years later as a soldier in the Special Air Service. What a man!

14

Peace at Last! : Homeward Bound

Within days of winning the Presidential Election, General Eisenhower fulfilled his electioneering promise and made a clandestine visit to Korea in order to make a personal assessment of the situation.

He returned determined that a war that had already cost his country some 30,000 men killed and over 100,000 wounded, together with about 20,000 non-battle deaths, should be brought to an early conclusion with honour. As things then stood, this could only mean that it would end virtually as it had started, with Korea still divided.

Peace could only be achieved by diplomatic means. If those failed, the alternative had to be a massive military operation to clear the Chinese right out of Korea, an operation that might well involve penetration of the Chinese mainland by both air and ground forces. If need be, nuclear weapons would have to be employed. There were immense political objections to that second course but, as a threat, it could prove decisive, making the first course successful.

Meanwhile, steps were being put in hand to increase the strength of the ROK Army so that the US presence could be substantially reduced once an armistice had been achieved and the Chinese had begun to withdraw from North Korea.

In March 1953, the Americans achieved a most important breakthrough in the nuclear field by producing a warhead that could be fired in an artillery shell or a small missile. The first tactical nuclear weapon had arrived.

John Foster Dulles* was despatched to India in May to inform the Indian Prime Minister, Pandit Nehru, that the American National Security Council had resolved that, if peace could not be achieved at Panmunjom,

---

* The American Secretary of State.

they would put in hand the massive military operation described above and that it could involve the use of nuclear weapons. Nehru was asked to let his Chinese and Soviet contacts know this and to emphasise that it was no idle threat. It did the trick! The Soviet and Chinese leaders took fright and the talks at Panmunjom came to life remarkably quickly, although the Chinese attacks along the line of contact continued up to the end of June. By the same token, the bombing of North Korea by the US Air Force went on.

By June, the vexed question of the voluntary repatriation of prisoners had been resolved and on 27 July an armistice was signed, based upon a new permanent demarcation line on the Kumsong river. The South Korean government was furious that Korea was to remain divided but a little political strongarm work, leaving them in no doubt about the consequences of failing to support the UN line, brought them to heel. So ended one of the most extraordinary and least understood wars of the Twentieth Century.

★　　　★　　　★

Monday 27 July 1953, and peace at last! This was good news for sure, but we had seen the carrot so many times in this game, we were still waiting for the salt!

However, things *did* begin to happen. A batch of sick men was taken from our camp and, two days later, another lot. Oddly enough, they were travelling north – a mystery that we would not resolve until our own release some time later.

Meanwhile, the locals began to celebrate and at the weekend there were junketings in the town. An old peasant, who was a bit of a character, made regular Sunday visits there and passed through the camp, a path which he sometimes found hard to negotiate on his return, weaving his way from one side of the road to the other, encouraged by our shouts of 'Go on, Grandad!'

With his arms flailing and a big smile on his face, between hiccups, his brass-plated teeth shining like the sun, he took it all in good part. Many of the older Koreans had those cappings on their teeth. We called them brass but, in truth, it only looked like it. The caps were very badly stuck on and those teeth must surely have been more trouble than they were worth.

Despite it being Monday, our old friend appeared before us on the 27th, as drunk as a fiddler's bitch. It was a case of, 'Here's me legs. Me head's following!' Then, on his return, it was the other way round! Suddenly, with his hands waving above his head and gabbling away about we knew not what, he advanced upon me and fell into my arms. The spit which flew from his mouth reeked of garlic as he rambled on. Though he was speaking Korean, his meaning became clear enough.

'OK, Pappasan, you've had a good day!'

As I held him at arm's length and supported his shoulders, he pointed at me and went through the motions of a bird flying.

'Yeah, if we're lucky!', I responded.

Just as he was about to fall backwards, a guard came along and led him away.

As the days passed and there was no further sign of our own departure, we played such games as volleyball and table-tennis to keep our minds occupied. In the evenings we played Tombola with home-made cards but, as the stress inevitably mounted, we found it increasingly difficult to concentrate.

Then one day, about ten trucks, travelling south and carrying ROK prisoners, came through the camp, followed intermittently on the following day with open trucks with prisoners from No. 5 Camp on the Yalu, some of whom we knew. Strangely enough, there was no shouting and waving between us; it was all very much like men going into battle and showing a quiet restraint. Of course, the plain fact was that we were still surrounded by an aura of uncertainty, which after nearly two and a half years was not going to go away overnight. We were caught up in a tense game of 'wait and see'.

That night we went up through the town to the top company for a game of football, followed by a dance. Over the years, the sight of blokes dancing together had become quite normal, although there were still some who wouldn't be seen dead with their arms round another man. Everyone enjoyed the light-hearted fun and singing with the accompanying band of mouth organs and a home-made bass, made of tin, string and a stick. Danny and Stan Lee were in that company so a visit up there was something to look forward to and a great opportunity for a get-together.

That night the Chinese gave us each a bottle of beer. Mistrusting the effect it might have upon me, I gave mine to Tom, who enjoyed it.

Eleven days after the signing, on 8 August to be precise, my name was drawn to be one of the first batch from our company to leave for Kaisong. We were given a celebration bottle of wine and, once more, I gave it to Tom. Later, it took three of us to hold him down and stop him from going out to strangle 'that slant-eyed bastard of a guard.' The wine had really gone to his head, which was exactly what I had feared would happen to me. The last thing I wanted at that moment was trouble. I had no hatred for the Chinese in me. All I wanted was to get out of that camp.

Next morning, Reveille was at 03.30, so we had little sleep. A meal was dished out at 05.00. However, the original start time of 06.00 was cancelled because the Red Cross were due to visit the Camp. They duly turned up at noon, but we never saw them as we had been taken down to the cinema and formed into mixed companies. I found myself with two blokes from my home town, Jimmy Birt and Des Mansfield. Those two were inseparable. They had been together in the Army for years and had always managed to keep together – out to Jamaica and back, in various camps in England, on courses and so on. Then, of course, out to Korea.

There was only one Chinese English-speaking instructor in our party; the rest, each of whose English was limited to a few words, were designated as company leaders and it quickly became obvious that the only answer was for us to organize ourselves and to liaise directly with the instructor to get our orders. Ding, our company leader, looked completely disorientated so we found ourselves telling him what to do!

At last the journey started. As we left, I could hardly believe that I was looking at that camp for the last time. It had begun to rain. After three hours, we reached the Yalu River and the drivers had a rest. Like that party of sick men, we were travelling north! Why, in God's name? As with so many mysteries, there was a simple reason which we would discover later. Meanwhile, we remained a bit bothered and bewildered.

Two hours later, on a mountain road which had been washed away in places by the heavy rain, we were running parallel to a fast-flowing, flooded river. If this was the Yalu, we must be on the north side and in Manchuria. Where were they taking us?

On we went throughout the night. Progress was slow as our convoy was being led by a squad of Chinese on foot who were checking the state of the road.

As dawn broke, we finally came to a complete halt for the road in front had simply been washed away. We could not go forward nor could we turn and go back. There was nothing for it. The road had got to be rebuilt. Fortunately, there was a good supply of fallen rock available and, with many willing hands, the shoulder was rebuilt. We clambered back on board our trucks which now crept cautiously along that precarious stretch with its steep, grassy slope on one side, falling down to the raging torrent of a river below.

An empty truck, manned just by its driver and his mate, now led the convoy to test the road. As what now occurred showed, it was a prudent step without which we would certainly have had a disaster. Within minutes that truck was beginning to slide as the road, which was like wet concrete, began to break away on the driver's side. The driver, who reacted quickly to the impending disaster, turned his wheels into the slide and, like the captain of a ship, stuck to his guns, desperately pointing the front of the truck into the drop and bravely negotiating the tree stumps which now confronted him. It was to no avail. Shovels and

165

a spare wheel flew out of the back, the wheel overtaking the truck, bouncing in great arcs into the river, followed by the truck which had now gone into a side roll.

With just the front of the truck showing above the raging water, first the driver and then his mate surfaced and could be seen clinging to the vehicle. As they appeared, half a dozen quick-thinking Chinese who, providentially, had a rope, had reached the spot and very soon the two men were sitting on the bank. Fortunately, they were without a scratch – a near miracle. As they were helped up the slope, they were greeted by our loud cheers.

Once more we set to and repaired the road, working together as a first-rate team. Almost at once, the road now straightened out and left the line of the river, sloping down into a lush green valley. In the distance we could see a line of gently sweeping hills.

The rain had stopped, leaving a fresh, slightly misty morning. The sky was still rather overcast but we now had a fine panoramic view of what had once more become a peaceful scene. Not knowing where we were, some of us even thought we could see the Great Wall of China in the far distance, spanning the horizon. All that was missing was a couple of yaks!

By late afternoon, we had reached what looked like a small industrial town with four-storey buildings like mine workings. The few people we could see were fur-hatted with knee-high leggings. At the outskirts of the town, we dismounted at an open railway station. We were clearly at some sort of railhead and the reason for our coming north was at last explained. What we now needed was a train! We did not have very long to wait.

Before we left Chongsong we had all been given what might be called a 'packed lunch' which, as far as I can remember, consisted of steamed bread and peanuts. As we sat there waiting, we made some sort of a meal, though the experiences of the night and the continuing ignorance of our whereabouts and what was supposed to be happening to us, left me, at least, feeling pretty low and apprehensive and not very inclined to eat.

Up to that point I had been keeping a diary in my little red book but now I just could not bring myself to bother with it. Short of sleep and exhausted by the events of the night, frustrated by the lack of any idea where we really were or where we were going, depression wasn't far away. All of a sudden, the sound of a very large, dark-coloured railway engine, drawing a line of goods trucks, which now loomed towards us, hit my jangled nerves and I had a feeling of inward fear. Having been away for so long from the realities of the outside world, living in a comparatively protected environment and suffering from whatever phobia that experience had induced, I had to pull hard on my common sense and get myself collected. Common sense prevailed as the train

166

pulled up and we could see the heavy sliding doors of the goods trucks – shades of '8 horses or 40 men'!

To our intense relief, we now learned that this train would take us all the way to Panmunjom. Launching ourselves through those doors into the cattle trucks, for that was what the stench soon told us they were, we found we had ample room for ten – everything went in tens still!

That stench simply did not bother us as we sprawled on the sparsely strewn straw on the wooden floor. My only thought was of sleep and a chance, hopefully, of disentangling my tired, bewildered mind.

Still not yet feeling safe, our thoughts were on what lay ahead and our hopes for a swift return home, the strain driving each of us into his own shell at times.

As for me, all I wanted was to get away from Korea and out of the Army, so that I could start some kind of decent, stable existence. I should have realized that my mates were all going through the same sort of trauma.

I had lost touch with Tom but I believed he was on the train some- where so, hopefully, we could meet up at the far end. Meanwhile, at least I was with two blokes from my own town.

As the train rumbled on, my natural introversion took over and set me reflecting on my early life and my family. Although as a youngster I had always had many friends, I had been a shy, highly-strung, rather aggressive kid, with an inferiority complex.

My happiest times had been in my early youth, especially at Christchurch Junior School and in the 16th Cheltenham Scout Troop, which I and my mates had joined after a snowball fight and a talk with the Scout leader, who we had the impertinence to opine that his lads were 'a load of cissies'. As I have described in Chapter 1, I began to get into a lot of trouble and was sent to the Padcroft Boys' Home. There, after the initial settling in, I grew to love the place and it did a great deal for me.

My initiation into the workforce was with a firm of French polishers as a probationary apprentice. However, after six months of lugging great pianos, settees and the like around the town on a handcart, my Mum found that she simply could not keep me on the measly ten bob a week I got as a glorified labourer. After a couple of stints with aircraft facto- ries, of which there were a number in our area, I had settled down with a small builder, who turned his hand to just about anything. It was with him that I had spent long hours mixing cement and wheeling it about building sites, thereby building up my physical strength which had stood me in good stead these last three and a half years.

As I reflected on all this, I said to myself, 'If I ever do get out of this stinking place, I am going to try something new, something demanding a bit of intelligence, which I can get stuck into. No more mixing up barrowloads of sand and cement. I know what it's like to be poor. What's it like to be rich?'

Then I added, 'I'll get myself a nice girlfriend. That's all that I really want. Bugger the money!'

More mixed-up thoughts troubled my mind as we travelled along with open doors. The rattle of the train's wheels and the clinking of loose chains, the scenery passing by, all left me cold. All I was concerned with was getting over that demarcation line!

I tried to conjure up the picture of my sweet Korean girl, Heesoon, but it was no good, the picture just wouldn't come. Then I thought of Pete, my first and best mate in the army, lying buried God knows where, his shattered body mangled by those American bombs which had devastated Gloucester Hill.

At last the train stopped. Outside there were Chinese everywhere, front-line troops who gazed at us as we were herded onto trucks. The sky was overcast with what appeared to be a dull smog, like the pollution of battle.

As we moved off, packed in standing order, and were making our way across a piece of open ground, a truck full of GIs from our camp drew alongside. 'Hi Dave!' a voice shouted. It was the Mexican boxer. 'Look me up, Dave, if ever you come to the States!'

He was clearly in high spirits. 'Those Mexicans are pretty tough', I thought. 'Seem to take everything in their stride. Look him up? I hardly know the bloke and America is a pretty big place.'

We finally arrived at a large building which must have been a university or large school. This was the holding camp. The long straight road which ran past it led, we were told, to Panmunjom, the exchange point. A really great meal was produced for us but I had no stomach for it. Mine was in knots. My fuddled head and weary body would have traded anything, except my precious freedom, for a good night's sleep.

We had got so near and yet so far. The old game started again. Each day, British and American names would be called out in batches of fifty for release. It was our most traumatic experience to date for we knew that at any time, through a violation of the peace plan, the fighting could break out again. It was indeed a case of 'So near . . .' Much closer lay insanity, on the verge of which each one of us was continuously perched.

One day I saw Dick Sneider, who I had known in the SLU. He was sitting on a wooden step, his head in his hands, crying.

'I can't stand any more of this. I'll go crazy for sure.'

I sat myself down beside him, my arm round his shoulder. 'Come on, buddy. No worries, just hang in there', I said, imitating the GI lingo, as we all tended to do.

God, I wished I could cry on his shoulder but I was past that. Poor Dick. He told me that he had smoked the weed daily in captivity, when he could get it, and now what would his family think of him?

Similar thoughts had also entered my mind. But we would arrive home, if we were lucky, probably hailed as heroes. I felt no hero; most of those were dead. A survivor, so far, yes. Certainly no hero. Of the night? Hardly!

I tried to pacify Dick but in so doing only added to my own fears. I left him, his head still buried in his hands.

Nights were no longer anything you could look forward to but just another obstacle to be overcome.

On our fourth day, we stood grouped round a Chinese officer who was to read out the names for release. We were like wharfies seeking a day's work on the dockside in the depression.

Then I heard it, 'Glin'. There was only one and that was me!

A huge black hand of a friendly GI pulled me into the back of an American truck. Saint Peter had let me through the Pearly Gates!

Fully laden, that blessed truck traversed the lonely stretch of road to freedom. The flat, barren paddies on either side which had seen the changing fortunes of war were now abandoned.

Coming in the opposite direction, dressed only in their short underpants, was a truckload of Chinese prisoners. Their physical well-being was in stark contrast to our emaciated state.

We later learned that thousands of their countrymen had opted to join their cousins in Formosa but these hardcore believers of the faith, or those drawn by their family ties, were returning to their homeland unblemished, singing their Maoist songs as they hurled the hated prison khaki denim, which had so defiled their bodies, over the side, strewing the road.

At last we saw the outlines of our destination, Freedom Village, and then could make out the reception committee of British and American brass waiting to greet us. As the truck ground to a halt and we started to clamber over the tailboard, the friendly black GI asked me if I had any souvenirs. What on earth had I got to give him? I found the cheap biro pen given to us with the little red book and thrust it into his hand as I slapped his shoulder and thanked him for the ride.

Over the gateway to the camp hung 'Welcome to Freedom Village'. On each side of the gate, representatives of the Red Cross, the Women's Voluntary Service (WVS) and medical staff lined the approaches. I walked through that gateway in a daze. I just could not believe that that terrible uncertainty was over and that we were in friendly hands at last.

Keeping only our personal possessions, we bathed, were examined and issued with light tropical uniform. Hearing the chatter of our hosts,

I gathered that they attributed the better condition of the Turkish and British prisoners, in contrast to the Americans, to our having been given better food. Of course, I knew nothing about the Turks, except that they were a really tough lot, but as far as we were concerned that was a completely false assumption. The plain fact was that we had never allowed our situation to destroy our morale, though it was often under stress. Through the comradeship and natural sense of humour which so typified the British, our determined efforts to keep fit and the total absence of 'give up-itis', that morale remained remarkably high. In our camp at least, the example set by our companies, with our PT, football, sing-songs and entertainments, was infectious and the state of the Americans had improved markedly once they saw what we were up to; as was proved by their ability to join in the 'Olympics', something which would have been quite beyond those grey, dismal characters we saw on our arrival in Chongsong, with their daily trips to Boot Hill.

The village consisted of a series of wooden huts, with all the necessary facilities, including a bar. Everything was free and, if we wished, we could go anywhere outside. For three years we had not touched a drink, apart from those Chinese 'gifts' just before we left. Now that we had the opportunity to indulge, we were cautious about the effects and still uneasy about 'the other side'. From experience, we knew only too well that the Chinese could sweep down on us, incarcerating us once more, never to roam again.

That first night of freedom was a very uneasy, tense and sleepless one for me. My brain was racing and unable to tell my body to rest. Perhaps it would have been better if I had gone out with a couple of the lads. They had asked me to go with them but, as far as I was concerned, I had seen all I wanted to of Korea – much more than I had ever seen of my own country.

The WVS group in the village were marvellous, slaves to our every whim. Mostly middle-aged women who had brought up families and then, when their children had flown the nest, had decided that they wanted to see more of the outside world.

Chaperoned by one of these kind women, we were taken on the next day through Seoul to Kimpo Airport where we boarded an American Dakota.

With an overwhelming sense of relief, we at last felt that we really were getting somewhere as the rattling cargo plane took off and headed west. Within a couple of hours we saw the coastline of Korea fading away behind us as we set course for Japan in a clear blue sky with just a few motionless cotton wool clouds scattered around it. Far below us lay the pewter-coloured waters of the Straits of Korea with just an occasional ship, its course being indicated by its wake.

We sat on long wooden seats which ran down each side of the old kite. The outer skin vibrated with every thrust of the engines and we felt that it was more like riding in a tram than an aircraft. A middle-aged US Army air hostess, who looked more used to handling freight than humans, stood at the rear, keeping her balance with the aid of looped straps which hung from the ceiling.

As we approached Japan the aircraft lost height, giving us a good view of the little islands which dotted the Inland Sea. It was a typical Pacific scene and one of great beauty, the rich green vegetation contrasting with the light blue of the sea.

We landed at Osaka on Honshu, one of the four principal islands which together constitute Japan. From there we were ferried to Kure, the Commonwealth base, where we were picked up from the jetty by a military bus. The atmosphere was positively sticky – hot and humid.

We were driven through the outer city to a restaurant where a special meal of welcome had been arranged for us. Even though big ceiling fans were circulating the air, the humidity was such that the sweat dripped from my chin and my tunic clung to my body. Seated at tables laden with food that, a few weeks previously, we would have given our eyes for, did little to whet an appetite that had wilted. Food, however good and plentiful, did nothing to quell the mental stress from which we were still suffering.

The lovely sloe-eyed, kimono-clad waitresses were extremely pleasant to look at and I thought to myself that we would see more of their ilk over the next few days. On release I had weighed nine stone ten pounds, about two stone lighter than my normal weight before capture. Fortunately, this had done nothing to blunt my sexual desires.

The meal over, we embussed once more and were taken to the camp where we were to be billeted. There we were given a briefing on the facilities and left to our own devices. Although it was a military camp, it was clear that no one was going to be too hard on us. We were in a state of limbo, for most of us had finished our time. The swimming pool was an ideal place to spend a few hours on the following day, before our late afternoon invasion of the city.

Since leaving Chongsong, our transit had been a rather erratic business with little sense of order. The whole pack got reshuffled as we went from one point to another. Mates had moved on and others had been left behind. However, we were birds of a feather, known to one another, so new mates were easily acquired.

Downtown Kure had everything. Never have I seen so many beautiful girls. No sooner had we got off the army bus than they were seeking our company. To have a tall, slim, sloe-eyed beauty, with her arms wrapped round your waist, pleading for your favours, I found a bit embarrassing at that stage. Still virginal, I had no idea how I'd rate as a lover and would have liked to have said to her, 'Take me away and teach me.'

In the early years of my manhood, when I should have been acquiring those skills, I had been tucked away from these clutches. Now, in packs, we roamed the streets, savouring our first taste of freedom!

There is nothing resembling an English pub in Japan. If you want to buy a drink you go to any one of the numerous eating houses or beer halls. Having disengaged ourselves from the bevy of beauties, we decided to go to one of the eating houses for a quiet beer.

Ian Black, who answered to 'Jet', was a young National Serviceman, like myself, but from B Company. Both being separated from our mates by the great reshuffle that had gone on, we had sat down at a small table together. Jet was a good-looking kid with unusual brown eyes and, like us all, was very tanned. Whereas my hair was fair, his was white.

He ordered a bottle of beer from one of the two waitresses who were shuffling down the aisle in their wooden-soled shoes, catering for the rest of our mob.

As in Singapore, this was Tiger beer. Moisture from the quart-sized, brown, chilled bottle dribbled its way to the tabletop as it did from our two equally chilled glasses. That amber liquid melted our still troubled souls.

Having seen on the street a sample of what was to be had out there, we weighed up the pros and cons of our evening's entertainment.

'We'll be all right tonight, Dave!' said Jet, rubbing his hands. All those lovely women waiting! With a nod and a wink to our other mates, we left, twice the men we were.

'Where are they?' mouthed Jet, ''Alf a pint and I'm anybody's!'

A short walk up the street, a nice, spacious glass-fronted restaurant looked inviting. It was still early, so in we went to try a meal.

At the door, a young waitress bowed and then ushered us to a table. We ordered a beer in Japanese and she, answering, pointed to the side, indicating that when we were ready, we could order food.

On a long tabletop was a variety of glass tanks, some of which contained living sea creatures. Behind them, chefs prepared the food, cooking it on hotplates, charcoal grills and so on. The smell was pretty good. Knowing that 1,000 yen equated to a pound, we ordered there and then, picking a combination of seafood and steering well clear of any meat. There were a lot of Commonwealth troops stationed in and around Kure and the place was reasonably full. Even so, the girl stayed close to our table, waiting for our order to be cooked.

The meal ready, she brought it over, turning her head to smile. As we ate, it became obvious that we were getting more attention than the others. Our waitress stood, feet together, smiling at every glance. At the first opportunity she came over to us, wiping the table around our dishes. Pointing at our chopsticks, she gesticulated, laughing. She had obviously realised that we were no novices with those weapons and said, 'Koree soldee?' By now it would have been common knowledge that we were in town with money.

I smiled at her and said '*Watashi Anata*?' Literally 'You and me?' and asking if I could take her out. She looked thrilled. Just to be with a girl would have been quite enough for me. I did not just want to make love to her but to have her to show me around would have made me very proud. She went across to the chefs and spoke to a middle-aged, slightly built one, who, after a lengthy exchange, in which she was clearly trying to twist his arm, he came across to us.

'She *Ammaari Wakai*', meaning 'She is too young.' She was obviously his daughter and he, equally obviously, thought that I wanted to make love to her. So that was that!

Ah, well. We wouldn't be around long anyway. The poor girl was obviously upset, which boosted my self-esteem a bit. I wondered if she too had thought that I just wanted to make love.

Out on the street again, it was not long before we came to the entrance to a courtyard at the bottom of which was a bunch of our blokes, well on the way.

'Hey. Dave! Come 'ere.'

They were sitting round a table laden with luxurious food with Japanese hostesses plying them with morsels of watermelon and the like. They were clearly having quite a party – and no doubt paying for it too! What did they care about money? At this stage in our new-found freedom, it was immaterial to us.

These girls, their work as hostesses an art, would certainly get their cut and were genuinely enjoying doing it for their Madame.

Leaving them to their fate, Jet and I had wandered to the outskirts of the city. An aged woman, clip-clopping in her wooden shoes, was following us. Deciding that we had better find our way back to the centre, we stopped. With bowed head, the old woman approached us and said, '*Hajime machite dozo yoroshika, onegasishimasu*? which meant, 'How are you? I am pleased to meet you. Do you want a nice girl?'

Looking at each other, Jet and I said 'Why not?'

'*Ikura desu ka*?' i.e. 'How much?'

'1,000 yen.'

'OK!'

Beckoning us to follow, she clip-clopped on. We followed close behind. Out in the back streets, the clatter of her wooden clogs was signalling that the white fish were netted and all ready to be eaten alive in the piranha's lair.

At the end of a cul-de-sac we found that we had arrived. With bowed head she invited us to enter through the sliding paper-panel door. It was a spacious house with high ceilings and room adjoining room in all directions. A staircase led up to the first floor. Guiding us into an inner room, the old woman placed two bar stools beside us and indicated that we should wait there.

The anticipation of that wait was rather like going to the dentist. However, we had a pleasant surprise when she brought two beautiful girls in. They were a bit shy and I am sure did not do this sort of thing on a regular basis.

The ice having been broken, the two girls were fascinated by the colour of our hair, bleached by the summer sun and so different from the universal black hair of their countrymen.

The taller one, whom I thought the prettier, chose me. First we had to pay our money. That formality over, my girl led me upstairs to our room. There was a quilted bedspread on the floor. With a little smile, she said '*Feru-ba. Machimas*' which meant, 'Wait a minute, I am going to the bathroom'. She disappeared for some time but when she returned I could see that she had had a bath. Dressed in a purple kimono which reached down to the floor, she sat and then lay at my side, undoing the cord of the kimono.

It was all so sudden. Here was a beautiful girl just giving herself to me. I thought, 'How I would love to take you out and get to know you properly, not just to make love to you because I had paid money.' She was a thing of real beauty and not to be abused.

Slipping her clothing apart, she revealed her bare midriff and thighs, her skin a pale yellowish colour. The dark pubic hair between her legs thinned over her flat stomach, which I now kissed, raising my head to look into her eyes. Her lovely pale face broke into a smile as I gently stroked her. Her tummy trembled and she said, 'I like very much.' '*Koko iqirisu ka*?' or 'Are you English?', she asked.

As she spoke, a hell of a commotion broke out in the next room, quickly spreading through the whole building. Japanese voices were coming upstairs. Our door was almost lifted off its runners as it was slung open and Jet dived in.

'Quick, Dave! Let's go!', he said, handing me a knife, one of a set of three in a sheath which he had bought earlier in a gift shop. All I had on was a pair of boxer shorts. Struggling into my clothes, I trundled through the door with my boots unlaced.

'Move it, Dave!', Jet panted, 'Let's get out of here!'

Expecting sword-wielding Samurai warriors to come charging through every door, we fled, our unlaced, hob-nailed boots echoing throughout the street, like the sound of galloping Clydesdale mares.

Once clear of the cul-de-sac and back on the main road, at what we thought was a safe distance, we slowed down to a fast walk and I stopped to tie my laces.

I paid 1000 yen for that!, I gasped. 'What happened?'

All Jet would say was 'Stupid bitch!' and would not elaborate.

As I calmed down, I thought to myself, 'Well at least my girl made some money!' All I now had was sweet memories of what might have been!

No doubt similar scenes were being enacted all over Kure that night. When we got back to camp, we were warned to watch out what we were up to or we would 'catch a dose'. Smugly, I thought to myself, 'Well, at least I kept clear of that particular problem!' I had by no means forgotten the fright I had endured after that mad night out in Pusan.

We spent one more night in Kure. I still did not get a girl but had a great time with a mob of us going to a beer hall and thoroughly over-indulging.

On the following day we boarded a Hastings, a smallish passenger plane, to take us to Singapore, with a scheduled stop for refuelling at Okinawa, the scene of such bitter fighting in the Second World War and now a US air base.

After we touched down on that historic little Pacific island, we were allowed to stretch our legs on the tarmac whilst the ground staff checked our plane over. Then it was 'All aboard!' and we were off again. She was a comfortable aircraft, like travelling in a Black and White coach. A few hours later, after flying over Formosa, the weather began to get a bit bumpy. Sitting in my window seat, I suddenly saw sparks flying from one engine and then, a little later, flames!

The Captain assured us that there was nothing to worry about as the plane had four engines and the troublesome one had been shut down. As we banked to port, we sensed that we were going back the way we'd come. Sure enough, we put down in Formosa, making an unscheduled stop.

As we touched down, flames engulfed the entire engine, licking their way around either side of the wing. The problem was quickly brought under control by the fire crew as we disembarked on the other side. Typically British, calm and collected, our Captain and his aircrew had averted what had all the makings of a disaster.

Clearly, the old girl was due for a stay in the pits. However, lightning never strikes twice and we had no qualms about boarding a similar aircraft to take us to Hong Kong, just a short hop across the Formosa Straits. Singapore was out. Unlike Kure, Hong Kong had nothing to excite us apart from a couple of quiet beers.

To the British military stationed in Hong Kong we were heroes but,

175

believe me, I did not quite feel the part. In the two days we were there, the most exciting thing we did was to have a couple of tattoos, which had been done in Chongsong, coloured in!

Our happiest moment was boarding the troopship *Asturias*. Unlike the *Windrush*, with which I had fallen in love, this ship was bigger and more modern, but cold. It just lacked that warmth of character.

I had not felt too well in Hong Kong and got myself all scared when I saw the colour of my water in the loo – it had gone reddish brown. In my ignorance I wondered if I had a touch of gonorrhoea which had lain dormant since Pusan. However, when I looked in the mirror and saw how yellow my eyes had gone, I realized with considerable relief that I had jaundice. Throughout all that time in Chongsong I had kept in pretty good shape when compared with a lot of my mates, apart from occasional bouts of the mildest form of dysentery. Clearly, all the rich food I had had of late had upset my system. I went to the doctor who at once put me in the sick bay. This was located on an upper deck in the stern of the ship, well away from all my old mates with whom I had only just become reunited. However, that did not stop them and they visited me in droves.

I found it hard to stay in bed and would get up and wander round the ward, helping to sweep up and so on. At most times there were no nurses about once the doctor had done his rounds. He had told me to drink plenty of water and every day I was given a small dose of calcium.

I was not allowed ashore when the ship docked in Singapore so I asked Archie Coram who, in those circumstances, was the most reliable, to get me some presents for my family and mates at home. I had given him a list and he went about his task in style, spending about eleven months Army pay in one fell swoop! The silk kimonos, cigarette cases, camera lighters and so on were all wrapped up in a large leather suitcase which would last me a lifetime. Good old Archie! He was a real friend.

Apart from being unable to go ashore, just the jaundice itself was enough to induce depression, especially when Chris, the Sapper in the bed alongside mine, who was being sent home with some unidentifiable disease, told me that the only cure was rest and plenty of water!

Rest! I was still having a job at night, let alone during the day. Alcohol was out and my mates were having a whale of a time. However, I felt a bit smug when quite a few of them were making visits to the doctor to prevent their do-dahs dropping off! Guess who was one – Jet!

On our way out on the *Windrush*, the sight of foreign lands had fascinated me but now, as we approached Aden, everything looked flat and static. The only bit of light relief was watching some of the crew, who were queers, going down the gang-plank in their colourful shirts, jokingly swinging their bums to the whistles from the blokes on deck.

At about 1 am that night there was a heck of a commotion outside my ward.

'I want to see Dave Green!'

Tommy Clough was out there wrestling with a couple of Regimental Policemen. He was f. . .ing and blinding and as pissed as a newt with a bunch of bananas round his neck and a pineapple in one hand. Just as they dragged him away, the pineapple came flying down the passage for his old mate! Poor Tom, back to his pleasant self, though undoubtedly with an imperial hangover, came to see me next day.

As we made our way through the Suez Canal and began the home stretch, I was at last let loose, seemingly better, though still banned from alcohol. At least I could now wander freely around the ship. The last few weeks had been pretty traumatic but, in my depressed state, pretty uneventful.

I wanted to look my best when I met my family. At the moment, little worries all seemed to be big ones. Most of us were pretty skinny and my sojourn in the sick bay had not helped.

Clear of the Mediterranean and out in the open sea once more, we whiled away the days and nights with thoughts of home and wondering just what life there was going to be like after all we had been through. The ship had made good time to the Channel and, in order to be on schedule, had even cut down her speed. As we headed for Dover, the words of the song we had all sung so often came into my mind:

'There'll be blue birds over the white cliffs of Dover,
Tomorrow just you wait and see.'

Now our tomorrows had arrived. Through blood, sweat and tears, many of the latter would be shed that day, for joy and sorrow. If only Pete and a lot of my good mates, who we had left in early graves in Korea, had been there to wipe away the guilt I felt. But no such luck!

We anchored off Southampton, our kit packed ready for disembarkation. Then we lined the deck for inspection by Customs, each piece of baggage untied or opened. The Customs Officers came on board and walked through our ranks. To our joy, they did not delve into a single kitbag to find our carefully concealed contraband. Within minutes the inspection was over.

I was standing at the end of the line, close to the rope ladder down which they were disembarking. The Customs Officer in charge looked at me and winked. I found myself saying, 'Thanks, mate.' He replied, with obvious pride in his voice, 'My pleasure, soldier.'

As we made our way into the harbour, weaving our way through the big American ships at anchor, all the sirens were blasting and helicopters

177

hovered overhead with press photographers hanging out of them. A flotilla of small boats came out to greet us.

The Glorious Glosters were home!

We, 'the heroes of the night', lined the rails on every deck and sang our way in:

> *'There'll always be an England and England will be free,*
> *If England means as much to you as England means to me.'*

The ship berthed, the crowds milled around on the dockside as we disembarked, searching the hundreds of faces for those familiar to us and making our way through the mob away from the immediate area of the dock.

Finding a quiet spot, I took off my big pack, planting it together with my kitbags and lit a cigarette whilst I gathered my bearings.

I had not been there long before I heard a scream, 'There he is!' and my sister Muriel came running towards me, throwing herself into my arms and almost knocking me over, as the tears poured down her face. Then there was Dad and sister Ruth. Just behind them was my dear old Mum. I was shocked to see how much she had aged, her once light brown hair having turned silver white. She had been ill and felt so frail as I hugged her. But she was tough and hung onto my arm as if she would never let me go.

As we all stood there and I was talking to Dad, up strolled a one-armed Major Walwyn, as immaculate as ever, his empty sleeve pressed and tucked neatly into his belt. His thick grey moustache was carefully trimmed. He shook my hand saying, 'You made it Green. Welcome home. Sorry I was unable to be with you.' I had great admiration for this officer. A superb leader, able to mix and swear like the best of us. I proudly introduced him to my family.

Who could ever forget that morning on Hill 327 as, with that bullet-torn arm dangling on a few strands of flesh, he stood, fully exposed to the enemy's fire, defiantly reassuring what remained of our depleted company, 'Don't be afraid of these people' and then protesting vehemently when the medics dragged him away. Truly an Officer and a Gentleman, in capital letters.

All the Cheltenham families had hired a Black and White coach between them and they were all there. I sat by Mum for the journey home. As always, when other people were around, she was very quiet but I knew just how much it was meaning to her to have me beside her once more.

Our house was bedecked with flags and a big 'WELCOME HOME' was stretched across the gate, beside which stood my two mates, Ron

Carruthers and Mick Tarrant. I later discovered that these two had painted out my bedroom, papering the walls – the lot. I was deeply appreciative of that. They really were the best of mates and I was so delighted to be with them again.

So now I was home and ready to start the battle of settling back into civilian life and finding a worthwhile job. My nerves were still shattered. After two and a half years of prison life and that awful aura of uncertainty, through which we'd all come pretty well, thanks to our determination not to give in and the wonderful spirit of give and take amongst the finest bunch of mates you could wish for, the reaction was hitting most of us fairly hard. It was like staring into a bottomless pit of nothingness. Sleep had not been easy for some time and I found that lying in bed each night, in the peaceful surroundings of my own home, the silence was deafening. I longed to throw open the window and shout out 'Wake up!'

My brother Eric, who was still having problems in settling down to civil life after twenty-two years in the Navy and had just been released from Gloucester prison following one of his periodical bouts of drinking, called round at the house on the morning after my return. Muriel and I were in the scullery sharing a pot of tea, when he came in, looking a bit apprehensive and clearly not too proud of himself. But he had no need to feel that way, since we were birds of a feather, damaged by war and he, no matter what he might have done of late, was still my hero. When I was a schoolboy and Eric was fighting on a warship in the Mediterranean, we always sang 'For those in peril on the sea' at morning assembly and I would sing it with a good deal of feeling.

I was very touched when he confided in me that he had cried whilst being locked in a prison cell for breaking a second hand dealer's shop window, when he had heard that I was 'Missing In Action'.

I was astonished how many people stopped me in the street, some of whom I hardly knew, to tell me of their concern for me whilst I was in Korea.

That awful restlessness just would not go away. I found I could not sit in a cinema and see a film right through. The only relief from stress that I could find was to tour the pubs – which really only made things worse. I just couldn't handle too many beers, neither could some of my mates. Mick Thomas, from Gloucester, had been arrested for holding up the traffic with a red flag in the middle of Cheltenham High Street!

The great Army machine ground slowly on sorting us all out for 'demob'. At last the day came and I was out on the street in a cold hard world, with a job to find and not knowing really what to do next.

Two months later, I had seven jobs tucked under my belt, the shortest of which had lasted all of two hours. This had been in a dark, artificially lit foundry. I had had to kick the security guard's grappling hands off me as I tried to escape over the gate. Finally, I was offered a job as a trainee machine operator in an aircraft factory. This one I was determined to keep, especially as there were three other young ex-servicemen on the same course. Whilst there, I was introduced to a really nice girl, whose guiding light worked wonders.

One morning, I caught the same No. 2 bus that I had taken on that day when I was off to Bulford and met Pete for the first time. Getting off at the LMS Station, I got a platform ticket and made my way to the buffet for a cup of tea. The whole scene was re-enacted. There were the usual two train crewmen, the tea urn that rattled as a train came in and even the slab cake that I had so fancied as a boy.

Off went the driver and his mate and the whistle blew for the departure of their train. I walked onto the platform and watched it pull away. As I did so, the words of the old ticket puncher, three and a half years back, echoed in my head. 'Good luck to ya son.'

I thought of Pete and those others who died with him and a tear rolled down my face. I walked away with a lump in my throat and the minute hand on the big clock went 'CLUNK!'